MORE PRAISE FOR

Extraordinary, Ordinary People

"Engaging . . . A coming-of-age story during the final years of segregation and its aftermath . . . complicates what many think they know about one of the most prominent women in recent history and provides a compelling portrait of the life of a middle-class Southern black family." —*Washington Post*

"Vivid and heartfelt writing . . . Rice's graceful memoir is a personal, multigenerational look into her own, and our country's, past . . . Highly recommended." —*Library Journal*

"Pays tribute to the people who truly shaped her . . . sets the record straight on aspects of her life that often flirt with myth." —*USA Today*

"A thrilling, inspiring life of achievement." —*Publishers Weekly*

"Though politically Rice may be a moderate to conservative hawk, *Extraordinary, Ordinary People* is the work of a dove—an ode to her parents, with sweetness and love." —*Christian Science Monitor*

"A frank, poignant, and loving portrait of a family that maintained its closeness through cancer, death, career ups and downs, and turbulent change in American society." —*Booklist*

"In this remarkably clear-eyed and candid autobiography, Rice focuses on her fascinating coming-of-age during the stormy civil rights years in Birmingham, Alabama." —*BookPage*

Extraordinary, Ordinary People

A MEMOIR OF FAMILY

CONDOLEEZZA RICE

THREE RIVERS PRESS · NEW YORK

Reading Group Guide copyright © 2011 by Three Rivers Press, an imprint of the
Crown Publishing Group, a division of Random House, Inc.

All rights reserved.
Published in the United States by Three Rivers Press, an imprint of the
Crown Publishing Group, a division of Random House, Inc., New York.
www.crownpublishing.com

Three Rivers Press and the Tugboat design are registered trademarks
of Random House, Inc.

Originally published in hardcover in slightly different form in the United States
by Crown Archetype, an imprint of the Crown Publishing Group,
a division of Random House, Inc., New York, in 2010.

Grateful acknowledgment is made to the following for permission to reprint
previously published material:

Alfred Publishing Co., Inc.: Lyrics from "Take My Hand, Precious Lord,"
words and music by Thomas A. Dorsey, copyright © 1938 (Renewed) by
Warner-Tamerlane Publishing Corp. All rights reserved. Reprinted by
permission of Alfred Publishing Co., Inc.

Hal Leonard Corporation: Lyrics from "Theme from 'The Greatest American Hero,'"
from the television series, words by Stephen Geyer, music by Mike Post, copyright
© 1981 by EMI Blackwood Music Inc., Dar-Jen Music, EMI April Music Inc. and
Stephen Cannell Music. All rights for Dar-Jen Music controlled and administered
by EMI Blackwood Music Inc. All rights reserved. International copyright secured.
Reprinted by permission of Hal Leonard Corporation.

Library of Congress Cataloging-in-Publication Data
Rice, Condoleezza, 1954–
Extraordinary, ordinary people : a memoir of family / Condoleezza Rice.—1st ed.
1. Rice, Condoleezza, 1954—Childhood and youth. 2. Rice, Condoleezza,
1954—Family. 3. African American families—Alabama—Birmingham.
4. African Americans—Alabama—Birmingham—Biography. 5. Birmingham
(Ala.)—Biography. 6. Birmingham (Ala.)—Race relations—History—20th
century. 7. Stateswomen—United States—Biography. 8. Women cabinet officers—
United States—Biography. 9. African American women—Biography. I. Title.
E840.8.R48A3   2010
327.730092—dc22
[B]   2010021645

ISBN 978-0-307-88847-1
eISBN 978-0-307-71960-7

Printed in the United States of America

Unless otherwise indicated, all photographs are courtesy of the Rice Family Collection.

BOOK DESIGN BY BARBARA STURMAN
COVER DESIGN BY WHITNEY COOKMAN
COVER PHOTOGRAPHY COURTESY OF THE AUTHOR

8 10 9 7

First Paperback Edition

To my parents,

JOHN AND ANGELENA RICE,

and my grandparents:

MATTIE AND ALBERT RAY,

and

JOHN AND THERESA RICE

CONTENTS

AUTHOR'S NOTE

JOHN AND Angelena Rice were extraordinary, ordinary
people. They were middle-class folks who loved God, family,
and their country. I don't think they ever read a book on par-
enting. They were just good at it—not perfect, but really good.
They loved each other unreservedly and built a world together
that wove the fibers of our life—faith, family, community, and
education—into a seamless tapestry of high expectations and
unconditional love. And somehow they raised their little girl in
Jim Crow Birmingham to believe that even if she couldn't have a
hamburger at the Woolworth's lunch counter, she could be President of the United States.

As it became known that I was writing a book about my parents, I received many letters and emails from people who knew
my mom and dad, telling me how my parents had touched their
lives. In conducting this journey into the past I had the pleasure
of returning to the places my parents lived and talking with their
friends, associates, and students.

I was also contacted by people who *didn't* know my parents
but recognized in my story their own parents' love and sacrifice.
Good parents are a blessing. Mine were determined to give me
a chance to live a unique and happy life. In that they succeeded,
and that is why every night I begin my prayers saying, "Lord, I
can never thank you enough for the parents you gave me."

Extraordinary,
Ordinary People

CHAPTER ONE

Starting Early

MY PARENTS were anxious to give me a head start in life—perhaps a little too anxious. My first memory of confronting them and in a way declaring my independence was a conversation concerning their ill-conceived attempt to send me to first grade at the ripe age of three. My mother was teaching at Fairfield Industrial High School in Alabama, and the idea was to enroll me in the elementary school located on the same campus. I don't know how they talked the principal into going along, but sure enough, on the first day of school in September 1958, my mother took me by the hand and walked me into Mrs. Jones' classroom.

I was terrified of the other children and of Mrs. Jones, and I refused to stay. Each day we would repeat the scene, and each day my father would have to pick me up and take me to my grandmother's house, where I would stay until the school day ended. Finally I told my mother that I didn't want to go back because the teacher wore the same skirt every morning. I am sure this was not literally true. Perhaps I somehow already understood that my mother believed in good grooming and appropriate attire. Anyway, the logic of my argument aside, Mother and Daddy got the point and abandoned their attempt at *really* early childhood education.

I now think back on that time and laugh. John and Angelena were prepared to try just about anything—or to let me try just about anything—that could be called an educational opportunity. They were convinced that education was a kind of armor shielding me against everything—even the deep racism in Birmingham and across America.

They were bred to those views. They were both born in the South at the height of segregation and racial prejudice—Mother just outside of Birmingham, Alabama, in 1924 and Daddy in Baton Rouge, Louisiana, in 1923. They were teenagers during the Great Depression, old enough to remember but too young to adopt the overly cautious financial habits of their parents. They were of the first generation of middle-class blacks to attend historically black colleges—institutions that previously had been for the children of the black elite. And like so many of their peers, they rigorously controlled their environment to preserve their dignity and their pride.

Objectively, white people had all the power and blacks had none. "The White Man," as my parents called "them," controlled politics and the economy. This depersonalized collective noun spoke to the fact that my parents and their friends had few interactions with whites that were truly personal. In his wonderful book *Colored People,* Harvard Professor Henry Louis "Skip" Gates Jr. recalled that his family and friends in West Virginia addressed white people by their professions—for example, "Mr. Policeman" or "Mr. Milkman." Black folks in Birmingham didn't even have that much contact. It was just "The White Man."

Certainly, in any confrontation with a white person in Alabama you were bound to lose. But my parents believed that you could alter that equation through education, hard work, perfectly spoken English, and an appreciation for the "finer things" in "their" culture. If you were twice as good as they were, "they" might not like you but "they" had to respect you. One could find space for a fulfilling and productive life. There was nothing worse than being a helpless victim of your circumstances. My parents were determined to avoid that station in life. Needless to say, they were even more determined that I not end up that way.

My parents were not blue bloods. Yes, there were blue bloods who were black. These were the families that had emerged during Reconstruction, many of whose patriarchs had been freed well before slavery ended. Those families had bloodlines going back to black lawyers and doctors of the late nineteenth century; some of their ancestral lines even included political figures such as Hiram Rhodes Revels, the first black United States senator. There were pockets of these families in the Northeast and a large colony in Chicago. Some had attended Ivy League schools, but others, particularly those from the South, sent their children to such respected institutions as Meharry Medical College, Fisk, Morehouse, Spelman, and the Tuskegee Institute. In some cases these families had been college-educated for several generations.

My mother's family was not from this caste, though it was more patrician than my father's. Mattie Lula Parrom, my maternal grandmother, was the daughter of a high-ranking official, perhaps a bishop, in the African Methodist Episcopal Church. Though details about her father, my great-grandfather, are sketchy, he was able to provide my grandmother with a first-rate education for a "colored" girl of that time. She was sent to a kind of finishing school called St. Mark's Academy and was taught to play the piano by a European man who had come from Vienna. Grandmother had rich brown skin and very high cheekbones, exposing American Indian blood that was obvious, if ill-defined. She was deeply religious, unfailingly trusting in God, and cultured.

My grandfather Albert Robinson Ray III was one of six siblings, extremely fair-skinned and possibly the product of a white father and black mother. His sister Nancy had light eyes and auburn hair. There was also apparently an Italian branch of the family on his mother's side, memorialized in the names of successive generations. There are several Altos; my mother and her grandmother were named Angelena; my aunt was named Genoa (though, as southerners, we call her "Gen-OH-a"); my cousin is Lativia; and I am Condoleezza, all attesting to that part of our heritage.

Granddaddy Ray's story is a bit difficult to tie down because he ran away from home when he was thirteen and did not reconnect with his family until he was an adult. According to family lore, Granddaddy used a tire iron to beat a white man who had assaulted his sister. Fearing for his life, he ran away and, later, found himself sitting in a train station with one token in his pocket in the wee hours of the morning. Many years later, Granddaddy would say that the sound of a train made him feel lonely. His last words before he died were to my mother. "Ange-lena," he said, "we're on this train alone."

In any case, as Granddaddy sat alone in that station, a white man came over and asked what he was doing there at that hour of the night. For reasons that are not entirely clear, "Old Man Wheeler," as he was known in our family, took my grandfather home and raised him with his sons. I remember very well going to my grandmother's house in 1965 to tell her that Grand-daddy had passed away at the hospital. She wailed and soon said, "Somebody call the Wheeler boys." One came over to the house immediately. They were obviously just like family.

I've always been struck by this story because it speaks to the complicated history of blacks and whites in America. We came to this country as founding populations—Europeans and Africans. Our bloodlines have crossed and been intertwined by the ugly, sexual exploitation that was very much a part of slavery. Even in the depths of segregation, blacks and whites lived very close to one another. There are the familiar stories of black nannies who were "a part of the family," raising the wealthy white children for whom they cared. But there are also inexplicable stories like that of my grandfather and the Wheelers.

We still have a lot of trouble with the truth of how tangled our family histories are. These legacies are painful and remind us of America's birth defect: slavery. I remember all the fuss about Thomas Jefferson and Sally Hemings a few years back. *Are we kidding?* I thought. *Of course Jefferson had black children.* I can also remember being asked how I felt when I learned that I appar-ently had two white great-grandfathers, one on each side of the family. I just considered it a fact—no feelings were necessary. We all have white ancestors, and some whites have black ancestors. Once at a Stanford football game, my father and I sat in front of a white man who reached out his hand and said, "My name is Rice too. And I'm from the South." The man blanched when my father suggested we might be related.

It is just easier not to talk about all of this or to obscure it with the term "African American," which recalls the immigration narrative. There are groups such as Mexican Americans, Korean Americans, and German Americans who retain a direct link to their immigrant ancestors. But the fact is that only a portion of those with black skin are direct descendants of African immigrants, as is President Barack Obama, who was born of a white American mother and a Kenyan father. There is a second narrative, which involves immigrants from the West Indies such as Colin Powell's parents. And what of the descendants of slaves in the old Confederacy? I prefer "black" and "white." These terms are starker and remind us that the first Europeans and the first Africans came to this country together—the Africans in chains.

CHAPTER TWO

The Rays and the Rices

ONE DAY Granddaddy Ray, now a coal-mining engineer, passed a beautiful young girl drawing water at a well. He introduced himself, but when he learned that she was only sixteen, he refrained from trying to date her. When she was finally old enough, Mattie Lula Parrom and Albert Ray married. Albert was industrious and worked three jobs for most of his life. He labored in the mines during the week, a profession that saddled him with emphysema and heart disease and gave him a deep admiration for John L. Lewis and the coal miners union; he sheared horses in the evening, a skill that he'd been taught by Mr. Wheeler; and on the weekends he built houses. Granddaddy's day began every morning at four o'clock with Grandmother cooking a big breakfast of steak or bacon and eggs to sustain him through the hard workday ahead.

The Rays were proud people. They settled in Hooper City, Alabama, which in those days was pretty far outside the city limits of Birmingham. Even when I was a child, my grandparents' home felt as though it were in the country, not a city. Life was apparently pleasant, though there were some tensions between my mother and the daughter of the owner of the Italian grocery store, who seemed to have traded racial insults on a fairly regular basis.

Mattie and Albert Ray were landowners who built their house with their own hands. The white wood-framed home was large for its time, on a corner lot with a big pecan tree in the front yard. It had eight large rooms, including a music room where my grandmother taught piano. Grandmother loved fine things, and the heavy mahogany furniture, always purchased with cash, survives in various family members' houses—as well as my own—to this very day.

Still, Grandmother Ray was frugal. When Granddaddy lost his job at the mine, he worried that they might lose the house. But my grandmother had saved enormous amounts of money in a mattress, allowing them to pay off the bank and to acquire more land.

My aunts and uncle remember their parents' determination to maintain their dignity despite the degrading circumstances of Birmingham. The children were constantly reminded, "You are a Ray!" This was both an admonition to let nothing hold them back and occasionally a rebuke when my grandparents disapproved of their behavior. They were never allowed to use a "colored" restroom or water fountain. "Wait until you get home," they were told. And my grandparents always made sure that they had a car so that no one had to ride in the back of the bus.

My mother had five siblings. Albert junior, Mattie, and my

mother were born very close together in the early 1920s. Uncle Alto and Aunt Genoa, who went by Gee, made their entrance about a decade later. My grandparents were not themselves college-educated, but they were determined that their children would be. Though they believed in honest hard work, they wanted their children to have an easier life than they'd had.

As it turned out, this took some doing. The eldest child, Albert, was difficult to educate. Albert started school at Miles College in Fairfield, Alabama, not far from Birmingham. But my restless uncle left school and went north to Pennsylvania with his young bride and first child to seek his fame and fortune. When my grandfather learned that Albert was working in the steel mills, he got on the train, brought Albert and his young family back to Birmingham, and insisted he return to school. My grandfather had had to work in the coal mines, but the steel mills were not good enough for his son. Albert did eventually finish college and became a quite successful Presbyterian minister.

On the other hand, Mattie and my mother finished Miles in the requisite four years. They lived at home and drove to college each day. Both were stunningly beautiful. Mattie looked like her mother, sharing her rich brown complexion, high cheekbones, and long, wavy black hair. My mother looked like her father, fair-skinned with the same round face that I have and long, straight brownish hair. As little girls they were favored by adults because they were so cute. One of my most cherished photographs shows five-year-old Mattie and three-year-old Angelena as "calendar girls" for the local barbershop.

In college the "Ray girls," as they were called, were popular, with outgoing Mattie becoming a majorette and my more reserved mother breaking out of character by becoming a cheer-leader. Mattie, who played high school and collegiate tennis and basketball, was a real athlete. My mother, however, was not. In order to fulfill her physical education requirement, she created a scrapbook. Her teacher gave her a B for the beautiful work but told her he just couldn't give her an A when she didn't even break a sweat. This was very much my mother. She was an artist and a lady, and she didn't really believe that women should play sports or, heaven forbid, perspire. I can't remember my mother ever picking up a bat or a ball of any kind, and though she later learned to enjoy spectator sports with my father and me, she never fully came to terms with my tomboy tendencies.

After college Mattie and Angelena continued to live at home. My mother and her sister had many friends, but they were clearly each other's best friends. Life in segregated Birmingham was in some ways pretty simple: family, church, work, and a social life built around black fraternities and private clubs. Mother and her sister became well-regarded teachers at the same high school, though their perpetual tardiness led their father to set the house clocks far ahead to force them to be on time.

They'd been taught music by their mother and grandmother and on Sundays played organ and piano for Baptist churches. Although they were Methodists, the Baptists paid better. They had to learn to play gospel and improvise by ear, something that those who read music sometimes find hard. I certainly do. But it was apparently not so difficult for my mother and Mattie. I asked about this once when I played for a Baptist church and found myself unable to follow the preacher when he'd "raise a song." "Mother," I said, "he starts in no known key. How am I supposed to find him?" "Just play in C," she said. "He'll come right back to you." It was good advice, but I never mastered playing gospel the way my mother and Mattie did.

On the weekend, the girls went to fraternity and social club dances in dresses that Mattie, who could sew beautifully, made from whatever material they liked. They loved clothes. My mother once said that her meager teacher's salary was already owed to fine clothing stores such as Burger-Phillips and Newberry's the minute she got it. They took trips to shop in downtown Birmingham, where their really light-skinned acquaintances would "pass" as white so that they could go to lunch counters and bring hot dogs out to their waiting, darker-skinned friends.

I'VE HEARD many friends and family say that they never thought my mother would marry. She was so close to her family, extremely reserved, sharp-tongued, and, despite her beauty, headed for spinsterhood. But one day she went to work at Fairfield Industrial High, where she'd been teaching for several years. There was a lot of buzz about the new athletic director and assistant football coach. Tall, dark-skinned, and extremely athletic, he was powerfully built with a deep, resonant voice. And he was a preacher who happened to be single.

Mother claimed that John Wesley Rice Jr. first saw her walking down the hallway in a red polka-dot dress and red, very high-heeled strappy shoes. He was leaning against the wall, filing his fingernails and hoping to have a chance to say hello. He claimed that it was *she* who had made the first move, dressing that way to catch his attention.

Daddy had come to Birmingham after finishing Johnson C. Smith University in Charlotte, North Carolina. He'd started school at Stillman College in Alabama, but when World War II broke out, Granddaddy decided to send him to Smith, where he could attend college and then go on to seminary. For reasons that I don't know, Granddaddy didn't want his son to fight in the war. I don't think he had any political or philosophical objection to the war. Perhaps he was just fearful of losing his only son, whom he counted on to follow in his footsteps into religious ministry. Daddy wanted to go into the army but acceded to his father's wishes that he continue his work in the seminary. He did do some chaplain's work for soldiers returning from the front, but I think he always felt a little guilty for not having fought in World War II. He had enormous admiration for those who were in the military, particularly his first cousin, Philip, who served in Vietnam and retired as a colonel in the air force. They became exceedingly close and remained so until Daddy's death.

In any case, by the time Daddy arrived at Fairfield High School, he had already been pastor of his first church and had worked several jobs simultaneously. On the weekends he played and coached semiprofessional football in Burlington, North Carolina. Sometimes he worked as a waiter to supplement his income, and he even tried opening a restaurant, which failed miserably. Until the day he died he always tipped generously, saying that waiting tables was the hardest work he had ever done.

My father had grown up in a family dominated by his father, John Wesley Rice Sr. My paternal grandfather was born in Eutaw (pronounced "UH-tah"), Alabama. There were apparently three branches of the Rice family, each emanating from a different slave-owning brother in Greene County, Alabama, about an hour's drive from the Mississippi border. Not many blacks owned land in those days, so my grandfather's family worked the land of others as sharecroppers. Granddaddy's father was illiterate—and may not have been his biological father—but his mother, my great-grandmother Julia Head, was a freed slave who'd learned to read. It isn't clear who educated her, since it was illegal to teach slaves to read. But she was apparently a favored house slave, and there is a story, perhaps apocryphal, that Julia had run Union soldiers off the plantation and protected the horses during the Civil War. To the day she died, she would sit on her porch with a shotgun in her lap and a pipe in her mouth. Perhaps she thought she'd have to do it again.

According to my father, Granddaddy Rice was not a favored son because, unlike his siblings, he was very dark-skinned. You will notice that I have by now described the skin color of each of my relatives. Unfortunately, it mattered. One of the scars of slavery was a deep preoccupation with skin color in the black community. The lighter your skin, the better-off you were. This bias extended to other facial features: "thin and Caucasian" was preferred to "thick and Negroid," just as straight hair was "good" compared to kinky hair, which was "bad." The repercussions were significant in my parents' time, when no self-respecting black school would select a dark-skinned homecoming queen. There was even rumored to be a "paper bag test" for membership in the best clubs—if you were any darker than a paper bag, you needn't bother to apply.

By the time I came along, skin color and other physical features were less important, though not irrelevant. My father loved that I had my mother's long hair, despite the fact that mine, unlike hers, was a coarse, thick, and somewhat unruly mop. When I finally cut it in college, it was pretty clear that he thought I'd given up some sort of social advantage. But by then the "black is beautiful" aesthetic and Afro hairstyles had introduced a new concept of what was appealing.

One can imagine, though, what it was like for my very dark-skinned grandfather in the first half of the twentieth century. He was given the worst land to work and not much encouragement from his father. But his mother taught him to read and sent him to school. He had big dreams and loved books. So when he was about nineteen, he decided to get a college education. He asked people, in the parlance of the day, how a "colored" man could go to college. They told him about little Stillman College, which was about thirty miles away in Tuscaloosa, Alabama. He saved his cotton and paid the school.

After one year, though, Granddaddy Rice ran out of cotton and had no way to pay his tuition. He was told that he would have to leave. Thinking quickly, he pointed to some of his fellow students. "How are those boys going to college?" he asked. He was told that they'd earned a scholarship and that he could have one too if he wanted to be a Presbyterian minister. Without missing a beat, Granddaddy Rice replied, "Well, that's exactly what I had in mind." As they would do several times in my family's history, the Presbyterians educated this young black man.

John Wesley Rice Sr. soon met Theresa Hardnett, a pretty half-Creole from Baton Rouge. The Hardnett family produced educated girls, including two who were among the first black registered nurses to graduate from Booker T. Washington's Tuskegee Institute. My grandmother, though, left home when she was seventeen and married my grandfather shortly thereafter. She set out with him on his mission of church building and educational evangelism.

While my mother's family was landowning and settled,

Daddy's family lived the life of an itinerant preacher. As a result, my parents held very different views on the importance of land. Mother always wanted to own a house and sometimes, a little pointedly, reminded Daddy that he'd grown up moving from place to place and living in "other people's houses." Her family, on the other hand, had owned land. Daddy didn't really care and felt a bit tied down by the financial responsibility of home ownership. While they did eventually own property and a house, their differences in perspective on this matter remained a source of some conflict throughout their marriage.

In any case, Granddaddy Rice worked mostly in Louisiana, founding a church and a school next door. Sometimes he found it necessary to work in Mississippi and Alabama, leaving the family behind for a few months in Louisiana. Granddaddy's churches were successful because he was a powerful speaker. His sermons were intellectually sound and biblically based. He made it clear that he'd studied theology in seminary and was a fully ordained minister. In his sermons, there was none of the "whooping and hollering" emotion of the Baptists across town, who had no formal training. Granddaddy apparently delivered his sermons without notes. I once told my father that I was grateful that I'd inherited his exceptional ability to speak off the cuff. He told me that he was indeed good but not like Granddaddy. "You should have heard your grandfather," he said. "He spoke in whole paragraphs."

The Rice schools were even more successful than the churches. My grandfather believed that his schools could better educate black children than the miserable public schools of the day, and he sought funds from any source he could, whether it meant contributions from church members, a few cents from parents in the community, or fifty dollars from rich white people across town. Granddaddy Rice once told Daddy that "white guilt" was his best ally in funding his schools. But when a white church collected a bunch of old textbooks and "donated" them to my grandfather's school, he politely declined. It was important, he explained, that his kids have the most up-to-date reading materials, just like the white students.

John Rice's educational evangelism sometimes brought him into conflict with the Catholic hierarchy in Louisiana, which saw his efforts as competing with its own education ministries. Granddaddy Rice maintained that the Catholics had put some of his schools out of business in several parishes. This led to a kind of militant Protestantism in the Rice family. My father, a tolerant and educated man, opposed John F. Kennedy's presidential bid less because the Massachusetts senator was a Democrat and more because he worried that Kennedy, as a practicing Catholic, might need to answer to the Vatican.

When I went to Baton Rouge for my grandmother's funeral in 1986, I saw one of Granddaddy's surviving schools in Scotlandville, on the outskirts of the city. It had been remodeled, but it was still sitting in the same dusty field where it had been built. Several former students had come back to pay homage to what my grandparents had done for them. "Your granddaddy was a giant," one person said. Another, who was a schoolteacher, acknowledged that she never would have gone to college but for John Rice Sr. Her story was repeated several times. Granddaddy's educational evangelism compelled him to go door-to-door in the poor neighborhoods around him and impress upon parents the importance of sending their kids to college. Then he would go to colleges—usually Presbyterian schools such as Stillman,

Johnson C. Smith, and Knoxville College in Tennessee—and "make arrangements" for the kids to go there. In turn, he would recruit young teachers from the historically black colleges with which he had these relationships. He was zealously committed to education because he believed that it had transformed him, and he was determined to spread its benefits.

When it came to his own family, he was even more insistent. My father and his sister, Theresa, attended schools their father had founded. The family had little money and lived in any house the congregation could provide. Several times when Daddy was a child, Granddaddy decided that his work in a particular Louisiana community was done and the family would move on. If Daddy and his sister resented the upheaval, there was no trace of it in their recounting of their childhood. When it came time for high school, Granddaddy placed his kids in Baton Rouge's McKinley High, which in 1916 held the distinction of graduating the first class of black students in the state of Louisiana.

Growing up, my father was a very good athlete but not a great student, as he remembered. It was a struggle to get him to study, and he didn't love to read, though he loved history and politics. The whole family was taken with and followed closely the famed Louisiana governor and U.S. senator Huey Long. Daddy's uncle on his mother's side, Sylvester, would go down to the courthouse and sit in the "colored" section when Huey Long was a trial attorney. Family lore contends that Long wouldn't start a trial until Sylvester was seated. Daddy remembered the family gathered around the radio listening to Huey Long speak and the absolute devastation they felt years later when Long died after being shot at the state capitol building. "They turned on every light in the capitol that night," he recalled. "The funeral procession was miles long." I suspect this event loomed larger than life in my father's memory, as is often the case with childhood recollections. But the Rices really loved Long, a populist politician whom they saw as caring about common people—even black people.

For the most part, Daddy seems to have enjoyed less serious pursuits. He loved to play preacher. One day he and his sister re-created a funeral that their father had just conducted. They went to the church, set their dolls up in the pews, and laid one doll on the altar table to mimic a casket. Theresa was playing the piano, and my father had begun to preach when one of the dolls in the pews fell with a heavy thud. They ran out as fast as possible, sure that they'd somehow awakened the dead.

Theresa, unlike the young John Rice, was an intellectual and a somewhat somber personality from the day she was born. She read constantly and seemed to take personally the suffering and sorrow around her. My father illustrated this in a story about a certain Easter. The seven-or-so-year-old John was thrilled with his new suit for the Easter program and the basket of candy that the Easter Bunny had brought. But nine-year-old Theresa cried. When my grandfather asked what was wrong, Aunt Theresa said that she was reflecting on the bad things that had been done to Jesus.

That in a nutshell captured the difference between Daddy and his sister. Daddy was an easygoing personality who didn't always take life too seriously. He was a popular kid who would become an outgoing adult.

Theresa was reclusive, brilliant, and determined to follow in her father's intellectual footsteps. She would later go on to become one of the first black women to receive a doctorate in

English literature from the University of Wisconsin. Thus I am not even the first PhD in my family.

Aunt Theresa wrote books on Charles Dickens, including one called *Dickens and the Seven Deadly Sins.* When I was about eight years old, we were visiting Aunt Theresa in Baton Rouge, where she was teaching at Southern University. When I saw that she was reading *A Tale of Two Cities,* I asked whether she'd ever read that book before. "I have read this novel at least twenty-five times," she said. I remember thinking that this was a terribly boring way to spend one's life. For years it soured my thoughts of being a professor, since I associated the vocation with the drudgery of reading the same book twenty-five times.

CHAPTER THREE

Married at Last

I T TOOK my parents a long time to finally tie the knot. They began "courting," as my mother called it, almost immediately after meeting, but they did not marry for almost three years. I soon learned, both from their recollections and from the stories told by others in the community, that these young sweethearts were apparently the talk of the town.

While teaching their classes, my parents often passed notes to each other through student couriers whom I later met. The students kept the missives and were disappointed to find they usually just said, "Hi. See you tonight."

The two young teachers were fully committed to their work. Mother taught English. Her former students remember her as a teacher whom you didn't disobey despite her diminutive stature. She was a stickler for good grammar. I remember that she'd bristle whenever someone misused the subjunctive tense. "If I *were*," she'd shout when someone incorrectly said "If I was." She was the coach of the debate team and would enter her students in citywide "oratorical contests." She also directed student plays and musicals, gaining a sterling reputation throughout the city for her efforts.

Her most famous student, though, was neither a debater nor a thespian. Mother taught American baseball legend Willie Mays and, despite her lack of sports acumen, knew that he was special. He recently told me that he remembered her well and recalled that she had told him early on, "You're going to be a ballplayer. If you need to leave a little early for practice, you let me know."

During my parents' courtship, Daddy's workday was completely tied up with sports. Daddy had studied athletic administration at the University of Wisconsin and put that knowledge to work by creating a comprehensive sports program. He started a girls' basketball team, which he held to the same rigorous standards of technical excellence that he demanded of the boys. Doris Jackson Blue, who went on to become a registered nurse, remembered that Daddy liked the fact that she was strong and aggressive, but he told her that she couldn't just run over people. She needed to learn to ball-handle. He then spent hours teaching her how.

My father's players all remembered him as pretty tough—he'd call the boys "dirty dogs" when he was angry with them. Yet he was also caring. One young man who'd sustained a concussion remembers that Daddy sat at the hospital all night with him to make sure he was okay. Another of Daddy's charges, who had fainted during practice, remembered that my father stayed with him during a series of hospital tests. The results revealed an enlarged heart, which meant that he could no longer play football.

Nonetheless, he said, Daddy treated him like a member of the team and made him feel "all right" about his infirmity. The school did not provide health insurance, so if the parents couldn't afford to pay, Daddy would.

He obviously loved to coach, but he once told me that he didn't have the nerves for it. Explaining why, he described a basketball game during which his team was leading by eleven points with one minute to go. A series of mishaps led to a comeback by the other team, and Fairfield lost. Daddy said that he woke up with his pillow soaked from crying in his sleep. "I decided that night," he said, "that my career success was not going to be based on what seventeen-year-olds did in a game." Eventually he would leave the coaching profession for good.

After school, my father and mother often went to the Rays' house for dinner. My grandparents adored him, particularly my grandmother, who loved that he was a preacher. Grandmother prepared great meals, but once in a while my mother would try to prove that she too could cook. One night my father was at the Rays' for a quick dinner between school and a game that he had to coach that night. Mother, it seems, took forever to prepare the meal, only to emerge from the kitchen holding a plate of hot dogs. It turned out that frankfurters were one of only two things she could cook. The other was banana pudding, and after being presented with banana pudding for several weeks in a row, my father finally graciously declined, citing his expanding waistline, not his exhausted taste buds.

The young couple also enjoyed an expansive social life outside of school. Birmingham was so segregated that most middle-class social activities were private, taking place in private homes and private social clubs. The few public spaces for blacks weren't very desirable and were located in rough neighborhoods such as Fourth Avenue in downtown Birmingham. The area was known for drinking, knife fights, and "loose" women. Though my father seems to have gone to the movie theater in that part of town once in a while, my mother stayed away. In those days, there was a very clear distinction between "nice girls" and "bad girls," and one had to be very careful about one's reputation.

Fortunately, there seem to have been many private functions. Daddy was a member of Alpha Phi Alpha, the oldest black fraternity, and the brothers would sponsor dances and parties. Thankfully, Daddy was a *Presbyterian* minister, not a Southern Baptist, and dancing and even a little light drinking by the minister were quite acceptable to the congregation. To the end of his life, Daddy's eyes would fill with tears when a band played "Stars Fell on Alabama," which was always the last dance of the night.

My parents' lives, before and after they were married, were also taken up with my mother's younger siblings. Alto and Gee were high school students at Fairfield when Mother and Daddy were teaching there. Because of the age difference, my parents helped raise them. Gee, sandy-haired, pretty, and spirited, was a handful and challenged her parents, particularly her mother, about everything from what dress to wear to what party to attend. Daddy was often a shoulder to cry on and a wise counselor whom both my aunt and her parents trusted.

This was especially important when Gee abruptly left Spelman College in Atlanta without informing her parents. (They eventually learned of her departure from the school.) Gee, it seems, had decided to go to New York, where she planned to marry an Irish boy named Andy she'd met there. Granddaddy Ray boarded a train and, as he had done earlier with Albert, brought her back to Birmingham. My father, sensing that Gee could not at that moment live at home, arranged for her to go to Norfolk, Virginia, and live with his sister and mother. Gee says that she had never heard of Norfolk until she was told it would be her new home. She attended and graduated from Norfolk State University, where Aunt Theresa was a faculty member. Gee became a teacher and later principal at a school for children with special needs.

Daddy was also very close to Mother's brother Alto. He was unable to convince Alto to play football; Alto said that being hit once was enough for him. But the two became like brothers. Alto was incredibly handsome, with dark, wavy hair and an athletic build. As Gee would later do, he started college but soon quit. He joined the army, where he used his extraordinary talents as a trumpeter to play in the band throughout Europe and admittedly avoid the hard work of infantry duty.

That wasn't good enough for my grandfather, who was determined to see every one of his children get a college education. After selling insurance for a while, Alto was shipped off to Southern University in Baton Rouge, where Daddy's sister, Theresa, had been a faculty member before moving to Norfolk. Alto finished college and, like most of the Rays, became a teacher.

Thus, like most of their middle-class peers in segregated Birmingham, John and Angelena managed to live full and productive lives. Segregation provided in some ways a kind of buffer in which they could, for the most part, control their environment. Like their friends and neighbors, my parents kept their distance from the white world and created a relatively placid cocoon of family, church, community, and school.

But when my parents did have to venture outside of their

narrow world, shocking things happened. My uncle tells the story of the night that my father drove him back to college in Louisiana after a holiday at home. Their car broke down on a dark back road. That was in the days when a sign at the Louisiana border was said to have read, "Run, nigger, run! If you don't know how to read, run anyway." A highway patrolman came upon them and asked why they were there. They explained that their car had broken down. "All right," he said. "But you boys had better have your black asses out of here before I come back." Alto was a master auto mechanic and somehow, working in the light from matches that my father had with him, found a way to get the car started. The two young black men were grateful to be gone before the officer returned.

Another oft-told family story relates to my father's decision to become a Republican. Daddy and Mother went to register to vote one day in 1952. Mother sailed through the poll test after the clerk said to the pretty, light-skinned Angelena, "You surely know who the first President of the United States was, don't you?"

"Yes," Mother answered, "George Washington."

But when my dark-skinned father stepped forward, the clerk pointed to a container filled with hundreds of beans. "How many beans are in this jar?" he asked my father. They were obviously impossible to count.

Daddy was devastated and related his experience to an elder in his church, Mr. Frank Hunter. The old man told him not to worry; he knew how to get him registered. In those days, Alabama was Democrat country. The term "yellow dog Democrat," as in "I'd rather vote for a yellow dog than for a Republican," was often used during this era. "There's one clerk down there who is Republican and is trying to build the party," Mr. Hunter told my father. "She'll register anybody who'll say they're Republican." Daddy went down, found the woman, and successfully registered. He never forgot that and for the rest of his life was a faithful member of the Republican Party.

FINALLY, AFTER almost three years, my parents were married on February 12, 1954. Daddy was thirty and Mother twenty-nine, relatively old to be tying the knot in those days. Whenever I asked what had taken them so long, neither had a really good answer. I did not know until after my mother died in 1985 that my father had been married before. The woman had apparently told my father that she was pregnant when she was not. The resulting divorce or annulment—I am not sure which—was likely a chastening experience that prevented my father from wanting to quickly jump back into marriage.

At the time that Daddy married Mother, he was fully immersed in his pastoral responsibilities at Westminster Presbyterian Church in Birmingham. Granddaddy had chartered the church in 1944, but by 1952 he had resigned and moved to Mississippi with my grandmother, trying to revive a troubled congregation there. Westminster's new sanctuary had been completed and the church formally accepted into the presbytery by the beginning of my father's leadership. Maybe he just decided then that it was time to settle down.

So with both approving sets of parents present and Granddaddy Rice officiating, John and Angelena married in her parents' music room on February 12. Theresa, Alto, and Gee were the only others present. Mother wore a gray suit and spectacular smoke-gray shoes with rhinestones on them. There wasn't much

time—the wedding had to be squeezed in between Daddy's basketball game and an oratorical contest awards ceremony at which
Gee was receiving a scholarship. After the awards ceremony,
Daddy returned home to the church and Mother spent the night
at her parents'. She moved into the back of the church with her
new husband the next day.

Life wasn't so easy for the young bride, who became the
church congregation's new center of attention. Being a preacher's
wife ensures one of great scrutiny. And to be fair, Mother didn't
always exhibit much warmth with people outside of her family.
There was also some jealousy, particularly from the mothers of
marriageable-aged daughters in the congregation who'd hoped
the young preacher might become their son-in-law.

It probably didn't help that the young couple lived literally in
the back of the church. The little apartment consisted of a bedroom, kitchen, and bathroom connected by a small hallway to a
living room next to the pastor's office. Privacy was at a premium.
The church members had treated the living room as common
space before my mother moved in. They loved to gather after the
service, particularly when inclement weather drove them inside.

When my mother moved in and furnished the place with very
nice mahogany pieces, bought on time at Sokol's furniture store,
she put an end to the Sunday gatherings—or tried to, at least.
When members refused to honor her decision, Mother covered
her nice sofa in plastic and bought cheap chairs for the living
room. A minor scandal erupted in the church as members ex-
coriated Angelena for "not wanting them to sit on her furniture."
In retrospect I'm glad she was so protective of her possessions
because I am now fortunate enough to own those beautifully
maintained pieces.

In time, the congregation and Angelena began to make their peace. She stopped playing for Baptist churches and became the choir director at Westminster, which had been in dire need of one. Mother insisted that the church purchase an organ, which they did with the help of the Forbeses, a white family who owned the music store downtown and who adored my father. She formed a children's choir and started to direct holiday programs, endearing herself to parents with school-age kids. And soon my parents announced that Mother was pregnant and that the child was due in November. It is a good thing that I was not born early. The arithmetic worked well enough—nine months and two days—to prevent wagging tongues among nosy church elders.

My parents' marriage created one other complication. The school system had a nepotism rule that barred spouses from teaching at the same place. Daddy left the Fairfield system and got a job as a guidance counselor at Ullman High School in the Birmingham school district. Mother stayed at Fairfield. I once asked Daddy how they had made that decision at a time when the woman would have been expected to give up her job, not the man. He simply said that Mother had been there longer and it was only fair that he move. I still think that it was a very enlightened decision for that era.

BY ALL accounts my parents approached the time of my birth with great anticipation. My father was certain that I'd be a boy and had worked out a deal with my mother. If the baby was a girl, *she* would name her, but a boy would be named John.

Mother started thinking about names for her daughter. She

wanted a name that would be unique and musical. Looking to Italian musical terms for inspiration, she at first settled on Andantino. But realizing that it translated as "moving slowly," she decided that she didn't like the implications of that name. Allegro was worse because it translated as "fast," and no mother in 1954 wanted her daughter to be thought of as "fast." Finally she found the musical terms *con dolce* and *con dolcezza,* meaning "with sweetness." Deciding that an English-speaker would never recognize the hard *c,* saying "dolci" instead of "dolche," my mother doctored the term. She settled on Condoleezza.

Meanwhile, my father prepared for John's birth. He bought a football and several other pieces of sports equipment. John was going to be an all-American running back or perhaps a linebacker.

My parents planned to stay in the back of the church because there wasn't enough money to move. But Daddy convinced the congregation to paint the bedroom and bath, and Mother bought stuffed animals and a baby book to record every important event.

Tragically, these happy preparations were interrupted by the sudden death of Granddaddy Rice. Daddy and Alto had just made one of their periodic visits to my grandparents' in Mississippi, and right when they returned home, Daddy received a phone call from his mother. Granddaddy Rice had suffered a heart attack. They got back in the car and raced to Mississippi.

When they arrived, Granddaddy Rice was already dead, but my grandmother had been too shocked to do anything with the body, which was still lying on the floor. My father and uncle arranged to have Granddaddy's body brought back to Birmingham. A grand funeral was held for this exceptional man at Westminster Presbyterian, the last congregation that he had founded. My mother, seven months pregnant, played the organ, and my father officiated. The church was packed with people who had come from as far away as Louisiana.

My grandfather had been a giant in so many people's lives and in our family lore. He managed to get his college education and to educate his own children and many others as well. He never let anything get in the way of providing an intellectual environment for his family or pursuing the development of his own mind.

My father told me a story that seemed to sum up my grandfather's passion for learning. One day Granddaddy Rice came home very excited about a new purchase. It was during the Great Depression, and my grandmother was trying hard to manage expenses on their meager resources. My father remembered many days of eating bread sandwiches—bread with mayonnaise and nothing else. On Sundays Grandmother prepared "Sunday surprise," but there was no mystery since it was always red beans and rice with whatever creature Granddaddy and my father could fish from the creek.

Yet there was Granddaddy with nine leather-bound, gold-embossed books: the works of Hugo, Shakespeare, Balzac, and others. Each book began with a summary essay about the author and his work. My grandmother asked how much they had cost. Granddaddy Rice admitted they cost ninety dollars but told her not to worry because he had purchased them on time. They would only have to pay three dollars a month for the next *three years.* Grandmother was furious, but Granddaddy held his ground and refused to return the books. I am so grateful that he did not give in. One of the proudest days of my life was when my father gave me the surviving five volumes as I left for the ceremony to receive my PhD.

Granddaddy Rice died on September 14, precisely two months before I was born. I am told that he was thrilled when my mother became pregnant, saying that it would be really nice to have a child around the house. I deeply regret that I never knew him in the flesh, but I've always felt that I do know him in spirit. He has been a powerful guiding presence throughout my life. And I have those books: my bond with him. It is as if through them he has passed on to me the gift of transformation through education that he himself earned in the hardest of times and against very long odds.

CHAPTER FOUR

"Johnny, It's a Girl!"

M Y MOTHER thought that she felt labor pains on Friday night, November 12, and was rushed to the doctor. Dr. Plump, the black pediatrician who delivered most of the black babies in town, explained that it was probably just anxiety. He decided nonetheless to put Mother in the hospital, where she could rest comfortably.

The public hospitals were completely segregated in Birmingham, with the Negro wards—no private rooms were available—in the basement. There wasn't much effort to separate maternity cases from patients with any other kind of illnesses, and by all accounts the accommodations were pretty grim.

As a result, mothers who could get in preferred to birth their babies at Holy Family, the Catholic hospital that segregated white and Negro patients but at least had something of a maternity floor and private rooms. Mother checked into Holy Family that night.

Nothing happened on Saturday or early Sunday morning. Dr. Plump told my father to go ahead to church and deliver his sermon at the eleven o'clock service. "This baby isn't going to be born for quite a while," he said.

He was wrong. When my father came out of the pulpit at noon on November 14, his mother was waiting for him in the church office.

"Johnny, it's a girl!"

Daddy was floored. "A girl?" he asked. "How could it be a girl?"

He rushed to the hospital to see the new baby. Daddy told me that the first time he saw me in the nursery, the other babies were just lying still, but I was trying to raise myself up. Now, I think it's doubtful that an hours-old baby was strong enough to do this. But my father insisted this story was true. In any case, he said that his heart melted at the sight of his baby girl. From that day on he was a "feminist"—there was nothing his little girl couldn't do. I don't know if it was then or later that he decided that even if I could not be a linebacker, I could certainly learn to love football. Maybe the football he had bought for John wouldn't go to waste after all.

My mother and father plunged into parenthood with a vengeance. Early on they sought to build a good learning environment for me, reading stories to me every night until I was able to read myself. My mother was as determined to raise a musician as my father was to cultivate a sports fan. She bought my first piano when I was three months old, and I learned later that we would "play" songs together, Mother moving my fingers along the little keyboard.

Before I was one, my mother returned to teaching. There weren't any debates in my community about the relative merits of rearing children while working. Almost all of the women in my community worked, most as teachers. Teaching was such a prized profession that most who could teach did. There weren't many other options except perhaps nursing. Most men did the same, though occasionally they went to law or medical school.

There was a kind of hierarchy of employment among the school systems, the Birmingham public schools being the most sought after. The county schools, such as Fairfield, where my mother taught for the first few years of my life, were not as favored. I remember how thrilled she was when she finally landed a job at Western-Olin High School in Birmingham.

A white superintendent oversaw the entire Birmingham public school system, but there was also a director for the city's black schools, Dr. Carol W. Hayes, who, it is said, personally selected his teachers. It was a big day when families learned that their daughter or son had been accepted into the profession. The Birmingham schools' convocation for new teachers was quite an event, with beautifully dressed young black professionals— women in hats and gloves, men in suits and ties—attending a daylong orientation at the civic center. Occasionally it was a good place to meet a mate—my uncle Alto met his wife, Connie, at one such event in 1962. Put simply, there were no more respected figures in the community than teachers and principals.

Extended families provided a good child care alternative for these working parents. It was convenient that the length of the school day as well as vacations was roughly the same for parents who worked in the schools and for their children. But often grandparents filled in with kids who weren't yet school-age. I was dropped off by my parents at my maternal grandparents' house in the morning and picked up after school. There was no safer or more nurturing environment than the one provided by Grandmother and Granddaddy Ray.

WHEN I was almost four, my father persuaded the church to build a proper manse so that we could move out of Westminster. I have only a few memories of living in the back of the church, but I remember very well the whole process of building the small gray house on a corner lot at 929 Center Way Southwest. The manse was located about five minutes from the church in Birmingham's black middle-class neighborhood of Titusville.

My parents tried to involve me in family decision making from a very young age, and the impending family move was a perfect opportunity. There were so many decisions to make about paint colors and the functions that would be assigned to various rooms. I personally picked the pale green for the bathroom, the yellow for the kitchen, and a rich blue for my playroom. Mother decided on "Chinese" red for the living room. Since I was an only child and had no competition from siblings for space, I had a pink bedroom in addition to the playroom. But I was afraid to sleep in it alone, having shared the bedroom in the church with my parents. My bedroom was soon turned into a small den and a second bed was put in my parents' room. This was the arrangement for a few years until at about eight I declared the need for my own space and reclaimed my bedroom.

But then there was the question of what to do for a den. Again here was an opportunity to involve me in decision making. By now I was president of the family. We held an election every year. My father insisted on a secret ballot, but since my mother always voted for me, I was assured of victory. There were no term limits. My responsibilities included calling family meetings to decide matters such as departure times for trips, plans for decorating the house at Christmas, and other issues related to daily life. So I called a meeting, and after some discussion, we all agreed that the playroom should become the den.

The move to 929 Center Way had been one of the most exciting times in our lives and included the family's first TV purchase, a little thirteen-inch Zenith black and white set. We watched a lot of TV. I have many intellectual friends who either don't watch TV or pretend they don't. Some go so far as to refuse to own one. And I know that parents today restrict television watching for their kids.

My parents didn't set limits on how much TV I watched. To be fair, television was a lot more wholesome in the late 1950s. But there was more to it than that. I have always thought that it's harder to be the parent of an only child than to be an only child. Someone has to entertain the little one when night falls and playmates go home. In that regard, television was one of my parents' best friends. We watched TV together just about every night, and I often watched alone too.

The only black people regularly on TV were the characters on *Amos 'n' Andy*, and while we watched their antics, my parents went out of their way to point out and correct their butchered English. Mostly I watched cartoons such as *Popeye* and situation comedies such as *I Love Lucy. The Popeye Show* took place in a studio with Cousin Cliff, a big white man in a sailor suit, hosting an audience of schoolkids. Sometimes kids would bring their friends and celebrate a birthday on TV. The studio audience was all white, of course, until about 1962, when the show started devoting a few days each year to "Negro day." I actually got to go when I was about seven years old and one of my friends had her birthday party there. I remember finding the whole highly anticipated event rather disappointing. We drove up to Red Mountain, where Channel 13 was located, sat on bleachers in a studio, and went home. I never again held Cousin Cliff in high esteem.

My mother also made sure that I watched *Mighty Mouse,* in which the heroic mouse sang, "Here I come to save the day!" Mother explained that this was a form of opera in which dialogue is sung, not spoken. She seemed to find high culture in just about everything.

But my favorite show was *The Mickey Mouse Club,* which we watched as a family every day after school. All three of us would put on our mouse ears and sing, "M-I-C (See you real soon) . . . K-E-Y (Why? Because we like you) . . . M-O-U-S-E." It was a real family ritual, not to be interrupted by anything. One day Mr. Binham the insurance agent was in the living room pitching my parents on some new policy. He was the only white man that I can ever remember coming into our house in Titusville. In any case, it was about time to sing the Mickey Mouse song, and I was becoming agitated that my parents were otherwise occupied. Daddy politely told Mr. Binham that he'd have to wait. We put on our mouse ears and engaged in our family ritual. I felt very proud that my parents had put our time above whatever business it was they had with Mr. Binham. This small gesture was simply one of the many that communicated they always had time for me.

After *The Mickey Mouse Club* we would take a break from television for reading time and, as I became older, doing homework together. We would then tune in to the nationally televised news program *The Huntley-Brinkley Report*. My father would comment on each story, explaining the historical significance of big events. I remember watching John Glenn's historic mission to space, which preempted all other programming for the entire mission. For a while I wanted to be an astronaut, as did most of my friends. We'd load up our "space capsule" out in the backyard, with some lucky kid getting to be the astronaut and others being confined to earth as ground controllers.

But one of my most vivid childhood memories is the Cuban missile crisis in October 1962. We were glued to the set every evening during the thirteen-day standoff. It was a very scary time. We'd never bothered with a bomb shelter in the house, even at the height of the Cold War. But some of our friends did have them, fully stocked with provisions to survive a nuclear exchange. In school, we went through duck-and-cover drills. When the alarm sounded, all the children fell to the floor, huddling under their desks. My friends and I even played bomb shelter, crawling into the little space just beneath the house in response to a "nuclear attack."

But the standoff in Cuba was no drill. Because the missiles were deployed just ninety miles from the Florida coast, the newscasters reported, probably incorrectly, that Birmingham was in range. They showed big arrows pointing right at us. I could tell that my father was worried, and I realized that this was something my parents couldn't save me from. It was the first time that I remember feeling truly vulnerable.

Daddy explained that our country had never lost a war, and

he was sure we weren't going to lose this one. He was nevertheless visibly relieved when the Soviet ships turned around, ending the crisis. The whole episode had a surprisingly strong impact on me. I once told an audience of Cuban Americans that Fidel Castro had put the United States at risk in allowing those missiles to be deployed. "He should pay for it until he dies," I said. Even I was surprised by the rawness of that comment.

CHAPTER FIVE

"I Need a Piano!"

AFTER OUR move to 929 Center Way, my parents set about building a solid and enjoyable life for our family. Each day my father would drop me off at my grandparents' and Mother and Daddy would come together in the afternoon to pick me up. Granddaddy still worked a pretty full day, and my grandmother was a full-time homemaker. I'd "help" her around the house and watch soap operas with her. She loved *As the World Turns,* and I loved the commercials, especially for Tide and Mr. Clean, which made stains disappear right before your very eyes.

Sometimes Daddy would pick me up early to go to a high school football game at Rickwood Field, the somewhat dilapidated stadium at which black high school teams played their games and which the city of Birmingham today calls, with a touch of irony, "historic" Rickwood. According to Grandmother,

I would become so excited at the prospect of going to a game that I would pester her all day about the time. "When is it going to be two o'clock?" I would ask over and over. My exasperated grandmother finally showed me a clock and the position of the hands at 2:00 p.m. so that I could track the time myself. I guess I can thank football for helping me learn how to tell time.

But the activity that I enjoyed most was watching my grand-mother teach piano. Grandmother Ray had about twenty students, ranging from beginners to quite advanced pianists. Her lessons started at about three o'clock every day, and she taught for a couple of hours, charging twenty-five cents a session. When the students would leave, I'd go to the piano and pretend to play, banging at the keys and "reading" the music. Then I'd ask to take some sheet music home so I could "practice." Each day I'd leave with music, usually forgetting to bring it back the next day. To preserve her music collection, Grandmother finally gave me a regular book to take home. "Grandmother, this isn't music!" I told her.

Grandmother Ray decided that it was unusual for a kid to know the difference and asked my mother if she could start giving me piano lessons. I was three years old, and they wondered if it might be too early but decided to give it a try. Unlike the early experiment with first grade, this worked. I loved the piano.

Grandmother started every student in a series called *The Standard Revised* (I still don't know what exactly had been revised) that trained young fingers to do progressively more difficult things. Each student also learned a prescribed series of increasingly more difficult hymns, starting with "What a Friend We Have in Jesus." Because I was so young, I don't remember learning to read music, so today it is like a native language for me. This made it much easier to master sight-reading, something that I do well to this day.

My parents had bought a little electronic organ for our new house, and I'd play for hours when we got home. They claimed that it was hard to get me to do anything else, including read books or watch television. But a problem emerged as I began to play hymns: the little organ did not have enough keys. Each time that I wanted to play low notes in the bass, I was out of luck.

"I need a piano," I told my parents several months into my lessons. Daddy made me a deal. "When you can play 'What a Friend We Have in Jesus' perfectly, we will buy you a piano," he said. Everyone in the family has exactly the same memory of what transpired. The next day I went to my grandmother's and sat at the piano for eight hours, not even wanting to break for lunch. I practiced and practiced, and when my parents came to pick me up I played "What a Friend" *perfectly!*

As they'd do many times in my life, John and Angelena found a way not to disappoint. They didn't have the money to buy a piano, but they rented one the next day from Forbes Piano Company. By the end of the week I had a brand-new Wurlitzer spinet piano.

I became good at the piano very quickly and started to play publicly. Mother found opportunities for me to play at various church functions as well as citywide events. I played several pieces at the gathering of new teachers in 1959, where I was decked out in a gray polished cotton dress with pink flowers, black patent shoes with rhinestones, and, curiously, a white fur hat. I don't remember being nervous and have always thought that these early experiences helped me to overcome any sense of stage fright. My parents also called me into the living room to play whenever there was a visitor to the house. I hated that, perhaps sensing that the poor captive audience wasn't really all that interested in seeing little Condoleezza perform.

My mother reinforced my inclination toward music in multiple ways. She'd buy books written for children about the great composers. I imagined what it would have been like to meet Beethoven, who scribbled musical notations on tablecloths, or Bach, who fathered twenty children. My favorite story was about Mozart's life. I was totally enchanted by this man who had written so much and died so young at the age of thirty-five. I even developed a little crush on him, imagining myself as his wife, Constanze. Admittedly, this was a strange infatuation for a little black girl in Birmingham. Most of my friends were in love with Elvis Presley.

Mother also brought home records, which we would listen to together. One day, when I was about five years old, she brought home *Aïda,* the Giuseppe Verdi opera. My little eyes were as big as saucers as I listened to the "Triumphal March" for the first time, and I played the record over and over. And on Saturdays we listened to radio broadcasts of the New York Metropolitan Opera, "brought to you by Texaco." Opera and classical music were totally and completely my mother's domain. My father loved jazz but had no interest in or taste for classical music. Even so, he displayed admirable patience when my mother and I took charge of what was playing on the car radio as we ran errands on Saturday afternoon.

Daddy *was* the one, however, who taught me to dance. He'd put on a record by jazz singer Dinah Washington or play the big-band music of performers such as Duke Ellington. Then I would stand on his feet as he walked me through the box step or the fox-trot.

But Daddy's real territory was sports, and I took to it with great fervor. We watched the National Football League on television every Sunday after church. In those days, there was one game and no halftime studio show. Daddy wanted me to really understand football and would analyze the plays, explaining what the defense was doing to counter the offense and vice versa. As the season approached, we would go to the drugstore and buy magazines previewing the matchups. Our favorite was *Street & Smith's* pro football report.

Our team was the Cleveland Browns, and to this day I am a fan. This may seem puzzling given that I didn't visit Cleveland until the mid-1990s. The reason is simple: Birmingham had no NFL team when I was a child. It was one of only two cities in the South, the other being Memphis, that prohibited blacks and whites from playing together professionally. In 1954, Birmingham's city commission actually tried to amend the city's laws and relax its prohibition against integrated professional football teams. Outraged voters, however, reversed this decision by ballot initiative and reinstated segregation a few months later. By the late 1950s, the NFL was refusing to play in the South because segregation made it impossible for the teams to bring their players there.

My father told me that in the 1940s, before the League's epiphany, the first black players would stay with local families when games were played south of the Mason-Dixon Line since they couldn't stay in hotels or eat in restaurants. The last team to integrate was the Washington Redskins, which had no black players until 1962. Though Washington, D.C., was geographically the closest to us, my father hated the Redskins for their racist policies. They couldn't be our team.

But the Cleveland Browns had running back Jim Brown and the dominant teams of Paul Brown, their innovative coach. The Browns were on television almost every Sunday. Like my father, I was a Browns fan until Art Modell, the new owner, fired Paul Brown in 1963. At that point, I tore down the Cleveland Browns posters in my room and transferred my loyalties, temporarily, to the Baltimore Colts and Johnny Unitas. When Paul Brown founded the Cincinnati Bengals in 1968, I became a loyal fan. Many years later, when my friend Carmen Policy became the president of the "new" Cleveland Browns in 1999, I returned to my roots. The Browns—for better or worse—are my team today.

Each Thanksgiving, Daddy and I would watch the Detroit Lions, who by tradition played on that holiday every year. The next day, we would play the "Rice Bowl," a touch football game held at "Rice Stadium," known the rest of the year as the front yard. It was just the two of us, veering right and left and scoring touchdowns with the never-born John's football. Years later Mother got tired of being excluded from the fun and adopted a team of her own because she liked their uniforms. The undefeated 1972 Miami Dolphins would, at last, give my mother a reason to become a sports fan.

MY PARENTS may have doted on their only child a little more than their friends did, but they shared the same goals of other parents to provide a safe, nurturing, and stimulating environment for their kids. The task was hard and complex and yet straightforward at the same time. The hard part was obvious: Birmingham was the most segregated big city in America, and daily life was full of demeaning reminders of the second-class citizenship accorded to blacks. Whites and blacks lived in parallel worlds, their paths crossing uneasily in only a few public places.

So how can I say that there was a straightforward way for black parents to nurture their children? Well, ironically, because Birmingham was so segregated, black parents were able, in large part, to control the environment in which they raised their children. They rigorously regulated the messages that we received and shielded us by imposing high expectations and a determined insistence on excellence. It took a lot of energy for our parents to channel us in the right direction, but we became neither dispirited nor bitter.

The extended family, including grandparents, aunts, uncles, and cousins, provided the first layer of support and nurture. The community mentors were not far outside the family circle, and our little neighborhood of Titusville provided a strong network of black professionals who were determined to prepare their kids for productive lives. There were few single parents, and black men were a dominant presence in the community.

The schools too were completely segregated in Birmingham— there were no white teachers, no white students. Education in Alabama was well behind the rest of the country. For a number of years schools did not provide free textbooks to any student, black or white. Although my parents bought mine, some of my classmates were often forced to share one book. Sometimes teachers would pool their money to buy a few extras for their classes. The city put fewer resources into the black schools, so they were substandard in an already poor state system. But the teachers were dedicated and they produced remarkable results. In these circumstances, teachers could demand the best of their students without any racial overtones. Teachers had high expectations and were pretty tough on low performers. "To succeed," they routinely reminded us, "you will have to be twice as good." This was declared as a matter of fact, not a point for debate.

School principals were titanic figures, garnering respect and even awe. The most important of these men was R. C. Johnson, principal of Parker High School, the largest black school in the city. Johnson was Alma Johnson Powell's father and later Colin Powell's father-in-law. Ullman High, where my father taught, was run by George C. Bell, Alma's uncle. P. D. Jackson at Western-Olin High and even elementary school principals such as W. W. Whetstone and his successor Parnell D. Jones at Brunetta C. Hill, where I went to school, were household names. I remember well the grand funeral for Mr. Whetstone when he died suddenly of a heart attack. The service was on a scale that today would be accorded to an important political figure.

The churches provided a final pillar of support. There was no question as to where you should be on Sunday morning. There were no atheists and no agnostics in my middle-class community. The two largest churches, Sixth Avenue and Sixteenth Street, were Baptist. The Reverend John Goodgame Jr. at Sixth Avenue and the Reverend John H. Cross Jr. at Sixteenth Street Baptist were treated like celebrities in Birmingham.

The Presbyterian churches were quite a bit smaller, since fewer blacks belonged to that denomination. In fact, even the regional governing body of the Presbyterian Church was segregated. The church had split over slavery prior to the Civil War: the United Presbyterian Church in the USA in the North and south of the Mason-Dixon Line what was commonly called the

Southern Presbyterian Church. The southern branch of the church maintained separate black and white presbyteries. When the black presbytery came to meet in Birmingham, Westminster's members housed the participating ministers in their homes, and the women cooked sumptuous meals for them. There were, after all, few places for the visitors to stay and eat in our segregated city.

Birmingham's churches were competitive with one another for members and vied for the reputation of having the most compelling services and outstanding music. It also helped to have influential members, particularly those lured away from other congregations. But the churches were more than a place to worship on Sundays. They were also the locus of much of the community's social life and a safe place for kids. Later, some would also become centers of political mobilization.

All of these elements—extended family, community, schools, and churches—conspired together to convince me and my peers that racism was "their" problem, not ours. Whatever feelings of insecurity or inadequacy black adults felt in the appalling and depressing circumstances of Jim Crow Birmingham, they did not transfer it to us. For the children of our little enclave, Titusville, the message was crystal clear: We love you and will give you everything we can to help you succeed. But there are no excuses and there is no place for victims.

CHAPTER SIX

My Parents Were Teachers

THIS WORLD of family, community, school, and church was the larger environment in which I grew up. But my circumstances were also special because I was an only child. My parents were sensitive to this and strove to make sure that I had plenty of contact with other children. Apparently, I didn't want siblings. Mother told me that I asked repeatedly whether she intended to have any more kids, making clear that I would not be supportive of that decision. Most likely, my parents just decided that one was enough, since at the time of my birth Mother was already older by the standards of the day.

In lieu of siblings, I enjoyed several close friendships with

Vanessa Hunter, Margaret Wright, and Carole Smitherman; Carole was older but would play with us from time to time. I was also close to my cousins Lativia, Yvonne, and Albert. Our grandfather was insistent that the cousins spend time with one another, and even after Uncle Albert and his family moved to take up a congregation in Thomasville, Georgia, our families made certain to pay each other holiday and summer visits.

When I was about to turn five, my parents decided that it would be good to enroll me in kindergarten. My father thought that I needed to engage with other children in a more structured environment. Throughout my childhood, Mother always contended that I was well adjusted and got along well with other kids. My father, though, had a different take. He thought I was not at ease with other kids, and enrolling me in kindergarten became one of his many attempts over the years to make sure that I was competent socially. I struggled at times, exhibiting a bit of a thin skin and a tendency to retaliate when I felt slighted by my friends.

One such incident occurred when I was about seven. My neighborhood friends decided not to invite me to play with them for a couple of days in a row. I always had the latest dolls, and I loved to line them up and "teach" them, especially my favorite one, Baby Dear, who was a very good student.

So on the third day I gathered up all of my dolls and took them out to the front lawn, where, in view of my little friends, I began to play. When my friends came over, I informed them that I really didn't have time to spend with them, that they were at my house and these were my dolls and they should go home. My father said that he watched with pride but also with a bit of horror. On one hand, I proved able to stand up for myself in a pretty clever way. On the other, he didn't quite like the retaliatory impulse that came so naturally to me. He told me that it wasn't always good to try to get back at people, though he understood why I was hurt by what they had done. My friends and I eventually made up, of course, and years later my parents and I laughed about the incident. I told my father that I had received his message—but I also noted that my friends didn't ever do that to me again.

In any event, with an eye toward reining in my less sociable tendencies, my parents began in 1959 to look for a good kindergarten in which to enroll me. The school system didn't have kindergarten classes, but there were a few private alternatives, including at a local Catholic school. In fact, my father's church had sponsored a kindergarten a couple of years earlier. One of its students was Denise McNair, who was later killed in the bombing of the Sixteenth Street Baptist Church in 1963. But when that class went on to first grade, the kindergarten was disbanded.

Daddy decided to restart the program and recruited a retired teacher, Mrs. Louise Hunter, to teach the children. Mrs. Hunter was a member of Westminster and the widow of Frank Hunter, who'd helped my father register to vote in 1952. Several families signed their kids up for the program, which accepted children ages four to six.

The kindergarten program was largely academic, emphasizing reading, writing, and arithmetic. But there were also lots of fun activities as well, including stickball and singing. I loved kindergarten and eagerly went every day. I was a chubby little kid and sometimes bore the brunt of teasing about it. My head was kind of big, and some little kid started calling me "watermelon head." I retaliated with a comeback that I can't remember now, but in general, I got along better than expected with my classmates.

Florissa Lewis was my best friend in kindergarten. She remained so even after an incident of overstepping on my part that could have ended our friendship early. At the Easter program at church we were each assigned a speech to deliver. Mine was "Ring, Easter bells. Ring, ring, ring. Tell the glad tidings of Christ the risen King." Florissa was supposed to follow with her own part. I don't remember the words now. But I did on that day. When Florissa hesitated, I started delivering her speech too. My parents and hers were thoroughly embarrassed. My father explained that it would have been better to let Florissa have the time to see if she could remember her speech. "But Daddy, she wasn't going to remember it," I said. I thought I was just helping out.

After a year, we "graduated" from kindergarten in a ceremony complete with white robes and diplomas held in the church sanctuary. All of the other kids were on their way to first grade, but I wasn't. I was very sensitive about this and didn't want the other children to know. The problem was that I would not turn six until November, too late to meet the October 31 cutoff set by the school system.

My parents were determined to see that I not miss an entire year of school so that I would not fall behind in my education. They tried to get the school system to count my time in kindergarten and let me "test" into first grade. The Board of Education would not budge, so they came up with another idea. Perhaps I could "test" into second grade the following year. Having received permission for this unusual maneuver, they set about making certain that I would pass the test.

My mother decided to take a year's leave from teaching to coach me in preparation for the exam. Years later when the home-schooling movement became more visible, I belatedly realized that I had been a part of it, if only in an ad hoc way. Mother was very systematic about my school day. We'd get up and see Daddy off to work and then start "school." She ordered the first- and second-grade texts in math, science, and reading and took me through them in a very rigorous fashion. I'd take tests every week to chart our progress. This flexible schedule also allowed time to practice piano, and as a result, I advanced significantly during this time.

Occasionally, if I did well in my schoolwork, we would knock off a little early and go shopping in downtown Birmingham. One such trip yielded my first Barbie doll, dressed in the iconic black zebra-striped bathing suit. But for the most part, my mother was all business and very demanding.

I didn't mind having my mother teach me at home, except for one thing: I wanted to be like the other kids who would go to school every morning and come home at the end of the day. I felt so different and I hated it. So I invented a story that I was going to another school outside the community. Each morning as the kids were leaving, I'd get my books and go outside, pretending to wait for a ride to school. When they returned, I'd "come home." This subterfuge didn't last long because the other kids began to ask too many questions about my other school. My parents didn't particularly like this deception, including my desire to fit in, and convinced me that I had to tell the truth. So I admitted to my friends that I was studying at home. "Next year," I proclaimed, "I will be in second grade!" I was very proud when I passed the test, scoring at a third-grade level of competency in arithmetic and at a fifth-grade level in reading. I entered Lane Elementary School as a six-year-old second grader.

Though my neighborhood school was Center Street Elementary, I was enrolled in Lane Elementary because it was across the street from Ullman High, where Daddy worked. He would drop me off and then, at the end of the shorter elementary school day, leave work early and pick me up. After that I'd stay with him, doing my homework in his office (he was the guidance counselor) and getting to know the "big kids."

After launching me academically, Mother returned to work. Each morning she'd carpool to school with other teachers. She had received a credential to teach science and was assigned to Western-Olin High School. Parker High School was the flagship black school, located in mostly middle-class Smithfield. Ullman High School was the other prized place to work, located a few blocks from our house in middle-class Titusville.

Western-Olin was located in Ensley, squarely in the middle of steel-mill country and known as tough territory. The students were mostly from the projects, and knife fights and violence inside and outside school were frequent. Even in those days there were a fair number of single mothers and children being raised by grandparents. Ensley was not considered a desirable place to work. I remember my father's concern about Mother's working in such a tough environment.

Western-Olin was one of two schools that had a divided curriculum. Some students attended Western, the academic high school, full-time, while others would complete a half day of academics and spend the balance of the afternoon in vocational programs at Olin. The campuses were collocated, but it was as if the students lived in parallel universes. The vocational school students were seldom encouraged to even think of attending college; they were just expected to acquire minimal competence in reading and arithmetic and then specialize in a skill such as cosmetology or auto mechanics.

Needless to say, this produced some "attitude problems" in the student body. Mother believed that the vocational kids weren't taken seriously enough and that this, in part, produced the behavior problems that were so prevalent. She went out of her way to serve these kids, making some her "assistants" and giving them tasks such as cleaning the science lab so that they'd feel their contributions were valued. She would then make sure that they received certificates at graduation. These kids likely would have received no honors at graduation but for those that my mother invented. I remember one student in particular, a young woman who was tall and heavyset with dyed flaming red hair, who had built a track record of chronic behavioral issues. Each day she would come to work for Mother, eventually becoming trusted enough to open and close the science lab with her own key. She and my mother cried when she graduated, having beaten the odds that were clearly stacked against her.

Mother also believed that the arts could make a difference for these kids and for this underprivileged community as a whole. In 1962 she decided to produce a full-scale operetta with the students. The kids performed *Chenita,* a story of a Gypsy family, which used the music of Franz Liszt. The next year they were much more ambitious and performed George Gershwin's *Porgy and Bess.* The lead actress in both productions was a student named Carol Watkins. Carol remembers how my mother stood up for her when some of the teachers thought her skin too dark for the roles. "I don't care about her color," Mother said. "She can really sing."

Rehearsals would start just after Christmas for a performance in the spring. Parents were required to buy the material for the costumes, which were made in sewing classes. If a student couldn't afford the fabric, the teachers pitched in and purchased it. The scenery was made in the carpentry shop.

These events were always exciting for my family. As the production approached, Mother was at the school almost every evening, and I would often go to the rehearsals. Aunt Connie, who was also a teacher at Western-Olin, assisted my mother. The shows were on Friday and Saturday nights, and I got to take Friday off from school to help Mother with the final preparations. Parents, grandparents, students, and the rest of the community would show up for the performance, dressed in their finest as if they were attending the Metropolitan Opera.

My mother's productions were more elaborate than most but not unlike what was going on throughout the Birmingham public schools. These segregated schools were determined to provide these kinds of opportunities to develop their students' artistic talents. The centerpiece of these efforts was the role of instrumental music and band. Today everyone marvels at the extraordinary band performances of historically black colleges such as Grambling or Florida A&M. This tradition ultimately traces its roots, however, to the commitment of elementary schools of the segregated South to early band instruction.

Band was an important part of the curriculum. In addition to attending a formal class period during the school day, band members would practice after school during both the marching band season in the fall and the concert season in the spring. As band members, students were required to read music. There is a scene in the recent movie *Drumline* about a black college band that drives home this point. The instructor learns that his young and exceptionally talented drummer cannot read music, and the teacher insists that he learn to do so. While it's true that many great musicians play by ear and cannot read music, this was not sufficient for the more structured programs in black Birmingham. Learning to read music well was the most important task.

I joined the Lane Elementary School band. Obviously, there was no place for a pianist in a marching band, but I read music and easily qualified. The lingering question was what instrument to play. I wanted to learn the flute, but my father believed an old wives' tale that doing so too early in life would distort the shape of one's lips. My parents suggested the bells (also called the glockenspiel), which had the advantage of being very much like playing the piano using a mallet. I wasn't convinced until my father told me that the bells could be heard above every other instrument in the band.

With the band, the excellent choirs and glee clubs, plays, and variety shows, students in Birmingham's black schools had many opportunities to perform. The music teacher was always one of the best-known and most-valued members of the faculty. In some cases they were legends, such as Mrs. Gregory Durr White at Ullman High, who also taught many of the neighborhood's piano students. No one saw these activities as extracurricular or add-ons. They were an essential part of transforming students into more cultured people with well-developed artistic talents.

The performances were also occasions for the community to come together. A play or concert at one of the high schools was a highly anticipated social event. So too were the periodic visits of acclaimed choirs and bands from the historically black colleges. The best-known choir was the Fisk Jubilee Singers, but almost every college had one. We'd travel to Stillman College in

Tuscaloosa for special performances from artists such as the great black opera singer Marian Anderson in 1964. These activities were a key part of our social life at a time when it wasn't possible to go to a concert downtown or even to a proper movie theater. They were an important and satisfying element of our parallel universe in segregated Birmingham.

CHAPTER SEVEN

Something in the Water

T HE OTHER great social outlet was the church. My father's church, Westminster Presbyterian, was centrally located on Sixth Avenue not very far from downtown Birmingham. The neighborhood was solidly middle-class, and this was reflected in its congregation. There was one doctor and one lawyer, but the bulk of the membership consisted of teachers.

Services were formal and short, no more than an hour. Black Presbyterian services were a world apart from the emotional and high-energy services of the Baptist churches. The term sometimes applied to Presbyterians, "frozen chosen," would have described black church-goers as well as their white counterparts. Gospel music was rare, replaced with anthems written by composers from Bach to the modern, mostly white ones. There was no "call and response," where the preacher would say, for instance, "Do you hear me?" and the congregation would reply, "I hear you." There wasn't even a stray "amen."

I don't mean to make the services sound boring. In fact, they were beautiful, even inspiring. Mother was the organist and choirmaster, pushing the small choir to sing ever more complex anthems. My favorites, "God So Loved the World" and "The Heavens Are Telling" from Haydn's *Creation,* are still standard fare in most large Presbyterian churches. But they were a stretch for the Westminster Presbyterian Church choir, and it would sometimes take many weeks to learn them. Yet the choir usually managed to do a respectable job, and it grew in size owing to the pride people felt at being able to sing sophisticated music.

The Christmas and Easter holidays were particularly busy and enjoyable, celebrated with plays for the children and special music that took months to prepare. I loved to go to the church and help decorate, particularly on Easter, when the altar was adorned with three crosses that my uncle Alto built in his shop. There was a glorious sunrise service at six o'clock and then the regular one at eleven.

I didn't care much, though, for the Easter egg hunt the Saturday before. I thought it was kind of pointless to hide eggs and then try to find them. I was particularly put off when I caught my parents putting an egg in my basket so that I would not be embarrassed if I failed to find one. I asked them to stop doing that, protesting that I was smart enough to find a stupid egg if I wanted to. I just didn't want to.

My father was a terrific preacher, though he rarely raised his voice above a normal speaking tone. "He was known as a pastor who made you think before you could feel," to quote one of his elders. This "lecture style" of preaching brought in many new members, particularly teachers who identified with my father's more cerebral approach to his ministry.

I can still remember some of Daddy's sermons, and some of the outlines for them have survived. He preached often about the uncertain times for the disciples leading up to and after Christ's crucifixion. He had great sympathy for Thomas and the other disciples who were so unnerved by Christ's death and disbelieving of the resurrection. One of Daddy's most controversial sermons involved a rather nuanced approach to Judas, who, according to my father, felt that *he* had been betrayed. He told the very human story of these men who had given up everything to follow Christ and the confusion, anger, and fear they felt when it turned out that Christ could be killed like a common criminal. Their skepticism about what would happen after Christ's death was, he said, understandable. Daddy used the stories to say that questions and doubts were to be expected. Jesus would not condemn his followers for these human responses to the mystery of faith.

From the time I was very young I loved to engage in theological debates with my father. This started at the age of four when I insisted that my father was mispronouncing the name Job. It was the book of "Job," I insisted, not "Jobe"! My father, ever tolerant of my dissent, argued patiently and I guess decided that eventually I would know better. Our theological debates became a bit more sophisticated over the years. We exchanged views on everything from the teachings of Paul, about which my father had some reservations, to the horrors of Revelation. We discussed the relationship between the angry God of retribution in the Old Testament and the God of redemption in the New. I always felt that my father wanted me to use my intellect to help build my faith. I was never told to simply accept anything on the face of it, and my constant questions were always engaged. Because my father never made reason and faith enemies of each other, my religious conviction was strengthened. I am grateful for that because in the many intellectual environs in which I have found myself, I have never suffered the crisis of faith that so many do. I have always *believed,* fully and completely. My challenge has been to avoid complacency in my faith and to remember to struggle with its meaning as my father taught me to do.

Westminster grew rapidly under Daddy's leadership, with new members joining frequently. Toward the end of the Sunday service there was a "call," where the pastor stands in front of the congregation and invites "anyone who has decided today to declare for Jesus" to come forward and join the church. This is still done in many Presbyterian churches today. I hated that moment because it seemed really awkward if no one came forward. Therefore, when I first learned, at about seven, that Christian doctrine expected Christ's return to earth, I had a good idea. I prayed each night that if Christ was coming again anyway, perhaps he could come to Westminster. I knew that membership would soar if he did.

In fact, my father built the church in more conventional ways. He knew that it was important to make his church more than a place of worship on Sunday. Most churches had a social component, but Daddy's church was ahead of its time, providing a place to gather all week long. Choir practice was on Wednesdays, Bible study on Thursdays, and on Tuesdays and Thursdays church members who were teachers offered tutoring in algebra, science, and foreign languages. Mrs. Margaret Cheatham, who was my father's colleague at Ullman, was recruited to tutor and attended services at Westminster, though she did not join the church for several years.

Dr. Duval, a white dentist, would come to the church once a month to conduct checkups and perform dental work. There were also typing classes and etiquette lessons that taught young people such things as which fork to use at the dinner table. Friday night was "flop night," a time when kids could come to the church for everything from chess lessons to movies, watched on a projector borrowed from the school. In the summer we looked forward to church-sponsored cookouts as well as volleyball matches and track meets.

These activities were open to the whole community, not just to the church members. This was somewhat controversial, particularly when Daddy insisted on including the kids from Loveman Village, the government housing project behind the church. There was considerable class stratification in segregated black Birmingham. I remember being told by my mother, for instance, that my friends from Lane Elementary could come to visit me but I could not go to visit them. Their neighborhood was "too rough."

Many of our church members were not comfortable with Daddy's outreach activities. I recall one attempt at inclusion that backfired when during a picnic some of the kids from Loveman Village were caught teaching children from the congregation to shoot craps behind the church. "Reverend Rice, I told you they weren't ready to be with us," an elder told my father. Daddy came home and told Mother about the episode. He was really hurt and defended his program. But he was always struggling to reconcile his desire for the broadest outreach with what his church's middle-class membership would tolerate.

Relations were sometimes very strained when my father pushed church members beyond their comfort zone. At one meeting of the Board of Elders, the powerful governing committee in Presbyterian churches, members decided to deny money for Daddy's "missionary work." My father became so angry that he turned over a table and stormed out, my uncle Alto trailing behind. Daddy was a big man and could be physical in his expression of anger, though never with my mother or with me.

Daddy decided to seek support among the women of the church, getting the Presbyterian Women's Circle to fund his activities. Stalwart supporters such as Mrs. Florence Rice (a cousin by marriage), Mrs. Hattie Conrad, Mrs. Lillian Ford, and Mrs. Marie Bracy helped him overcome opposition. These women shared his vision of the centrality of a ministry for children—everybody's children. Daddy, in turn, tried to get the presbytery to ordain these women as elders. When the Presbyterian Church of the late 1950s refused to do so, he created a special category for them. They were allowed, for instance, to serve communion, likely in violation of church policy. He didn't ask permission, and in the end, no one objected.

My father's somewhat controversial youth ministry became central to Westminster. The links between the church and the community were nurtured through the Youth Fellowship program and a club that Daddy formed for young black men, the Cavaliers, who were teenage boys with whom my father met weekly. They wore yellow hats with "Cavaliers" written in purple across the front. Daddy involved several other men from the church and the community in what is now called mentoring.

Youth Fellowship met every Sunday afternoon at four in the church with social activities for high school kids. At its height there were more than forty students. My father recruited Ms. Julia Emma Smith, an unmarried parishioner, to be his partner in the program. They arranged panel discussions and tutoring sessions as well as a one-week summer leadership conference at Stillman College.

Daddy wanted the kids to know that there was a bigger and different world outside of their immediate environment. He befriended a rabbi and took his students to Temple Beth-El or Temple Emanu-El to learn about Judaism. The temple was not in use on Sundays, so the Youth Fellowship would go there to listen to lectures arranged specifically for them. Looking back on it, I rather doubt that the congregation at Beth-El or Emanu-El realized that a group of black high school students was taking instruction at their synagogue. I later learned that blacks were not the only ones targeted in Birmingham; fortunately, a heavy rain doused a burning fuse leading to fifty-four sticks of dynamite intended to blow up Beth-El in 1958.

The young people of Westminster also participated in an "exchange" program with a large white church, South Highland Presbyterian, during the early 1960s, when segregation was still almost total. The minister and my father decided to do this despite trepidation on the part of both congregations. According to several participants, such as Harold Dennard, a retired Birmingham teacher, their parents were wary of having their children attend these excursions but trusted Reverend Rice to take care of their kids. Harold remembers that the white kids sometimes seemed to come without their parents' knowledge. It appears that the exchanges happened only a few times, likely owing to growing opposition in the congregations. The soon-to-come violence also put a damper on the idea.

In addition to these educational and cultural opportunities, my father could also provide something that the Baptists couldn't: dances and parties. Some members complained that the church should not be used for dances. Daddy countered that the church was the safest possible place for kids to have their parties.

Moreover, parents trusted him, and the dances he arranged were always heavily attended. One night some of the kids decided to hold a house party and tell their parents that Reverend Rice would be there, which was not true. When Daddy found out just before the party was to take place, he went to the students and told them to recant their story or he would go individually to their parents and explain the truth. I rode in the car with him as he confronted each student. Playing the role of a vindictive little sister, I lobbied to have him tell their parents. Daddy refused, saying that it was important that the students come clean themselves. He left it to the parents to discipline their children. He never had that problem again.

In fact, Youth Fellowship and the Cavaliers were vehicles for my father's educational evangelism. Much like his father before him, he would insist on strong academic performance and counsel each student toward college. Daddy's "kids" turned out to be a remarkable lot.

Before he died, Daddy talked about writing a book called *Something in the Water* that would reflect on the exceptional achievements of the young people with whom he had worked. Freeman Hrabowski III (a black teenager, apparently with Polish ancestry) lived at the corner of our street. My father called him his "little math genius." Freeman went to college at fifteen and received a PhD in higher education administration and statistics from the University of Illinois at Urbana-Champaign. He now serves as president of the University of Maryland, Baltimore County, where he became well known for his pioneering work in inspiring young black students, particularly men, to pursue careers in math and the sciences.

The National Merit Scholarship organization named Sheryl McCarthy one of the first National Achievement Scholars in Birmingham. I remember a Good Friday service at which Sheryl, still in high school, wrote and delivered a "newscast" of the crucifixion. She ended her commentary on Christ's death on the cross with a beautifully constructed line that I'll never forget. "Well," she said, "I'm going to sign off. The weather is starting to look pretty threatening. Looks like a real storm is moving in. It has been a day to remember." Sheryl was a brilliant writer and went on to become an award-winning journalist at *Newsday* and the New York *Daily News* as well as a national correspondent for ABC News.

Amelia Rutledge was studious and quiet. She was the valedictorian at Ullman and eventually earned a PhD in medieval studies from Yale. She now teaches at George Mason University.

Larry Naves, a member of the Cavaliers, became chief judge for the Denver District Court in Colorado after my father recruited him for the University of Denver. Mary Kate Bush finished Fisk magna cum laude, received an MBA from the University of Chicago, and became a Treasury official in the Reagan administration as well as the first black woman to serve as the U.S. government's representative on the board of the International Monetary Fund. Carole Smitherman served as president of the Birmingham City Council and became the first black woman to serve as a circuit court judge in Alabama.

These were the children of middle-class Titusville. But the

success stories extended to less advantaged kids. Gloria Dennard became director of library media services at the Jefferson County Board of Education. I cried at Daddy's memorial service when Gloria said that but for my father's intervention with her parents, who were not college-educated, she would never have gone on to college. Barbara S. Allen, who served as interim superintendent of the Birmingham public schools, was one of the children of Loveman Village whom my father sent to college. She too says that it was my father who insisted that she get a degree. And Harold Jackson, a Pulitzer Prize–winning journalist and editorial editor at the *Philadelphia Inquirer,* was a Youth Fellowship kid from the Village. As the next-to-youngest of the five Jackson brothers, Harold credited Daddy for laying the spiritual foundation for his life and inspiring his older siblings to pursue a college education.

These were just a few of the scores of teachers, doctors, lawyers, and other professionals who grew up at that time in deeply segregated Birmingham. They clearly took the right messages from their parents, teachers, and mentors such as my father and mother who emphasized excellence and hard work and never tolerated victimhood.

These future professionals were, in turn, role models for younger kids like me. I wanted so much to be one of the "big kids." My father would always say of Mary Bush, "That little Bush girl is pretty, and smart too." I wanted to be Mary Bush. When Sheryl McCarthy won a National Achievement Scholarship, I wanted to be Sheryl McCarthy. When Amelia Rutledge was voted valedictorian at Ullman, I pretended to be the valedictorian. And whenever someone went off to college, I'd pretend to be on my way too.

Over the years, I have come to understand that it must have been much tougher for these older kids to stay focused and positive. I was very young in segregated Birmingham and perhaps easier to insulate from its negative influences. But these teenagers were well aware of their circumstances. They must have felt the sense of injustice and harm more intensely than those of us who were younger. That they still succeeded and internalized the positive messages of their teachers and parents is a great testament to their focus and perseverance.

CHAPTER EIGHT

School Days

BECAUSE I so wanted to emulate the older kids, my parents found it rather easy to discipline me. I can only remember being spanked once. That was when I ignored my parents' order not to climb up on a chair to get my Halloween costume from the top shelf of the closet. I almost fell, and my father had had enough. Usually, though, they only had to say something about being "disappointed" in me. I hated that phrase because I did not want to let them down. They could also say simply, "You're acting like a child." I hated that even more. Perhaps as an only child I was driven to be more like the adults with whom I spent so much time. I even refused to eat the "child's plate" at A. G. Gaston's, the only nice black restaurant in town. And when we went to the Presbyterian ministers' retreat in Tennessee's Great Smoky Mountains in 1959, I insisted that my parents pay full price for my meal when the cashier tried to discount it. Obviously, "You're acting like a child" was a real insult.

In fact, my childhood was quite normal. I liked but didn't love school. When Lane Elementary closed after third grade, I enrolled at Brunetta C. Hill. Again, it was not in my neighborhood, but my parents chose it because my uncle taught there. After school he would take me to my grandmother's, where I would stay until my parents could pick me up on the way home.

I was taught by superb teachers, particularly in fourth and fifth grade, where Mrs. Hagood and Mrs. Colquitt were able to convince me that I really was good at math. Mrs. Hagood even played to our competitive instincts by seating in the front of the class those students who did best on the weekly test. This made me a lot more careful about avoiding errors because I really didn't like being in the back of the room.

My parents were very involved too, mostly for the good. Like their friends, they were members of the PTA and attended the meetings. They checked my report card and discussed my progress with me at the end of each grading period. They were especially interested in my conduct grade because disrespect for my teachers was simply not tolerated. My parents were, after all, teachers. But occasionally when they thought that I had been treated unfairly they took my side. One day the home economics instructor sent me home with a note saying that I was uncooperative. I had simply observed that the project of making bathroom curtains from towels with lace sewn on them seemed rather ridiculous. "You can buy them at Sears," I said, "and they look much better." My mother told the teacher that I had a point but insisted, nevertheless, that I make the curtains.

Then there was the time that I received a C in music. My

mother was furious and confronted the music teacher, Mrs. Gertie Battle, who backed down and changed my grade to a B. She wouldn't give me an A, though, saying that she expected more of me since I was such a talented musician. I later suspected there might be something more to this when I learned that my mother and Mrs. Battle had disliked each other since college.

Though I did well, I have to admit that my study habits left something to be desired, given my strong tendency toward procrastination. Unfortunately, my parents, eager to help me succeed, probably reinforced this problematic instinct. One morning when I was in third grade, I woke up and realized that I'd forgotten to do a class assignment for that day. The task was to make a book with pictures that illustrated the story we were reading that week. Perhaps my parents should have just let me face the consequences. But they didn't. The three of us rushed around, cutting pictures from magazines, books, even the encyclopedia in order to finish the assignment. I got an A. All through school and college I was given to last-minute completion of my assignments and cramming for tests in all-night sessions. I'm afraid that procrastination remains a problem for me to this day. It's one of the few bad habits that my parents failed to cure me of when they had the chance.

I know this admission stands in contrast to the image that has emerged of me as a "grind"—someone who early in life studied all the time and did assignments well ahead of due dates. That description better fit my best friend, Velda Robinson, whom I adored but envied for her organized approach to her schoolwork.

The fact is, I was always more interested in other activities such as piano. My parents were especially concerned that I did not love to read, as they did. They enrolled me in every book club known to man, but the books would just pile up unread. At one point they resorted to something called "Classic Comics," which were comic-book versions of works by authors such as Daniel Defoe and Mark Twain. I read principally when my schoolwork compelled me to do so. Eventually I discovered biography and found that I loved to read the stories of real—as opposed to fictional—lives. That is true to this day, though I still feel outmatched by the volume of books my friends and colleagues consume.

Despite my uneasy relationship with reading, my parents thought that I was a genius; they even arranged for me to take an IQ test at the age of six to prove it. When my score came back at 136—good but not Mensa level—they were convinced something was wrong with the test. But when I told them how hard I had found it to match the squares, circles, and stars with the correct hole in the puzzle, they calmed down. They hid whatever disappointment they might have felt at discovering that their daughter was, after all, a fairly normal little girl.

Yet there was no shortage of opportunities to develop the strengths that I did have and even some that I didn't. My Scouting career, for instance, was not wholly satisfactory. I was a Brownie and then a Girl Scout for a few years, and I was doing pretty well—until we got to the part about camping. One trip to the wilderness outside of Alabama convinced me that I was not the outdoors type. In fact, the mosquitoes, heat, and warm Kool-Aid were enough to make me call my mother and tell her I wanted to go home. My parents picked me up, and to this day I've never tried camping again.

There were certain school activities I would have liked to do, but my parents quickly vetoed those ideas. When organizers of the school variety show cast me as one of the Supremes singing "Stop! In the Name of Love," my father decided that it would be undignified. Instead my parents hired Mrs. Clara Varner, the cosmetology teacher at Ullman, to teach me a tap-dancing routine to "Sweet Sue (Just You)" and "Sweet Georgia Brown." I was dressed in a blue leotard with tap shoes and a top hat, which my uncle had spray-painted gold. The routine was awful, but I gamely went out and performed. My father stood on the side of the stage, just in view of the audience, his arms folded sternly so no one would laugh. Given his imposing size, no one did. The end of my performance was greeted with applause. I was just glad it was over.

Outside of school, my parents provided me with a prodigious number of extracurricular opportunities. In addition to piano, I took all kinds of lessons: ballet, gymnastics, and even baton twirling, of all things. My mother decided that every well-bred young girl should speak French, so when I was eight my parents hired Mrs. Dannetta K. Thornton, who'd earned a master's degree in Romance languages and taught at Ullman, to give me French lessons on Saturdays. She transformed her basement into a French "salon" with all sorts of French pictures and artifacts. I liked Mrs. Thornton, but I didn't care much for the French language. Nonetheless, I kept plowing ahead and acquired enough of a foundation to continue my studies through high school and well into college. My parents also thought it important that I learn to type, "just in case you need to know how," and enrolled me in Saturday lessons with a teacher down the street.

In time, my mother and her friends formed a chapter of a club called Tots and Teens to structure the many lessons they were providing to their children. In addition to field trips, parties, and modeling lessons for the girls, the organization offered cultural programs in music and art appreciation. I learned much later that my mother and her friends had formed Tots and Teens because there had been a disagreement with the leadership of Jack and Jill, the oldest black children's organization in America. Ask almost any black person my age whose family was upper-middle-class and you will learn that they belonged to Jack and Jill. I do not know for sure, but I suspect that our families in Titusville lacked the blue-blood credentials to be welcomed into Jack and Jill. The local ladies were highly critical of Jack and Jill and determined to do everything better.

I also played several sports. My friends contend that I was always a little lady in starched dresses, but I remember myself as bit of a tomboy who loved to tumble and run around. I ruined more than a few of those starched dresses, much to my mother's dismay and my father's delight. I also discovered that my parents' bed made a very nice trampoline. My folks tolerated my acrobatics as long as I jumped on the bed only when supervised. But they put an end to this when I fell off the bed during one of my "routines" when they weren't looking.

Trying to cope with my excessive energy, my dad tried to interest me in organized sports and finally found one that I liked: bowling. He loved to bowl, and when Star Bowl opened in the early 1960s it became a regular stop for us on Saturdays. Usually Daddy would bowl with his friends from church and school early in the morning, and then there would be lessons and tournaments for the kids. Star Bowl kept its premises clean and had a recreation room that became a favored place to hold birthday parties and even an occasional wedding reception. In segregated

Birmingham, gathering spaces were at a premium, so Star Bowl was a welcome addition.

I didn't, however, learn to swim. When I was six, I swam a few times, but the next spring, Mother said that there would be no lessons. In late 1961, Eugene "Bull" Connor, Birmingham's commissioner of public safety, had decided to close all recreational facilities rather than integrate them under court order. Not until I was twenty-five and living in California did I finally take swimming lessons. I suspect that there are a lot of black and white kids from Birmingham who learned to swim late in life thanks to Bull Connor.

The fact is, as hard as they tried, our parents could only partially succeed in building a fully adequate and parallel social structure. The time would always come when the children of Birmingham had to face the realities of segregation. For my friend Deborah Cheatham Carson it was when she asked if she could go to Kiddieland, an amusement park that her family passed on the way to her grandmother's house. Her father did not want to tell her that she couldn't go because she was black. So he said that Kiddieland wasn't good enough for her and that they were going to Disneyland instead. He then scraped together enough money to fulfill his promise.

One of my earliest exposures to segregation came when our family went to downtown Birmingham at Christmastime to see Santa Claus. Only about five years old, I overheard my father commenting that Santa seemed to be treating the black children differently from the white ones. My past encounters with Santa Claus hadn't been the best anyway. When I took one look at this big white man with a beard—likely the first one I had seen up close—I slowly pulled away, eyeing him suspiciously. My parents had to intervene to get me to finish telling him what I wanted for Christmas.

But on this particular day, the Santa in question had been putting the white kids on his knee and holding the black children away from him, keeping them standing. "If he does that to Condoleezza," Daddy said to Mother, "I'm going to pull all of that stuff off him and expose him as just another cracker." I fearfully went forward, not knowing what to expect. Perhaps Santa felt the vibes from my father because he put me on his knee, listened to my list, and said, "Merry Christmas!" All's well that ends well. But I never forgot how racially charged that moment felt around, of all things, Santa Claus.

CHAPTER NINE

Summer Respite

THE ONLY break from segregation came when we left Birmingham, which tended to be in the summer. When we would visit my grandmother and Aunt Theresa in Baton Rouge, we took the train, which provided integrated facilities.

We'd board the Silver Comet at about five in the evening in Birmingham, eat in the dining car, and sleep overnight in a bedroom berth. I can still taste the pudding served in heavy silver ice cream cups and feel the excitement of getting into bed as the train rushed along the tracks. But when we returned to Birmingham, the only place to eat out was A. G. Gaston's restaurant, and Mother didn't like to eat there because it was next door to a funeral home.

Once in a while we'd travel to Atlanta, about 150 miles away, where there was a wider variety of black restaurants and a nice movie theater. I can remember seeing Jerry Lewis' *The Nutty Professor* on one such occasion, being treated to dinner at Pasquale's, and then driving home since there was really no place to stay.

In 1959, my father decided to start graduate school. He wanted out of the ministry and into college work and began to pursue a master's degree in student personnel administration. The University of Alabama wasn't an option since it was segregated. As a result, many black professionals of my father's generation received their advanced degrees from midwestern or northern schools. Daddy learned that New York University had a fine program, and in the summer of 1959 and again in 1960, we packed up the family car and drove to New York City.

The problem was that there was nowhere for blacks to stay or eat until you reached Washington, D.C. The only option was a picnic lunch of fried chicken, pork chops, bread, and potato chips to eat in the car. Mother would get up very early and prepare the feast. We'd leave before daylight, hoping to make it out of the deepest South before dark. This was in the days before the interstate highway system was completed, and for a black family some of the roads in Georgia and South Carolina could be pretty scary.

When we reached Washington, D.C., we were all excited to be staying in a new chain of hotels called Holiday Inn. The rooms were hardly luxurious, but they were clean and it was a relief to have a bathroom. My parents, particularly my mother, were not too keen to stop at the gas-station restrooms for "coloreds" because they were almost always putrid and foul-smelling. If we couldn't find a reasonably clean bathroom when nature called, we just, shall I say, went in nature.

New York was fun. We ate at Howard Johnson's almost every night and went to the movies, including one that everyone was buzzing about, *Ben Hur*. We stayed in a nice hotel called the Manhattan until we started to run out of money. For a few days we stayed at the house of my mother's cousin Kate in Orange, New Jersey. But my parents were too proud to accept Kate and her husband Nat's charitable offer to stay until we were ready to go home. Somehow my father managed to get a small apartment in the quarters for medical students near Bellevue Hospital.

The second time in New York we began our stay in that complex. My mother didn't like the arrangements, though, complaining that the students would sometimes come home with blood on their clothes. I remember that there were quite a few roaches in residence too. Our dwindling resources and the less than ideal accommodations were taking a toll. Even I was able to tell that things were pretty tense between my parents. It was the first time I'd ever heard them yell at each other, and I was quite unnerved by the whole thing.

The next year my father decided to look for a more suitable place to pursue his studies. He learned that the University of Denver had a new program offering the degree that he wanted. More important, it offered reasonable student housing for families. So for the next two summers, when I was six and seven, we set out for a new destination: the Rocky Mountain state of Colorado.

The trip to Denver was longer than the trip to New York, but traveling westward, we were able to find lodging just across the Tennessee border. After a stopover we would resume driving, trying to make it as far as St. Louis or Kansas City, where we'd stop again. The car wasn't air-conditioned, and Kansas was always flat and hot. We would play all of those games that families do: How many different state license plates can you identify? Or can you guess the number of miles to the next town? My parents developed another game: What colleges are located here? On one of these trips we actually went several hundred miles out of the way to see Ohio State. My parents counted the number of college campuses visited like some people count national parks.

But all in all I loved these trips. I'll never forget the first time we crossed the border into Colorado. When you reach Colorado, the horizon appears to rise and you know you're about to climb a mile high. My heart would beat faster as we drew closer to Denver, and to this day I am happiest in the high mountains of the western United States. I always felt that I should have been born in the West.

The move to Denver was a good one. The university had very nice accommodations for families in Aspen Hall, complete with a full kitchen. My mother was also able to enroll in classes. Her certifications to teach were in English and science, so, to capitalize on her music skills, she decided to pursue a third qualification in music.

The problem was what to do with me. There was a day camp to which I could and did go, but the activities ended in the early afternoon. One day we were passing by the campus ice arena, and I got an idea: ice-skating lessons. I'd seen two teenage figure skaters coming out of the arena in their little skating skirts. Since I loved watching figure skating on television, I was immediately taken with the idea. The Denver Figure Skating Club ran a full-day summer school at the University of Denver arena. Skating was therefore the perfect answer: an opportunity to learn something new *and* high-priced child care.

In short, the summers in Denver were perfect for the whole family, with clean, cheap accommodations, educational opportunities for both Mother and Daddy, and skating for me. We discovered all kinds of activities in the relaxed atmosphere of Colorado. Evening trips to Elitch Gardens, an amusement park outside the city, were my favorite. I loved to ride the carousel and to play the game where one throws balls at bowling pins, winning prizes for knocking them down. We went to see movies and discussed them afterward at a nice pizza parlor near the campus. When it was time to go home, I was really sad to leave and sorry to say goodbye to my new skating friends. Funny enough, I don't remember reflecting much on the fact that, for the first time in my life, my little friends were white.

CHAPTER TEN

Turning Up the Heat in Birmingham

WHEN WE returned home late in the summer of 1962, tensions were rising in Birmingham. Slowly but surely, the firewall separating the races was crumbling. Segregation was being challenged—and challenged hard—by the growing momentum of the civil rights movement, creating an atmosphere in Birmingham that was increasingly charged.

Over the years, officials in Birmingham had flagrantly ignored a series of landmark federal-level decisions. In 1957 Central High School in Little Rock, Arkansas, had been integrated with the help of federal forces. In Birmingham, however, *Brown v. Board of Education* had had little effect: the schools remained segregated. Similarly, the law requiring blacks to sit in the back of the bus had been declared unconstitutional after Rosa Parks raised national awareness with her refusal to give up her seat to a white man in 1955 in Montgomery. Still, Birmingham officials dragged their feet in desegregating the buses.

Several citizens' committees had tried to promote racial justice over the years. As far back as 1951, there had even been an Interracial Division of the Jefferson County Coordinating Council of Social Forces that was funded by the Birmingham Community Chest. But in 1956 the Division was disbanded in the face of increasing hostility and violence. Several other efforts emerged during that period but quickly lost steam. When Alabama outlawed the NAACP that same year, the Reverend Fred Shuttlesworth formed the Alabama Christian Movement for Human Rights. Segregationists responded by bombing his house on Christmas night.

Throughout the late 1950s and early 1960s challenges to the system were met with growing violence. Nat King Cole was attacked during his performance at Birmingham's Municipal Auditorium in 1956. In 1958 the Ku Klux Klan lit eighteen crosses throughout Jefferson County, and the next year they paraded through black neighborhoods. The Klan burned eleven schools the year after that.

There were decent people, many of them white, who were trying to do the right thing. In 1997 I was very proud to accept an honorary degree at the University of Alabama alongside Mrs. Virginia Durr, who, with her husband, had publicly challenged Bull Connor and other segregationists. The Russakoffs were among the many Jewish families who tried to cross color lines. And of course Judge Frank Johnson was a pioneering figure whose rulings started to bring change but also drew sharp criticism and put him and his family in danger.

In the face of these challenges, Birmingham's authorities

remained steadfast in their insistence on segregation. Bull Connor became the fist of Jim Crow in the city and Governor George Wallace its soul in the statehouse in Montgomery. We watched on television as Wallace stood in the doorway of the University of Alabama to prevent its integration. I'll also never forget his infamous words during his inaugural address: "Segregation now, segregation tomorrow, segregation forever."

To be fair, around that time, my family had begun to experience small cracks in the walls separating the races. When I was about seven my mother developed a very bad bronchial infection. Nothing seemed to make her better. Desperate to find her proper care, my father asked Dr. Clay Sheffield, a white colleague who was director of guidance counseling and had taken a personal interest in my father's career, to recommend a physician.

And so on Saturday afternoon my parents and I went to visit Dr. Carmichael, an ear, nose, and throat specialist. We were escorted into the Negro waiting room, located up the back stairs above the pharmacy. The paint was peeling, the benches were pretty hard, and the wait was very long.

After Dr. Carmichael finally saw my mother, he called my father aside. "When you bring Angelena next week," he said, "come after five p.m." The next Saturday we arrived after five o'clock and were escorted into the now empty white waiting room with large leather chairs and plenty of magazines to look at. Dr. Carmichael broke the rules because he respected my father as a human being. He was ready for change. Over time, the two waiting rooms merged and more black families joined us "up front."

I can remember too another act of "white kindness" that occurred when, at age seven, I wanted desperately to go to the circus. Again, Dr. Sheffield came through, somehow wangling tickets and a pass to get in. My family made its way past the ticket taker without incident. Unfortunately, I hated the circus and wanted to go home after a few minutes. My father, who'd moved heaven and earth to get the tickets, was furious. We stayed until the end.

Then there was the white saleslady who also found a way around the rules. One day Mother and I went to buy me an Easter dress. We often shopped in Mountain Brook, a very exclusive white enclave outside of the city. At the Canterbury Shop for Children they didn't seem to care what color you were as long as you were willing to pay the exorbitant prices they charged. But on this day, we were downtown at Burger-Phillips and a clerk whom Mother did not know said that I would have to try the dresses on in the storeroom. Blacks were not permitted in the fitting rooms. I remember it as if it were yesterday. Mother looked her dead in the eye. "Either she tries them on in the fitting room or we won't buy a dress here," she sternly replied. "Make your choice." The poor woman shooed us into the dressing room and stood guard outside, hoping that no one would see us.

But of course these breaks in segregation were isolated incidents. They were small cracks in the façade of a relentlessly unequal and demeaning system of racial separation. Parents in Birmingham made their children's opportunities as equal as possible and their worlds as pleasant as they could. Segregation did not intrude every day and people lived good lives. We found a way to live normally in highly abnormal circumstances. But there was no denying that Birmingham eclipsed every other big American city in the ugliness of its racism.

The history of the civil rights movement has been chronicled many times, no more movingly than in Taylor Branch's extraordinary studies. As a student of politics, I'm able to read these accounts with some measure of detachment. But I lived in Birmingham, and by 1962 my parents' attempts to shield me from the hostility of the place in which we lived were no longer succeeding. Birmingham would shortly become "Bombingham"; it was a very scary place.

CHAPTER ELEVEN

1963

IT'S FUNNY what impresses you as a child. For me, the first salvo, the first shock of recognition, was learning of the boycott of the downtown stores in 1962. The action was organized to bring pressure on the stores to hire black clerks and to take down racial signage. Because an Alabama state law effectively prohibited boycotts, organizers called it a "selective buying campaign" and provided buyers with a list of black-friendly merchants and those stores who hired and provided good working environments for black employees. The idea was that people should buy from those stores rather than be prohibited from shopping elsewhere. That Easter everyone made sure to wear old clothes just to demonstrate that they were supporting the campaign.

But it was Christmas when I realized that something truly serious was under way. It had been our tradition to go downtown to see the elaborately decorated store windows at Pizitz and Loveman's. Much like Macy's in New York, the stores had animated mannequins in beautifully staged Christmas scenes. After viewing the windows, we'd always go into the stores and buy gifts for family, teachers, and friends.

But in 1962, my parents explained that we couldn't go to the stores because of something called a boycott. Black people were standing up for what was right, and we would too. I was terribly disappointed but old enough to understand the larger issues at stake. Strangely, we did go to visit Santa that year, though we didn't buy anything in the store.

Clearly, the boycott was succeeding. Sales declined 11 percent that year, leading the city of Birmingham to threaten to cut off a surplus food program servicing about nineteen thousand poor black families if the boycott didn't stop. The churches, including Westminster, responded by conducting a food drive to make certain that those families wouldn't be hurt.

Though they supported the boycott, my parents didn't want me to go without toys that Christmas, so they arranged for Aunt Gee to bring them from her home in Norfolk, Virginia. Santa Claus, therefore, showed up as expected with a Charmin' Chatty doll that spoke multiple languages. Like the iconic Chatty Cathy, the doll spoke when you pulled the string in her back. You could insert records in the side of *this* doll, however, and she would speak French, Spanish, and German. I loved her and got an early lesson in the fun of being multilingual.

Then came the crucible year of 1963 with its escalating challenges and violence. Throughout the winter and early spring, voting rights actions, sit-ins, and large protests removed any sense of normalcy in the city. In March two black candidates competed for spots on the Birmingham city council, and one of them received so many votes that he forced his opponent into a runoff election. And in April, Albert Boutwell won the mayor's race, handing a defeat to Bull Connor as the city switched to a mayoral form of government. Connor refused to step down, and for almost two months Birmingham had two governments. I'd never heard my father speak about any other human being the way he spoke about Bull Connor. He was, according to my father, the personification of evil. I hated him too and remember him as really ugly with a scowling, wrinkled face. I recoiled every time I heard him talking on television about the "negras" who needed to be separated from honest white folk.

That same month, the Southern Christian Leadership Conference (SCLC) launched demonstrations to end segregation. George Wallace sent a hundred state troopers into Birmingham to reinforce the police. And on April 12, Good Friday, Martin Luther King Jr. was arrested in downtown Birmingham. From there he wrote his famous "Letter from Birmingham Jail."

In the midst of this turmoil, people had to make decisions about what role they would play. The epicenter of the civil rights movement became the black Baptist church, and the working classes served as its foot soldiers. The Reverend Fred Shuttlesworth, who had led the local chapter of the NAACP and eventually served as president of the national SCLC, left for Cincinnati in 1961 but returned frequently to Birmingham during the tumultuous days of 1963. Reverend Shuttlesworth has not, to my mind, received his due in the stories of these turbulent years. People in Birmingham know that it was he who was the heart and soul of the civil rights movement. The great national leaders,

Martin Luther King and Ralph Abernathy, built on what Fred Shuttlesworth began.

My father and Reverend Shuttlesworth would sit on the front porch at our house and talk late into the evening. I can remember bouncing over to them and climbing on Daddy's lap. He would shoo me off since they were often deep in conversation. We visited Reverend Shuttlesworth in Cincinnati in 1972, and the two men again spent long hours revisiting old times.

Nevertheless, I had always wondered if Reverend Shuttlesworth harbored any resentment toward my father for refusing to march with him. The Reverend has said that he thought that my father would not march because he feared his church would be bombed. While that doesn't really sound like Daddy, perhaps concern for his parishioners was indeed a consideration. And Reverend Shuttlesworth has always said that he knew that Reverend Rice was "there for him."

I gained a deeper appreciation for the respect the two men had for each other during a recent visit with Reverend Shuttlesworth, who, due to a stroke, can barely speak. He nodded when his wife asked if he remembered my father. "Were you good friends?" she asked. He nodded again. Then, when I handed him a picture of my father, he smiled broadly and kept running his hand across my father's face. "Oh, Condoleezza," he said. I cried because it spoke volumes about how he felt about my dad. They might have disagreed about tactics, but they cared for each other as friends.

Today there is a narrative that the middle classes who would eventually benefit disproportionately from desegregation did little to actually bring it about. It is true that few adults in my

community marched with Martin Luther King. But the story of
the choices that people made is far more complex than the cari-
cature that neatly separates those who marched from those who
didn't.

First, if you were black in Birmingham in 1963, there was no
escaping the violence and no place to hide. What I remember
most from this time is the sound of bombs going off in neighborhoods, including our own. Clearly, leaders of the movement
such as attorney Arthur Shores were singled out. His home was
bombed twice in 1963, and his neighborhood became known as
"Dynamite Hill." But the white "night riders" and the KKK cared
little about the role you played in the struggle; they were content
to terrify any black family they could.

I can remember coming home from my grandparents' one
night. We'd just gotten out of the car when we heard a loud blast
down the street. In Birmingham that spring, no one had to think
twice: a bomb had exploded in the neighborhood. In fact, it had
been a gas bomb, hurled into the window of a house about a block
or so away. My father hurried my mother and me back into the
car and started to drive off. Mother asked where he was going.
"To the police," he said. "Are you crazy?" she asked. "They probably set off the thing in the first place." Daddy didn't say anything but drove to the Rays' house in Hooper City instead.

Several hours later we returned home and learned that a second bomb had gone off. As terrorists still do today, bombers exploded the first device in hopes that a crowd would gather. They
detonated the second bomb—filled with shrapnel and nails—in
order to injure as many innocent onlookers as possible. Fortunately, people knew better, and no one went out into the streets
after the first explosion. Still, no one slept that night. When we

got home, Daddy didn't say anything more about the bomb. He just went outside and sat on the porch in the springtime heat with his gun on his lap. He sat there all night looking for white night riders.

Eventually Daddy and the men of the neighborhood formed a watch. They would take shifts at the head of the two entrances to our streets. There was a formal schedule, and Daddy would move among them to pray with them and keep their spirits up. Occasionally they would fire a gun into the air to scare off intruders, but they never actually shot anyone. Really light-skinned blacks were told to identify themselves loudly upon approach to the neighborhoods so that there wouldn't be any "accidents."

Because of this experience, I'm a fierce defender of the Second Amendment and the right to bear arms. Had my father and his neighbors registered their weapons, Bull Connor surely would have confiscated them or worse. The Constitution speaks of the right to a well-regulated militia. The inspiration for this was the Founding Fathers' fear of the government. They insisted that citizens had the right to protect themselves when the authorities would not and, if necessary, resist the authorities themselves. What better example of responsible gun ownership is there than what the men of my neighborhood did in response to the KKK and Bull Connor?

A second point worth making about the Birmingham movement was that Dr. King's strategy was hardly uncontroversial. Daddy sometimes derided those who later said they'd marched even though many had not. "If everyone who says he marched with King actually did," he once told me, "there wouldn't have been any room on the streets of Birmingham."

My father had his own reasons for refusing to join King in

his acts of civil disobedience. I can remember as if it were yesterday a conversation between my parents about how to react to the call to take to the streets and behave nonviolently. I stood in the hallway of our house, listening as my parents conferred in the living room. "Ann, I'm not going out there because if some redneck comes after me with a billy club or a dog, I'm going to try to kill him," he said. "Then they'll kill me, and my daughter will be an orphan."

Years later I asked my dad if I had heard him correctly. He wasn't defensive about his refusal to march with Dr. King; in fact, he told me definitively that he didn't believe in being nonviolent in the face of violence.

He also hated the use of children and teenagers in the march. Out of frustration with the slow response to the protests, Martin Luther King and the movement preachers called children into the streets on May 2 for what became known as the "Children's Crusade." Some of my friends were involved. James Stewart, George Hunter III (called "Third"), Raymond Goolsby, and Ricky Hall, all students of my father, were told to go out first and distract the police. Others were to follow and get as close to city hall as they could before being stopped. As they approached city hall from Sixteenth Street Baptist Church, Bull Connor yelled over the bullhorn, "Do you have a permit?" When they said that they didn't, he opened paddy wagons filled with police who arrested the kids. When the kids kept coming and Connor could not stem the tide of protesters, he called in police dogs and turned fire hoses on the marchers. These young kids had been led straight into the teeth of Bull Connor's henchmen. The rightness of their cause aside, my father was appalled at what he saw as endangering innocent children.

Daddy nonetheless did what he could to support his students. On that day and several to follow, large numbers of high school students left school and joined the marchers. My father, their teachers, and for the most part their parents tried to dissuade them, saying they should fight racism with their minds, not their bodies. But when the Birmingham Board of Education demanded that the teachers report "absences" so that the kids could be disqualified for graduation, they refused. Students were encouraged to come to school, be marked present, and then leave for the protests. The teachers would turn their heads while the students left.

By the afternoon of May 2, policemen had arrested hundreds of students, and when the jails couldn't hold the protesters, the police shipped them off to the fairgrounds. My father received permission to go and walk among the kids so that he could report to their parents that they were safe. I went with him and walked among the throngs of students. After a couple of days of crowded conditions—so crowded that the students had to sleep in shifts because there was no room to lie down—the adults had had enough. They mobilized lawyers to get the kids released.

The images of Bull Connor's dogs and fire hoses confronting unarmed, peaceful protesters in Kelly Ingram Park, located in downtown Birmingham directly across from Sixteenth Street Baptist Church, are some of the most indelible in American history. During that long, hot summer of 1963, Bull Connor even brought "irregulars" from the backwoods of Alabama to do the dirty work that even the police would not do. My folks and I would watch them streaming down Sixth Avenue in pickup trucks adorned with Confederate flags. Trying to intimidate us, they hung out of the windows and brandished sawed-off shotguns. The protesters met even these goons with dignity and reserve and refused to be provoked.

But on the night of Saturday, May 11, Bull Connor's militia met up with a different kind of black protester. A full-scale riot erupted after the Ku Klux Klan bombed the A. G. Gaston Motel in an attempt to assassinate Martin Luther King, who had left the city hours earlier. Black protesters threw bricks at officers and attacked police cars in the area around the motel. Another large group of young men had gone drinking at an establishment on Fourth Avenue. "Lit up," as southerners put it, with various strains of alcohol, they joined in the riot and marched on Kelly Ingram Park. The marchers encountered an armored personnel carrier parked there, and rumors spread that Bull Connor was in it. The men set fire not only to the carrier but also to nearby patrol cars and pickup trucks. Members of the mob were arrested and hauled off to jail, but the "resistance" had an effect. My parents wanted me to feel safe, but they also wanted me to see what was going on. The next morning, we drove down to Kelly Ingram Park, where one could see the carnage of burned vehicles and quite a few irregulars heading for home.

Ironically, we should have been in Denver as these events unfolded. I've often wondered why my parents were so insistent on staying home in 1963. If ever there had been a time to go to Denver for as long as possible, this would have been it. But we didn't and thus witnessed the violence and turmoil. When I later asked them why, they didn't really have a good answer. After I pushed, my father finally said that he had to be with his congregation. Perhaps it just seemed wrong to abandon Birmingham in the midst of the struggle.

. . .

THE SUMMER of police dogs and fire hoses finally captured the attention of the nation. Birmingham was clearly exposed as a city of appalling hatred, prejudice, and violence. That hatred found full expression on September 15, 1963, when a bomb at Sixteenth Street Baptist Church killed four little girls who were on their way to Sunday school.

Services hadn't yet begun at Westminster that Sunday, but the choir, elders, and ushers were already in the sanctuary. I was there with my mother as she warmed up on the organ. All of a sudden there was a thud and a shudder. The distance between the two churches is about two miles as the crow flies. But it felt like the trouble was next door.

I remember Mrs. Florence Rice rushing in to say that it must have been a bomb. Everyone immediately wondered if the explosion was in our neighborhood, about five minutes away. Within what seemed like hours but was probably only a few minutes, someone called the church to say that Sixteenth Street Baptist had been bombed. No one knew how many other churches might have been targeted. People needed to get to safety.

My father didn't try to conduct the service but somehow thought it safer if people remained together in the church. An hour or so later word came that the bomb had killed four little girls who were in the bathroom. I don't remember how long it was, but we soon knew their names: Denise McNair, age eleven, and Addie Mae Collins, Cynthia Wesley, and Carole Robertson, all age fourteen. Two other black children would die that day in racially motivated attacks. Everyone was scared, and parents just wanted to get their children home.

Back at home we turned on the television. Footage from the bombed-out church was all over the news along with the unbelievably sad pictures of little bodies being removed from the wreckage and taken away in hearses. My parents were constantly on the phone with members of the family and their friends across Birmingham. The men of the community took up the neighborhood watch. But I remember feeling that they were really powerless to stop this kind of tragedy. I just sat and watched television. When it came time to go to sleep, I asked if I could sleep in my parents' bed.

I stayed home from school the next day, as did all of my friends. My father and mother went to work, but I went to Grandmother's house. She was as dazed as everyone else and just kept saying that the Lord worked in mysterious ways. I remember thinking that these mysterious ways were awfully cruel, but I didn't say anything to my devout grandmother.

The outrage would settle on our community, but at first we were just sad. Birmingham isn't that big and everyone knew at least one of those little girls. This was a deeply personal tragedy. My friend Vanessa Hunter remembers that she saw Denise in the hallway that Friday. They had talked about not having any homework that weekend. Cynthia and Denise were from the neighborhood. I knew Denise best; though she was older, we would still play with dolls together. Her father was our milkman and a part-time photographer who worked at everyone's birthday parties and weddings. Denise had been a student in my father's first kindergarten.

My uncle had been Addie Mae Collins' teacher, and he cried like a baby when he saw her picture on the news and again when he saw her empty chair the next day. Mr. John Springer, one of my father's closest friends, lived next to the McNair family. He had not left for church that morning. A while after the bomb went off he saw people running toward the McNairs' house. "I just heard Maxine wail," he told me later. "The door was closed but she cried out so loud that I just knew what had happened."

We tried to go to the funeral at which Dr. King officiated, but by the time we arrived at the church it was filled to capacity. Three of the girls were eulogized on the Wednesday after the bombing, and the other, Carole, on Tuesday at the Methodist church. Her parents had not wanted to eulogize their daughter in a mass funeral.

We stood outside on the steps at the funeral for the three. Some of my father's students—fifteen-year-old James, Ricky, and Third—were pallbearers. Ricky almost collapsed, but James held him up. I don't remember much except the recessional of coffins. They were small and white. In my mind's eye, though, one of the coffins was pink.

The homegrown terrorism against Birmingham's children seemed finally to rock the nation's conscience. On June 11, President John F. Kennedy had delivered a historic address calling for an end to segregation and introduced a legislative package in Congress to do so. The proposed Civil Rights Act sought to atone for the systematic prejudice and oppression that characterized the South by banning segregation in public accommodations and allowing the federal government to join in state lawsuits to integrate public schools. Although this effort had begun months earlier, we believed the tumultuous summer of 1963—culminating in the horrific deaths of four little girls at the hands of violent extremists—would give the young President greater impetus to act.

I can remember my father, who hadn't voted for John Kennedy, saying that he hoped the President had the muscle to carry through. If this attempt failed, he told my mother, the segregationists would be emboldened and life in Birmingham would be intolerable. He said that now that the hornets' nest had been stirred, white supremacy would either die or triumph completely. There was no middle ground because the last card was about to be played.

Daddy said that there had always been the belief that when the federal government finally decided to intervene to change the South, it would win decisively; the Feds had just never chosen to do so. If Washington now proved powerless, there was no recourse left. We followed events in the nation's capital through the daily reporting of Chet Huntley and David Brinkley. For us this wasn't just some academic political debate; it was personal. We felt that our fate was completely in the hands of the Kennedys.

That Friday, November 22, 1963, began like any other. In the most remarkable way, life had become more normal again after the awful events two months before. I was in Mrs. Riles' geography class, which would be followed by recess and then history, which Mrs. Riles also taught.

Suddenly one of the other teachers rushed in to tell her that the President had been shot in Dallas. It was nearly time for recess anyway, so Mrs. Riles shooed us out onto the playground and headed to the teachers' lounge to watch the reporting. I stood around with my friends on what was a pretty warm day for late November, not really knowing what to do.

Eventually the bell rang. We went back into the classroom, and Mrs. Riles started to teach again. A few minutes later, she stopped and went to the door. I heard her wail. "The President's dead," she said, "and there's a southerner in the White House. What's going to become of us now?"

School was dismissed, and I went to my uncle Alto's classroom. We got in the car and headed to Grandmother's house as we always did. He turned to me and said, "How do you feel?"

"Do you mean about the President?" I said. He nodded, and I told him that I was very sad. "And scared," I added. Alto didn't ask why, but Mrs. Riles had given me a reason.

It's true that all Americans of a certain age remember where they were when they heard that President Kennedy had been shot. That night's evening news and the constant replaying of the motorcade, the moment of impact, and the slumping President are images so vivid as to seem like yesterday. So too are the dignity of Jacqueline Kennedy, the swearing in of Lyndon Johnson, and the funeral cortege making its way mournfully through Washington, D.C. But for black citizens of Birmingham, John Kennedy's assassination was personally threatening. I doubt if many children outside of the South would have described their reaction to his death as fear.

Fortunately, though Lyndon Johnson was a southerner, he carried through on Kennedy's promise to end segregation. As a political scientist, I have read scores of academic papers on Johnson's legislative approach. Some believe that Johnson was able to do what Kennedy could not have done: assemble a coalition of northern Democrats and liberal Republicans to ram through landmark legislation. Donald Rumsfeld, then a young congressman from Chicago, was one of the Republicans who supported the President. I can dispassionately analyze Johnson's strategy and the shameful reaction of the Republican Party that resulted in the "Southern strategy," a conscious attempt to court white voters disgruntled by desegregation. But I have to step out of my own experience to do so because this was not just any legislation— it produced fundamental changes in my family's lives. And it did so almost immediately.

On that hot July day in 1964, we watched Huntley and Brink- ley deliver the news that the Civil Rights Act of 1964 had passed the U.S. Congress and had been sent to the President for his sig- nature. Johnson would sign the legislation on July 2. The local news anchor repeated the story after the national news. "The so- called Civil Rights Act passed today," he intoned, adding a rather telling qualifier to his description of the legislation.

But it didn't matter. A couple of days later, my father said, "Let's go out to dinner." We got dressed up and went to a rela- tively new hotel about ten minutes from our house. We walked in and people literally looked up and stopped eating. But after a few minutes, perhaps recognizing that the law had changed, they went back to eating, and we were served without incident. A few days after that, however, we went to a drive-through hamburger stand called Jack's. It was nighttime, and as I bit into my ham- burger, I told my parents that something tasted funny. Daddy turned on the car light. The bun was filled with onions: nothing else, just onions.

Nonetheless, de jure segregation was over. Decent people, not extremists but ordinary people, would start to adapt to that fact. Much is rightly made of the historic significance of the Voting Rights Act of 1965. But in terms of daily life, the Civil Rights Act of 1964 was at least as important, striking down legal segregation.

Many years later, when I was national security advisor, I was shocked to learn that this wasn't universally understood. One day in a meeting to plan the President's calendar, we reviewed a request to commemorate the fortieth anniversary of the Civil Rights Act. The consensus was that the President could issue a paper statement without much fanfare; the fortieth anniversary of the 1965 Voting Rights Act was to be celebrated the next year, and that legislation was considered to be the real breakthrough. I hit the roof and, more pointedly than perhaps I should have, told my colleagues that they'd better understand that the 1964 act was the one that had made it possible for me to eat in a restaurant in my hometown. Taken aback, they relented, and we had a very nice celebration in the East Room. We invited Lynda Bird Johnson Robb, whom I had the chance to thank personally for the courage and commitment her father had shown in bringing about dramatic changes in my life.

CHAPTER TWELVE

Integration?

To be honest, some things remained the same after the 1964 legislation. The schools, for instance, remained segregated in all but name. Yet interaction between white and black students began to occur. In the fall of 1964, our school was selected to participate in the first integrated book fair where students displayed books that they'd read along with little synopses of the stories.

Mrs. Hattie Witt Bryant Green, who was the library teacher and was very demanding, carefully prepared us for the big day at the Tutwiler Hotel. We weren't going to embarrass ourselves, she told us, in this first academic encounter with white people. Mrs. Green paid attention to every detail, insisting that the girls wear bows in their hair and that the boys wear ties. When we arrived at the hotel we found that we had been assigned to a separate room, but whites came through and looked at our projects, and we looked at theirs. After the event, Mrs. Green proudly pointed out that she never would have allowed her students to display projects as shabby as the ones the white students had created.

There were new opportunities for my parents too. The black and white presbyteries merged, and my mother's choir had an opportunity to sing at a white Presbyterian church. Daddy had tried to break down racial barriers much earlier and had befriended a number of white ministers. A few Sundays after the Civil Rights Act passed, he got an alarmed call from one of these pastors. "Reverend Rice," he said, "there are some Negro people out in front of the church and it seems they want to worship. What should I do?" My father replied that they probably weren't there to make trouble, just to worship, and that the best thing to do would be to greet them and seat them. His friend called after the service to say that all had gone well.

A few days later, my father came home from school really excited to say that Dr. Sheffield wanted him and another guidance counselor, Mrs. Helen Heath, to be the first blacks to work for the state of Alabama at the employment office downtown. They would be trained at the University of South Carolina and spend the summer counseling in vocational education. He added that the clients and their fellow workers would be black *and* white. Mrs. Heath remembers that Dr. Sheffield also said that he wanted them to teach the white people how to say "knee-grow." The time for saying "negra" had long passed.

I was really disappointed that we would not be going to Denver for the summer, but the trip to Columbia, South Carolina, was fun, especially since we got to fly on an airplane for the first time. I bought a new pink and white checked dress to wear aboard the Southern Airways flight.

That summer featured another highlight as well. I was almost ten and had begun to tire of the piano. Grandmother had stopped teaching, and Mother took up the role of my music instructor. This was not a good development. I can remember Mother yelling out from the kitchen as I practiced. "That's not right," she would call out.

"You're not supposed to be listening. I'm *practicing*," I would respond.

Somehow we just didn't have the right chemistry for this endeavor. I was also no longer the cute little kid very much in demand to play at various functions in the city. I told my mother I wanted to quit. I can remember her response as if it were yesterday. "You are not old enough or good enough to make that decision," she said. "When you are, you can quit." I was shocked, but I could tell that there wasn't any room for debate.

Mother and Daddy decided that I needed a change to reinvigorate my interest. As it happened, Birmingham-Southern College had a very fine conservatory of music, but to date its student body had been exclusively white. My father called and said that he had a child who was an accomplished pianist and wanted to study at the conservatory. Several weeks passed, but I was granted an audition. I was to play for Professor Hugh Thomas, the head of the Music Department, and Ms. Daphne Grimsley, who headed up the precollegiate pedagogical department.

On the day of the audition I admitted to my parents that I was nervous. They were surprised because I had always displayed rock-solid nerves while performing in piano recitals or concerts.

After all, I had been doing so most of my life. They asked if I needed more time to prepare. I finally admitted that I didn't want to embarrass anyone. I'd be the first black student in the Birmingham-Southern program. I felt that I was carrying the weight of needing to be twice as good. They reassured me that I was indeed twice as good. Looking back, it is striking that they didn't say, "You *don't have* to be twice as good."

The audition went very well. Ms. Grimsley was impressed and said she would take me on as her student. I got back into the car completely elated. We went to Forbes Piano store to buy the prescribed curriculum, and I was soon reenergized in my pursuit of a career as a concert pianist. Years later, my father said that he was really glad that he and my mother took the chance of letting me try to break this color barrier. He then laughed. "They were probably just relieved that you didn't dance on the piano."

As desegregation continued to take hold, social life changed too. We went to restaurants frequently and were generally treated with respect. And we took in a movie once in a while and went twice to the traveling ice show Holiday on Ice.

Then, in 1965, the NFL played its first professional football game in Birmingham's newly desegregated Legion Field, pitting the Dallas Cowboys against the Minnesota Vikings. Even though my mother's father was gravely ill—he died the next day—Mother went to the game to keep from disappointing me. She knew I regarded it as a watershed event.

Mother and I bought new matching outfits: navy blue suits with gold blouses and gold hats. We sat in our seats and began to watch the game. Former Olympic gold medal sprinter Bob Hayes was a rookie wide receiver for the Cowboys, and he took the opening kickoff and ran it back ninety-plus yards. We cheered wildly. I don't think my parents knew that I heard the man behind us say, "Oooh-wee. Look at that nigger run!"

We stayed in Birmingham only one more year before moving to Tuscaloosa, where my father accepted a job as dean of students at Stillman College. Over the years, Birmingham has remained fixed in my mind as a place and an experience inextricably bound up with those troubled times. A great deal has changed, including the election of successive black mayors and city council members (not least my friend Carole Smitherman). Ironically, Bull Connor's successor many times removed was, until recently, a black woman.

The schools are completely integrated, and though neighborhoods are still largely segregated in the de facto sense, even that is breaking down. In the suburbs where we once shopped to purchase the higher-quality goods of white merchants, affluent blacks and whites, including Aunt Gee, live side by side.

When I visited Birmingham in 2003, my aunt Connie threw a party for me, inviting my friends from school and several teachers. Everyone was, of course, black. But the caterers were white. No one else seemed to notice. I asked Connie how she'd selected them. "The mother of one of my students started a catering service," she replied. "I thought I'd give her a chance." This was perfectly logical but out of bounds for the Birmingham that I had known and left as a child.

Back in 1961, CBS did a devastating documentary called *Who Speaks for Birmingham?* The film is filled with whites and blacks talking about life in "The Magic City," as Birmingham is called. Several white citizens explain why race mixing is against natural law and why the "negras" are happy with the way things are. My parents and I watched it at the time and were appalled, angry, and hurt.

I once again saw clips of the documentary in 2005 when I took British Foreign Secretary Jack Straw and his wife, Alice, as well as British Ambassador David Manning and his wife, Catherine, to the Birmingham Civil Rights Institute. My father's longtime friend and colleague, Dr. Odessa Woolfolk, walked us through the exhibits that chronicled segregation. I was proud of what we had overcome, but as I noticed the horrified looks on the faces of my guests, I became deeply embarrassed. How could it be that so much hatred and prejudice had been lodged in one place? And how could it be that this was the place from which I had come?

In recent years I have been spending more time in the city with my family and friends, getting to know the "new Birmingham." Birmingham's efforts to emerge from the dark shadows of that time are now decades old. Yet I want to be a part of that emergence because somehow it is important for me to come to terms with and feel good about the city of my birth.

CHAPTER THIRTEEN

Tuscaloosa

MY FATHER came home one day and he and my mother went into their bedroom, closed their door, and began talking. I couldn't hear the words but it sounded like a very serious discussion. I wasn't used to being shut out of my parents' deliberations. We talked about everything—or at least I thought we did.

When they emerged, my mother was crying. Daddy wanted to take a job as dean of students at Stillman College, in Tuscaloosa, sixty miles from Birmingham. My mother, whose life had been spent in Birmingham and whose recently widowed mother was there, did *not* want to move. My parents had finally bought property, a plot of land adjoining one owned by my uncle Alto and his wife. They were planning to build there in a kind of family compound.

Moreover, Mother was gaining more and more acclaim for her cultural productions at school and for the excellence of Westminster's choir. In fact, during the summer of 1965 in Denver, Mother had taken a workshop offered by the faculty of Westminster Choir College. The head of the famed music school in Princeton, New Jersey, had worked with and encouraged my mother, and she'd returned to Birmingham with new, challenging music for her small choir. She was at the top of her game. What's more, she told my father, "Tuscaloosa is in the boondocks."

I wasn't thrilled with the idea of moving either. What about my piano lessons at Birmingham-Southern? What about my friend Velda Robinson, whom I saw at school every day, and Margaret and Vanessa, with whom I played in the neighborhood every evening?

My father was unmoved. For twelve years Daddy had juggled two jobs simultaneously—guidance counselor at Ullman High School and pastor of Westminster Presbyterian Church. Both were really full-time jobs and he worked all the time. Now, he wanted desperately to get out of the pulpit and into college work, and he was determined to take this opportunity. This was, for him, a logical extension of his commitment to youth in his ministry.

It seems that he had never really intended to preach for very long. He was taken with the study of theology and with the social ministry of the church but not with all of the duties that a senior pastor performed. The job of leading a church congregation is filled with politics, and putting up with slings and arrows from disaffected parishioners (and someone is always disaffected) was no longer fulfilling. Many years later he told me that he had felt pressured, if only by his own sense of obligation, into taking

Westminster when his father had left for Mississippi and then died not long after founding the church. He had come to care deeply for his congregation, but he really wanted to be in a college. His studies at the University of Denver had confirmed that his passion was higher education. When Stillman called, he felt it was time to go.

I was shocked to learn that he had already decided to accept the job before asking my opinion. I challenged him about it, saying that it was my life too. He actually apologized but said that it was time to leave Birmingham. We would come back every Wednesday so that I could continue my lessons at Birmingham-Southern. And I could call Velda every night if I wanted to.

Several days later we went down to visit Tuscaloosa. My mother was reassured when she was offered a job teaching at Druid High School. Daddy had been given a large house on Geneva Drive on the small, quiet campus. Pretty soon Mother set about having it redecorated, clearly impressed with the fact that it was much nicer than our little manse in Birmingham. The family was moving to Tuscaloosa.

Life in Tuscaloosa was very different, largely because our lives revolved around the college. Stillman was a small college then of about 650 students, but it had a very nice, well-appointed campus. For the first time, I could wander about unaccompanied because the campus was isolated and safe. I would often walk the quarter mile to the student union, where there was a bowling alley, or over to my father's office on the main quadrangle. My father even took advantage of the isolation of the campus to teach me at the age of eleven to drive along some of the back roads.

Stillman had no football team but an excellent basketball team, which we followed enthusiastically. We occasionally went to see the University of Alabama play football and began to develop an affinity for the Crimson Tide, which survives with me to this day. And of course we continued to watch the NFL, though poor reception in Tuscaloosa of the Birmingham stations made Sundays a bit of a challenge. I can still remember my father out in the backyard trying to adjust one of those huge ten-foot-tall antennas that were necessary to get long-distance reception in the 1960s. "No, Daddy, turn it the other way. The picture is even fuzzier now," I would yell out the den window. Daddy and I would laugh about this many years later as we watched multiple football games on satellite TV.

The University of Alabama, just a few miles from Stillman, also provided a whole new range of educational activities. My parents made certain that I spent a good deal of time on the newly integrated campus, attending the university's speakers series and touring science labs and the library. Sometimes after school we would just go up to the campus and walk around. The speakers series was particularly stimulating. We saw both Robert F. Kennedy and David Brinkley, our family's media hero, at the university's new field house.

When it came to my formal schooling, however, things were more complicated. In my last year in Birmingham, I'd been one of eight sixth graders who'd been merged into the seventh-grade classroom. This was something of an experiment that I never fully understood but which my parents had championed. We did our sixth-grade work but joined the seventh graders for their math, science, and reading curriculum. Our teacher, Mrs. Mallard, somehow kept all of this straight, and I remember the year as a wonderful academic experience. This "merged" classroom was to have continued until we finished eighth grade.

But when we moved to Tuscaloosa, there was no such program. Placing me in seventh grade would have meant repeating much of the curriculum. Yet skipping a grade meant that I'd be eleven in eighth grade until November and then only twelve.

My parents were worried because there is a huge difference between eleven-year-old girls and thirteen-year-old girls. Arguably, seventh grade was the worst possible one to skip. We discussed the issue as a family. It was the first time that I heard about something called puberty, my parents saying that I'd be behind my classmates in both physical and social development. I can remember sitting on the living room sofa, waiting patiently while my parents fumbled for the right words to explain what they meant. There were long pauses during which they'd look at each other. My father, who was one of the most articulate people I knew, was, for the first time in my experience, tongue-tied. He looked down and stopped trying. So Mother took up the task, delivering a rather opaque and disjointed lecture on sexuality. I was bemused, taking from her remarks something about needing to stay away from boys and their raging hormones, whatever those were. I didn't ask questions. I felt bad for my folks because they were so clearly embarrassed by the whole discussion. I didn't bother to tell them that I knew quite a bit about all of this from another source, my friends' older siblings. At the end I just said okay, and the conversation ended.

"Parents, talk to your children about sex" has been a part of our consciousness for some time now, and most schools have some form of sex education. But in the 1960s, many parents didn't really want to deal with the subject. For instance, my uncle once told my cousin Lativia, "Keep your dress down!" She had no idea what he meant.

Ultimately, I decided to go to eighth grade. I could tell that my parents wanted me to, but they really didn't push. They didn't have to because it was an easy decision for me. I had always wanted to be one of the "big kids."

It turned out, though, that fitting in was not as easy as I had imagined. I had only recently stopped playing with Barbie dolls, and now all my friends wanted to talk about were their boyfriends. I experienced early puberty, but I was still underdeveloped compared to my classmates. Eventually, though, I adjusted. I found a new best friend in Donna Green, who, like me, loved watching *Dark Shadows* on television after school.

In fact, my parents were a bit concerned when I suddenly announced that I had a boyfriend too. His name was Darrell Bell and he was a drummer in the Druid High School band. The bell lyre players, of which I was one, and the drummers sat next to each other, making it easy for Darrell and me to pass notes. My parents felt better when they learned that he was the son of the school guidance counselor. I guess they decided that with that parentage Darrell couldn't get too far out of line.

I came to enjoy Druid and did well academically. I became less conscious of the age difference with my classmates. But for my mother, things were not working out as well. The school principal, Mr. Hughes, and my mother clashed repeatedly. Mother had been a favorite of her principal at Western-Olin and wanted to produce at Druid cultural events like the ones she'd put on in Birmingham. She was rebuffed, though. It seems that Mr. Hughes was wary of my mother emerging as a competitor to the school's music teacher, who happened to be Mr. Hughes' wife. Mother felt stifled, and Mr. Hughes felt that my mother didn't respect him and his authority. I remember vividly the day that their conflict came to a head. It was in the spring and I was at lunch. My mother had been assigned one of the classroom annexes, actually a trailer, on the field next to the lunchroom. She had, of course, taken this as another affront.

Suddenly I heard a loud argument. I recognized Mother's shrill voice immediately as she screamed at Mr. Hughes, "Don't you ever come into my classroom unannounced and complain about my teaching!"

Mr. Hughes almost ran out of the room, yelling as he left, "That Rice woman is crazy!"

The kids in the lunchroom were laughing uncontrollably. Mr. Hughes was called "the bear" by the student body. "The bear got sent back to his cave," one kid said. I laughed too. Maybe I should have been embarrassed, but I loved it when my mother stood up for herself, even if she made a bit of a spectacle in doing so.

Obviously, Mother's relationship with Mr. Hughes was irrevocably broken after that. The next year, Tuscaloosa was opening two new middle schools, Woodlawn and Tuscaloosa Middle School, and the pressure was growing to integrate the schools and particularly the teaching staff. As it happened, my mother was assigned to the white school, Tuscaloosa. She was excited to be going there, breaking the color barrier, and teaching in a new environment. But before the school year started, she was reassigned to the black school, Woodlawn, without explanation. She was crestfallen, feeling that she'd been demoted. But she tried to make the best of it. She started a new arts program at Woodlawn and was put in charge of the opening ceremonies and cultural presentation for the school's inauguration. Still, working in a middle school was not nearly as fulfilling for her as teaching at Western-Olin had been. That was clear to me, and I felt very bad about it.

Daddy's career was flourishing in Tuscaloosa, however. He was right that college work suited him. Easily the most popular figure on the Stillman campus, he was also one of the movers in the city of Tuscaloosa. He was asked to speak everywhere, and everyone from the mayor to the leadership of the University of Alabama consulted him. Daddy struck up a friendship with the vice chancellor of the university, a man named John Blackburn, who would figure heavily in Daddy's career advancement for years to come.

I remember how busy my father was in those days. Daddy was determined to take advantage of the numerous new "Great Society" programs sponsored by the federal government. He was the acting director and a counselor in the Upward Bound program at Stillman, less than a year after the Higher Education Act of 1965 created it. And Daddy's church had housed one of the first Head Start programs back in 1965, so now in Tuscaloosa he was asked to chair the advisory board of the program. I could tell that he was a very important man in the community and I was very proud of him.

Yet John W. Rice Jr. was never one to grow complacent, and Daddy decided that Stillman's students were hearing too little about the social and political events of the day. Daddy received permission from the new president, Harold Stinson, to start a speakers series. Dr. Stinson was shocked when he learned that Daddy had invited as the first speaker Stokely Carmichael, the firebrand radical leader of the Student Non-Violent Coordinating Committee (SNCC).

Alabama had just begun to settle down from the upheavals of the past years. Not surprisingly, the thought of having Stokely Carmichael in Tuscaloosa was jarring. Stokely belonged to the new breed of black radical leaders. It was a time when the Black Panthers were a real and violent force on the West Coast and Malcolm X and the Nation of Islam were coming into their own. Stokely was making waves with incendiary language about the Vietnam War and white America. These were not people in the mold of Martin Luther King Jr., who believed in integration and the U.S. Constitution. They spoke in terms of revolution and blood, not in the language of nonviolence and civil disobedience.

A couple of days before Stokely was to speak in the Stillman College gymnasium, the Tuscaloosa chief of police called my father and asked to see him. "Reverend," he said, "Tuscaloosa just isn't ready for Stokely Carmichael. What if he starts some kind of riot? I don't want to stir up the rednecks either." Daddy reassured him. He'd talked with Mr. Carmichael, who wanted only to be heard. It would be good for the students and, by the way, any University of Alabama students who wanted to come were welcome too. After Stillman agreed to some extra security arrangements, the chief of police decided to let the lecture go forward. "Reverend Rice," he said, "I sure hope you know what you're doing." When he came home, Daddy told my mother and me that he'd assured the chief that he did indeed know what he was doing. Then he said, "I sure hope I do."

On the night of Stokely's appearance, the gymnasium was filled to capacity. Students *had* come from the University of Alabama, but none were white. Stokely, dressed in green fatigues, gave a stirring critique of American policy in Vietnam, adroitly displaying his rhetorical skills. The speech was radical. At one point he said that he had told the draft board to go ahead and draft him. "But don't expect me to use the gun on Vietnamese," he told the audience, implying but not saying that he might shoot American soldiers instead. "They classified me 4-F," he said, making reference to the draft category that meant "unfit to serve."

At the end, the place erupted in applause. We went backstage to see Carmichael. He was calm and courteous and told my father that Stillman College had been the first historically black college that had asked him to speak. "Thank you, Dean Rice," he said. Daddy replied that he believed in letting people speak, and he invited Stokely to come back the next year. It was the beginning of what would become a long and unusual friendship.

CHAPTER FOURTEEN

Denver Again

AFTER SETTLING in at Stillman, my father wanted to continue his graduate work. Now that he was a college dean, the school was prepared to pay for it. So in the summer of 1967 we resumed the practice of going to Denver as soon as school in Alabama was out of session.

Travel was much easier since hotels were now integrated all along the burgeoning interstate highway system. I was older and family games were replaced with Motown grooves and the latest rock anthems on the radio. My parents didn't complain, though they seemed slightly hurt when I indicated more interest in listening to the Temptations and Cream than in guessing the mileage to the next city or what college was located in that town.

The University of Denver had built new and quite pleasant graduate student housing. Mother resumed her music classes and I returned to the ice-skating rink full-time, rising at four-thirty in the morning to make the first session at five. I'd taken something of a hiatus from skating during our time in Denver in 1965, attending music classes with Mother. Now in 1967 I dove into skating with renewed passion, spending the entire day at the rink and beginning to prepare seriously for tests and competition. I passed the first set of figure tests (the discipline of tracing a figure eight three times with the blade of the skate—no longer practiced by today's skaters). The skating school was populated by very serious skaters, including a few destined for the Olympics. This time, when it was time to leave Denver, I really didn't want to go home.

When we returned to Tuscaloosa, I continued to progress both in social maturity and in the classroom. Life was good at Druid. But I longed to skate and Alabama had no ice-skating rinks. So I'd practice jumping on the floor in the den to the music of Schubert's *Unfinished* Symphony or Dvorak's *New World* Symphony. I made up routines that I looked forward to perfecting on the actual ice when we returned to Denver. As the summer approached, I grew more and more excited.

One afternoon in April, Mother and I had just returned from the home of the seamstress who was making a whole new skating wardrobe for me. As we walked into the house, we heard the news. Martin Luther King had been shot and killed in Memphis. My father came home immediately and we sat in the little den with the red carpet, watching the assassination images play over and over on the television. No one could really believe it. My father had had his doubts about the strategy that King pursued in 1963, but he lionized King the man, like practically every other black person in America. I was sad. And I was angry.

The next day we went to school. I'd become a member of the Druid High School debate team and we were scheduled to go to Montgomery for the competition two days later. Our debate coach called the team together and told us that we'd make the trip despite Dr. King's death. She was the only white teacher at Druid, having been sent to the black school as the token effort at integration (there were still no white students), and for the first time in my life I had a strong political and racial reaction. How dare she be so clueless! My teammates and I asked her to leave the room and we held a meeting. We would refuse to go to Montgomery in honor of Dr. King. When the poor woman came back into the room she must have immediately sensed the hostility. She announced that participation in the meet would be voluntary. Of course, no one volunteered.

There was no school the day of the funeral. Again we watched television as a family, taking in the images of the fully veiled Coretta Scott King and the tiny King children. I cannot listen to "Precious Lord" to this day without a flood of emotion harkening back to that event:

> Precious Lord, take my hand.
> Lead me on, let me stand.
> I am tired, I am weak, I am worn.
> Through the storm, through the night,
> Lead me on to the light.
> Take my hand precious Lord, lead me home.

Though I was only thirteen, 1968 was the year of my political awakening. It was one of those years that seemed to change things forever. It was not just the assassination of Dr. King. There was the Tet Offensive and the horrible pictures of Vietnam that suddenly filled our living room every night. I started to care what happened in Vietnam and would anxiously await Chet Huntley and David Brinkley's analysis. Then there were the May riots in Paris that introduced me for the first time to student radicalism. And on June 4, there was the news from Los Angeles.

My father was a political junkie. As a result, we always watched election coverage, staying up all night, for instance, until a winner was declared in the Kennedy-Nixon contest of 1960. We watched convention coverage every four years, listening with great anticipation to the roll call of the states in the nominating process. So there we were, glued to the TV set on the night of the California presidential primary in 1968 that would likely decide the Democratic nominee.

My father was a Republican, but this time he was going to cross party lines and vote for Bobby Kennedy. We all loved the Kennedys, Bobby most of all. He was, according to my father, ruthless in the pursuit of justice as attorney general and destined to be a great President. He just needed this victory in Los Angeles to defeat the "Happy Warrior," Hubert Humphrey, whom my father thought to be well-meaning but hapless.

The contest was very close and I was tired. As soon as Kennedy was declared the winner I went to bed, deciding to skip his acceptance speech. I'd just gone to sleep when my mother shook me and said, "Get up. Bobby Kennedy has been shot!"

My family gathered mournfully in the den. I sat on the red-carpeted floor, very close to the television set. We watched the footage of Bobby Kennedy lying on the floor, the huge football player Rosey Grier standing over him. We waited and waited. And then we heard. He was dead.

I had been sad and angry when Martin Luther King was shot. Now I was just devastated. What was happening to our country? That year would get worse. In August 1968, the Soviet Union invaded Czechoslovakia, thousands of miles away from Birmingham. But I watched that too in horror. I felt terrible for Czechoslovakia's leader, Alexander Dubček, and angry at the Soviet Union. My parents and I watched the Chicago convention too, with the whole controversy about the seating of the alternative delegation from Mississippi and the brutality of the police against the demonstrators in the streets. Nineteen sixty-eight was a tough year to come of age politically. I was too young to do anything about what was happening but old enough to know that the situation was very bad. There had been a *Time* cover in 1966 that asked "Is God Dead?" I didn't dare ask my parents about it then, but in 1968 the question seemed inescapable.

One night, not long after the Chicago convention, I went to my father's study, sat down with him, and asked what he thought of what was occurring. I told him that I felt like there was chaos all around us and I was scared. His response was, in retrospect, not surprising given his conservative, religious perspective. He said that the values of the country had gone off track. People didn't respect one another, the country, God, or anything else anymore. But America was going to survive, he told me, even though it might not appear that way right now. He was devastatingly critical of Lyndon Johnson, even though he admired him for his role in the passage of the civil rights legislation, and also disapproved of Hubert Humphrey. Daddy told me he would vote for Richard Nixon, who would bring order.

. . .

DESPITE ALL the upheaval, we did make it to Denver in that summer of 1968. When we arrived, I went immediately to the ice rink, not even waiting to unpack. The schedule on the board showed me taking seven lessons each week, preparing for the battery of tests that rank skaters according to national standards. This was momentous news. I was going to train in the elite program that prepared skaters for competition.

My parents were very proud but told me that they couldn't afford seven lessons. They went to one of my coaches, Diana Lapp, and asked to speak with her. I waited outside. I assumed that they were explaining that they just didn't have the money for a full program. But after a little while, they emerged. I'd have the seven lessons a week as prescribed. I was thrilled and resolved to work very hard. I have no idea where or how they found the money. It wasn't the last time that they would exhibit incredible selflessness where I was concerned—nor was it the last time I would take their sacrifice for granted.

That summer I became really serious about my skating and I got better fast. The problem was that we would soon return to Alabama, and one could only get so good practicing on the floor in the den. I couldn't believe my good fortune when my father asked me to call a family meeting: the subject would be whether to live in Denver for a full year.

My father had decided that he was never going to complete his graduate studies by taking two classes each summer. He had asked Stillman for a one-year leave of absence. Although he had been at the college for only two years, his request was granted. We would return to Alabama at the end of the summer, pack up what we needed, and return to Denver for the 1968–69 school year.

This all sounded great. But where would I go to school? And what about piano? I was doing very well at Birmingham-Southern. As it turned out, finding a piano program was easy. I would enroll at the University of Denver's pedagogical academy at the Lamont School of Music. The teacher gave me a full curriculum to study until I returned from Alabama.

The decision concerning my school was much harder. My parents weren't impressed with the Denver public school curriculum, which was at the leading edge of "experimental" education (read "not very structured or systematic"). Students were encouraged to be creative, even if they were wrong. "New math" was all the rage. My parents liked "old math" and thought that creativity was important but only after you knew the basics.

They learned, however, that there was a really fine college preparatory program at George Washington High School that was very rigorous. They tried to get me admitted there. But it was not in the neighborhood in which we would be living (on the university campus) and I was denied entry. In fact, they were told that there was a chance that I would be sent to Manual High School, located in what could only charitably be called "the hood," because Denver had begun a busing program to achieve racial integration. My parents found this idea preposterous. They questioned the notion that black kids would learn better just by sitting in a classroom with white ones. This perhaps reflected their experience with excellent but segregated schools in Birmingham. Now they were facing an almost laughable irony: their middle-class daughter could be bused across town to a poor black neighborhood in order to achieve desegregation. My parents decided to look for a private school alternative.

There were two possibilities: Kent Country Day School and

St. Mary's Academy. Both were all-girls schools. My parents were more attracted to Kent initially, although it was more expensive. But on further examination, it became clear that St. Mary's, one of the oldest educational institutions in Denver, had the really outstanding college preparatory curriculum. There was only one problem: it was Catholic.

I've noted earlier that my family, thanks to Granddaddy Rice's experiences in Louisiana, was militantly Protestant. My father could not believe that the best educational option for his daughter was a Catholic girls school. My parents visited the campus while I was skating. That evening we sat in the apartment to review their findings. They started slowly, making clear that the final decision would be mine. Still, the curriculum was excellent and there was no religious education requirement for non-Catholics. The last point sealed it, together with the fact that most of the nuns no longer wore habits.

The next day I visited St. Mary's. I liked the campus, whose entry was dominated by a stately convent and a circular driveway with a statue of the Virgin Mary in the center. The modern classroom building had a huge open space in the middle called the forum and beautiful classrooms and science labs. I was excited at the thought of enrolling there.

I filled out the application and was accepted before we left for Alabama. We also went to "The Denver," the large department store downtown, and bought my new uniforms: a navy and green watch plaid skirt; white blouses; blue, green, and white sweaters; a green blazer for special occasions such as assembly; green, blue, and white knee socks; and *saddle shoes*!

With everything in place, we prepared to return to Alabama to execute the move west. Daddy had agreed to get the school year started at Stillman, so we would not return to Denver until October. I'd start school a month or so late, studying the St. Mary's curriculum at home in Tuscaloosa and trying not to fall behind.

My parents were very anxious to get home to Alabama because there was a lot to do. I was scheduled to take a skating test on the Saturday morning that we were to leave. It would have necessitated a delay in our departure of about two hours. My father was adamant that we couldn't afford to wait. I could take the test when we returned in the fall. To this day, I still don't understand that decision. But grumpily I got in the car that morning and we set off for Alabama to prepare the move to Denver for one year. I secretly hoped that we'd never again live in Alabama.

Early in October, we loaded up the U-Haul and headed for Denver. Yes: the U-Haul. There wasn't much money since neither Stillman nor Denver was paying our moving expenses. We had to drive somewhat more slowly than usual, and there was the awful moment when the little trailer almost dislodged from the car somewhere near Kansas City. But we arrived with everything intact and moved into our new home: a two-bedroom graduate student apartment with rented furniture. From my point of view, it was the nicest place we'd ever lived. It was in Denver.

My new life in Denver was very structured. Every morning I got up at four-thirty and headed to the rink at five. At seven, I finished skating and went to school. After school I practiced piano, did my homework, and went back to the rink for another hour. Then I came back home and was in bed by nine-thirty. I had no free time and I didn't care. I loved the rigorous skating program, and my new piano teacher challenged me, insisting that

I begin to participate in piano competitions. I could tell that I was advancing more rapidly than I had at Birmingham-Southern.

St. Mary's was a good fit for me academically. Though I was several weeks late in starting, I quickly caught up and had little trouble with the work. Socially, though, I hated the school. I didn't make friends very easily, unlike at Druid, where I had been popular. I'd gone from Alabama, where I never had a white classmate, to St. Mary's, where there were only three black girls in my entire class of seventy. Yet there seemed to be a huge wall separating me from my black sisters. Maybe I was just the new kid on the block, or I didn't try hard enough, but I sure didn't feel welcomed by the few black students.

In general, I didn't care much for the social dynamics of an all-girls school. Life seemed to revolve around trying to attract the boys at our brother schools, Mullen Prep and Regis High. I explored becoming a cheerleader (one way to meet football players) but soon learned that the schedule interfered with skating. The only sport that St. Mary's played was field hockey, and after being hit with a stick by one of my sisters during tryouts, I decided that the ice was friendlier. Most girls skied, a sport that I had neither the money nor, at the time, the inclination to try, fearing an injury that would end my skating season. St. Mary's didn't have a band, so that was out as an activity. I finally joined the glee club and was installed as the accompanist. I didn't love that either, since I ended up playing for high school sopranos who sang "Climb Ev'ry Mountain" from *The Sound of Music* with equal measures of gusto and horrendous pitch.

My parents certainly sensed that St. Mary's was not a perfect fit. They asked repeatedly whether everything was going okay.

But that year I never confided my true feelings about the school. My parents were, after all, paying more than a thousand dollars in tuition—money they really didn't have. I wanted them to think that I liked St. Mary's and not worry. Moreover, it was just for a year, and my life revolved around skating in any case. I had plenty of friends at the rink, especially Debbie Mitchell, who was my closest buddy.

Debbie and I would skate every day and hang out together on the weekend. While we practiced, our fathers would stand and talk in the parking lot, and they got to know each other well. Debbie's father was Maurice Mitchell, the chancellor of the University of Denver. When my father finished his coursework that spring, Chancellor Mitchell offered him a job at the university.

Again we had a family meeting. I thought moving to Denver was a no-brainer. Though settling here would put my mother more than 1,300 miles from her mother, she too wanted to move and seemed confident that she could land a good teaching job. My father was a little worried because the financial package at the university wasn't quite as good as Stillman's. But after he worked out an arrangement for low-cost faculty housing, everything fell into place. My father returned to Alabama before the school year ended and resigned from Stillman. Mother and I followed as soon as school was out at St. Mary's. My dream had come true. We were going to live in Denver. Permanently!

CHAPTER FIFTEEN

Leaving the South Behind

WE MOVED into one of the modest three-bedroom homes that were rented to young faculty at a highly subsidized rate for a maximum of two years. My parents gave me the master bedroom because it had its own bathroom and I was getting to the age where that kind of thing mattered.

One of our neighbors was an Israeli family. Benzion Netanyahu, a professor of Hebraic studies, taught in the Department of Religion, giving him and my father common interests. The Netanyahus had three sons but only one was young enough to live at home. Their oldest son, Bibi, was in college, and their middle son was serving in the Israeli Defense Forces. Our families shared what I now understand to have been a Seder meal during the Passover holiday. Many years later when Bibi Netanyahu was elected prime minister of Israel for the first time, my father reminded me of this example of far less than six degrees of separation. I still send greetings to Professor Netanyahu when I see his son.

Daddy started his job as assistant director for admissions and assistant dean of arts and sciences. Perhaps not coincidentally, his friend and mentor from Tuscaloosa, John Blackburn, had also moved to the University of Denver as vice chancellor.

It didn't take long for Daddy to become a major figure at the university even though DU could not have been more different from Stillman. Denver University was private and very expensive. It was known as a bit of a party school populated by rich kids who either couldn't get into Ivy League universities or wanted to ski—or both. Denver itself was more homogenous than almost any other big city in the country. I remember noticing that it was possible to spend an entire day on the city streets and not see another black person.

One of Daddy's responsibilities was to increase the diversity of the student body, and he was given wide berth to do so. He traveled extensively to major cities, recruiting black students to the university, which wasn't always easy. The mountain West could seem a bit foreign to kids who had grown up in places such as New York and Chicago. Among those Daddy recruited were several students from Alabama, such as Larry Naves and Harriett Dale Rutledge, who had been members of Daddy's Youth Fellowship in Birmingham. "The university should commit itself to the proposition that it is possible to have varying entrance standards, but only one exit or graduation standard," he argued, speaking to the heart of the affirmative action debate.

After one year, my father increased the number of black students at DU to about one hundred in a population of seven thousand. The key, he believed, was adequate financial support. "What good does it do to locate a student, get him or her to apply for admission, and then have no funds available?" he asked. In search of a sustainable solution, Daddy created the Education Opportunity Program, which administered grants of up to eight hundred dollars to students who were receiving financial aid but needed additional help covering basic college expenses, such as books and rent. The program was unique not because of its intent but because of the funding source: parking meters on campus. The administration couldn't balk at such a creative initiative. Daddy also realized that the students had to have a few social outlets, and he successfully secured in the university budget an appropriation of $1,500 a year for black social activities.

But simply diversifying the student body was not enough. Daddy went to Chancellor Mitchell and Dr. Blackburn and told them that he wanted to develop a curriculum that would ensure that all Denver students fully understood black America. He envisioned an entire black studies program with a library that would be the envy of the nation. In an article for Denver's student newspaper, Daddy made an impassioned case, stressing the need for his new course: "We had to have a fire in Chicago before people realized ghettos existed there; we had to have a march on Washington before people realized discrimination existed in the U.S. This should not be necessary. We should do it out of an awareness of the needs of our fellow man."

Daddy was keenly aware that Denver, as a private school, had considerable latitude in developing a curriculum of the kind he envisioned. In addition to a course that he taught on the history of Africa until 1800, he wanted to offer a seminar that would launch an effort to create more minority courses and appoint black professors in regular departments. "It's incomprehensible that out of all of the schools at DU you have one Afro-American administrator and two part-time people on the Faculty of Arts and Sciences," he noted. Daddy hoped the seminar was just the beginning, and with its broad conception, the seminar encouraged students to combine academic coursework with public service and community involvement.

This Monday night class, "The Black Experience in America," for which students would receive two units of credit, was set to launch in the winter quarter of 1970. Daddy got into the car one day, almost giddy about the advertising fliers that he had just had printed. The fliers showed an American flag—with black stars and red and black stripes. "This will make them a little angry," he said. "That's good for this place."

The parade of speakers my father assembled for his seminar was extraordinary by any measure. Academics and educators, artists and activists, politicians and athletes, all came together to provide their perspectives on the state of black America. There were also some civil rights leaders such as Julian Bond, one of the founding members of SNCC, and Fannie Lou Hamer, the woman who led the fight to seat an alternative delegation from Mississippi at the Democratic National Convention of 1968.

Sometimes the course resulted in direct action. For instance, during her speech to the class in 1970, Hamer mentioned that she had been unable to get federal examiners into Sunflower County, Mississippi, to ensure fair voting practices. Chancellor Mitchell, a member of the U.S. Commission on Civil Rights, took up the matter with the Department of Justice, which finally sent federal examiners to Mississippi. Hamer's lecture also inspired a large service project that included a citywide clothing drive on

"Sunflower County Day," championed by Spencer Haywood and Larry Jones of the Denver Rockets professional basketball team. The entire Civil Rights Commission, headed by Father Theodore Hesburgh, the president of Notre Dame, came for a class session the next year.

Occasionally, cultural figures such as the Ramsey Lewis Trio or the poet Useni Eugene Perkins were invited to perform. But most speakers came from political backgrounds. A young Charlie Rangel, then a state representative in the New York Assembly, joined Ralph Metcalfe, U.S. congressman from Illinois and founder of the Congressional Black Caucus, in the lineup.

And many of the speakers were on the radical end of black politics, such as Dick Gregory and Louis Farrakhan. Lou House and Charles Hurst came down from Malcolm X College in Chicago, and the three track stars made famous by raising their black-gloved fists at the 1968 Olympics—Tommy Smith, John Carlos, and Lee Evans—also spoke. One course session consisted of a telephone hookup to the hunger-striking black inmates of Attica Prison in 1971. And, of course, Daddy invited his friend Stokely Carmichael to the podium several times.

Thus, "The Black Experience in America" had a pretty hard edge. This led my father, in a progress report on the class, to remind his unnamed critics in the university that the "deepest aims and hopes of the seminar are directed to the idea of reformation rather than revolution." "The seminar is *not* a staging ground for violent revolution," he emphasized. Daddy's point was that if the seminar encouraged greater demands from the black community, it should not be discounted as academically invalid.

In truth, my father was fascinated with the radical side of black politics. I was never taught that Farrakhan was a traitor or that the Black Panthers were terrorists. They were to be taken seriously on their merits. Years later, when so much attention was paid to then-Senator Obama's radical associations, I wondered what might have been made of the people who sat at our dinner table.

This was especially true of Stokely Carmichael, who came to Denver almost every year. Daddy even invited him in 1973 to speak at an adult education forum at the virtually all-white and quite wealthy Montview Boulevard Presbyterian Church, which we attended and where Daddy acted as a part-time assistant pastor. At the end of the session, Stokely, no longer in fatigues and now wearing tailored suits, received a standing ovation from the decidedly conservative membership. Afterward, my family and I were standing next to Stokely when we overheard a lady say, "Well, he wasn't so bad." Stokely turned to us without missing a beat: "What did she think I was going to do? Swing from the chandelier?"

Our association with Stokely Carmichael had an impact on me as well. When visiting the house, he referred to me affectionately as his *"petite soeur."* I remember sitting with him in the back seat of the car, singing along with the radio and witnessing his distress at lyrics that demeaned the black family. He hated the Temptations' "Papa was a rolling stone—wherever he laid his hat was his home." "Why do they send those messages to our kids?" Stokely asked.

Then, as I got older and my interest in Soviet politics grew, the two of us would debate his growing fascination with Leninism and socialism. He clearly thought that I was misguided in my rejection of communism and the teachings of Karl Marx. But Stokely Carmichael was a brilliant man and he made me hone my arguments. My father would beam as we argued, as he always enjoyed intellectual sparring and relished opportunities to "stir the pot."

Over the years I've reflected on what attracted my conservative, Republican father to radicals such as Stokely Carmichael. When I asked, he said that he liked the contestation of ideas. It's true that he loved to make people uncomfortable by testing the limits of their intellectual tolerance—whether with his congregation in Bible study or his students in the classroom.

But I've come to believe that there was more to it. Daddy would sometimes ridicule those who suggested that blacks find succor and support in a closer association with Africa. "America is our home," he'd say. "Africa doesn't belong to us or us to it." And he'd sometimes say to my horror that the tragedy of slavery had given us the chance to live in the freest and most prosperous country on earth. He loved the United States of America and was vocal in his appreciation for the good fortune of being American. Yet he clearly admired the willingness of radicals to confront America's racism with strength and pride rather than with humbleness and supplication.

Daddy was remarkably adept at navigating and charting a course for success in the white man's world. But there was, I know, a deep reservoir of anger in him regarding the circumstances of being a black man in America. On occasion it surfaced—for instance, when Santa Claus was about to mistreat his daughter. Sometimes, after integration took hold, he and my uncle Alto would laugh at the "shuffling" white service people who were grateful for a tip from them. "He ought to scrape and bow for how he treated my daddy," I overheard Alto say one day. My father roared his approval. But for the most part my father couldn't afford to let the bitterness interfere or to give expression to it. Maybe giving voice to black radicals in the midst of his very white world helped him to square the circle.

So just one year into his tenure at Denver, Daddy's career was flourishing, and his class was drawing crowds of more than five hundred people. I too was doing considerably better at St. Mary's, making new friends there. I won the state championship in Greek and Roman history, finding a new passion. Well, actually it was only a competition among parochial schools, so there weren't that many contestants. Nonetheless, my parents were very proud.

There *was* one unpleasant incident at St. Mary's, which did cause my parents to question their decision to send me there. After doing poorly on the Preliminary Scholastic Aptitude Test (I wasn't then and am not now a good standardized-test taker), the guidance counselor called me in to review the results. "You didn't do very well," she said, ignoring the fact that I was two years younger than my classmates. "Perhaps you should consider junior college." I just laughed at her, thanked her for her advice, and left. But when I went home and told my parents, they were *not* amused. They wanted to go to the school and confront her. I begged them not to, and I prevailed. I have told that story many times since, particularly when I was provost at Stanford, for several reasons. First, my own experience has led me to be rather suspicious of the predictive power of standardized tests. Second, I realize how lucky I was that my own sense of self—developed through years of parental affirmation—shielded me at that moment from self-doubt. I have always worried that there are many young people, particularly minorities, who might internalize negative messages like that and simply give up.

On balance, though, I loved my life in Denver. I kept the same rigorous schedule of piano and skating that I'd established the year before. I made rapid progress in piano in particular, competing in statewide and regional competitions. My first major competition was something of a disaster, though. Playing a Mozart piano sonata from memory, I lost my place a few minutes into the piece and wound up at the end before I'd played the middle. I was devastated, although the judges said that what I *had* played was very good. It was the first time I'd really bombed playing the piano. My parents tried to be supportive and kept talking about how good I'd sounded. I learned at that moment that some failures are best absorbed alone. I thanked them for their concern and spent the night replaying the disaster over and over. I knew that I had not really been prepared for the competition. Perhaps because playing the piano is both a physical and a mental challenge, it's not possible to "cram" for a performance in the same way one can for an exam. In other words, practicing eight hours one day will not produce the same result as practicing one hour a day for eight days. I'd left my preparation to the last minute and it showed.

A couple of days later I asked my piano teacher when the next competition would take place. It would be the Young Artists' regional competition in the winter. I entered immediately. When my parents asked if it would help to practice on a grand piano, I spent weeks visiting piano stores trying to choose the right one to rent. All that preparation helped, and when I won the competition, my parents bought the piano. I learned later that they had to take out a $13,000 loan in order to do so. To this day, I still own and play that Chickering grand.

But while Daddy and I were doing very well, Mother was

having a much more difficult time adjusting to Denver. She was unable to find a job right away, and for the first time I realized that my mother's sense of self was tied to her identity as a teacher. She really missed her family, particularly her mother, and we didn't have the money for frequent visits to Birmingham. To fill her days, Mother tried to throw herself into homemaking—even learning to make homemade bread, of all things. She made bread every week whether we ate it or not. At the age of fourteen I could see in my mother what it meant to make yourself content and happy, even if you were not fulfilled.

Mother also disliked the West's informality. Birmingham, and even Tuscaloosa, maintained a certain societal pecking order, and we'd always been high enough in it to satisfy my mother's social sensibilities. Denver was, in those days, a bit of a cow town with few cultural outlets. Skiing, hiking, and the rodeo provided much of the social activity. We weren't a part of whatever cultural elite there was in Denver. The people we knew rarely gave the fancy house parties or dances to which we were accustomed in the South.

One night shortly after moving we were invited to a cocktail party at the university. My mother dressed as she would have in Alabama, in semiformal attire. When we got there everyone was in pantsuits (polyester was the dominant fabric). Mother was clearly embarrassed, but when we got in the car she said, "Condoleezza, if you are overdressed, it is a comment on them. If you are underdressed, it is a comment on you." That statement has stayed with me over the years, and I have always dressed accordingly. But it said volumes about my mother and the importance she placed on social graces and nice clothes.

Despite this culture clash, the Rice family did settle into a rather comfortable life. Ice hockey became as important in our lives as football had been. The University of Denver had no football team, but it did have a tradition of championship hockey teams. We'd attended the games during our "temporary" stay in Denver the year before. Now we purchased season tickets and eagerly awaited the Friday-Saturday matchups of Denver against Western Athletic Conference foes. We especially loved the home and away series against Colorado College and would treat ourselves to a fancy dinner at the Broadmoor Hotel in Colorado Springs before the big game. Daddy became a member of the faculty athletic committee, which got us very good seats and a chance to get to know the hockey players. My parents liked the young men, most of whom were from western Canada, and treated them like surrogate sons, inviting them to dinner on many occasions. This was great for me since for the first time I was starting to react favorably to these creatures called boys.

CHAPTER SIXTEEN

Cancer Intrudes

WE WERE all looking forward to the coming hockey playoffs in March 1970. Denver was a powerhouse and stood a good chance of capturing their sixth national championship. I knew that Mother had a doctor's appointment that Friday but didn't think much of it. Daddy always dropped me off at school each day and picked me up afterward; school ended about three-thirty.

I waited and waited, and as more than an hour passed, I became concerned that something had happened to him. In those days, which were well before cell phones, there was no way to reach him. When he finally arrived, he explained that he'd been at the doctor's office. Mother had gone to Dr. Hamilton because she'd felt a lump in her breast, and she was still with the doctor, who was doing some tests.

When Daddy and I arrived at the doctor's office, the doctor

explained that he couldn't be sure but the lump felt like cancer to him. In those days, you didn't wait for second opinions and analysis. Mother would have surgery on Monday morning. It was likely that she would lose her right breast, and then we'd see what else could be done.

That weekend was consumed with preparations for her hospital stay. I'll never forget the sight of Mother cooking and cooking, making and freezing chicken and beef roast and vegetables so that we would have enough to eat while she was hospitalized. I suspected she was trying to get her mind off what she was facing. In 1970, cancer was considered a death sentence. I could tell that she was scared. I could tell that Daddy was scared. And I was terrified. Not frightened in the same way that I'd been by the bombings in Birmingham. This cut much deeper. I could not conceive of life without my mother.

Mother was admitted to the hospital Sunday night. My parents decided that I should go to school that Monday. I think that was the longest day of my life. By the time I reached my one o'clock Latin class, I just couldn't wait any longer for news. I asked Mrs. Winters if I could go to the office and call my father, explaining that my mother was having surgery. I waited for what seemed like an hour in the principal's paneled office. Finally, the nurses reached Daddy, and he said that the surgery was over and it was indeed a cancerous tumor. He asked if I wanted to leave school. I said yes, and he picked me up shortly after.

When we got to the hospital, Mother was awake and more relaxed than either my father or I. She was relieved to at least know the facts, and Dr. Hamilton was mildly encouraging, saying that the cancer had been caught early. "Early" in those days meant that it had already spread to at least two lymph nodes. She'd need to undergo radiation therapy, which would start in the hospital and continue when she came home.

My father called my grandmothers, aunts, and uncles with the news. A steady parade of family began to descend upon us. My mother's sisters, brother, and sister-in-law all arrived. Grandmother Ray wisely stayed home. I love my extended family and we needed them, but after a while it felt like a bit of an intrusion. Mother stayed in the hospital about ten days. On the day before she was to leave, I arrived home from school to see my aunt Mattie moving the bedroom furniture around. "What are you doing?" I said. She explained that it was good when people came home from the hospital to have things look different. Certain that my mother wouldn't appreciate coming back to a rearrangement of her carefully decorated bedroom, I protested and insisted that the furniture be returned to its original position. My relatives stayed a few days longer. They were trying to help, and for a while they did buoy Mother's spirits. But then it was time for them to go home. Mother and Daddy and I just wanted to get back to normal. We needed to do that as a family: just the three of us. We even went to the hockey game the night the last relative left—just two weeks after my mother's surgery.

But when your mother is diagnosed with cancer you have to find a new normal. Once cancer enters your family's life it is a constant and unwelcome presence. I prayed every night that Mother's cancer would not come back. And there were Mother's periodic checkups, first every month, then every three, then every six, which provoked an indescribable anxiety as they approached and only temporary relief when they passed without incident. I once asked my mother, just before one of these periodic trips to the doctor, if she was afraid. "It's not so bad. I'm only nervous just before the doctor gives me the news," she responded. After her five-year mark, which was once promoted as the moment when a cancer victim was considered cured, we all celebrated. But frankly I never believed that the struggle was behind us, and I was right.

As the daughter of a mother who had breast cancer I can confirm that the perpetual anxiety caused by a parent's disease is passed on to a child very directly. When Mother was first diagnosed in 1970, the genetic implications of the disease weren't as well understood as they are today. But over my lifetime the fact that my mother had breast cancer has persisted as a dominant factor in my own health prognosis. I started getting mammograms before I was thirty and have had several scary results leading to multiple biopsies. The promise of early detection (and the prayers that go with it) has become my talisman against this devastating disease. I am grateful for the advances that seem to give me a fighting chance, but I am ever cognizant of my vulnerability. I decided, nonetheless, to forgo the test for genetic markers of the disease. A positive determination would just be too heavy a burden to bear. I don't want to know the future.

The cancer altered Mother's life in other ways too. Though she never complained, I know that the drastic change in her physical appearance took a toll on her. Remember that this was a woman who took pride in her physical beauty and elegance. In 1970, cancer surgery was pretty blunt. The operation left a concave indentation where Mother's breast had been. It was not standard practice then to do immediate reconstructive surgery. Rather, the attitude was somewhat cavalier: *After all, what function does a woman's breast have past her childbearing years?* Mother lived the rest of her life with a prosthetic bra. Moreover, the removal of several of her lymph nodes caused her left arm to swell to almost twice the size of her right. She covered the swelling by always wearing long-sleeved dresses. I remember one day when Mother went shopping and tried on a dress, the sleeve of which was too tight for her disfigured arm. The saleslady innocently asked what had happened. Mother addressed the situation directly, explaining that the swelling was the result of breast cancer surgery. The startled woman fumbled for something to say and then just said, "God bless you." Mother, gracious and calm, simply replied, "Thank you."

I learned a lot about Angelena Rice from how she faced these challenges. She didn't allow anything "superficial" about her status as cancer victim to matter, sloughing off the physical disfigurement and the psychological toll of living with the disease. She was grateful to be a survivor and to continue her life as wife and mother. Mother was strong in ways that I cannot to this day fully fathom and am certain that I couldn't reproduce. Her strength allowed us to go on with our lives.

My father was deeply affected too. He told me that his prayers had been answered. When he'd learned of my mother's diagnosis he'd asked God not to take her, wondering, "How will I raise a fifteen-year-old alone?" He did not have to. Over the years, Daddy more often gave voice to his fears than Mother did, telling me, for example (but apparently not my mother), that the many doctors he'd spoken to had informed him that cancer never really goes away. "Those little seeds lie dormant and you never know when they'll strike again," he said. The fact is, from that brutal Monday forward our tight-knit family's sense of security was shaken by the infiltration of cancer into our consciousness. That was the new normal.

CHAPTER SEVENTEEN

Starting Early (Again)

THROUGH THE spring and summer of 1970 life was once again taken up with piano, skating, and school. My first major figure skating competition, held that August, was relatively successful. I had always been good at the compulsory phase of tracing school figures and found myself in first place. On the other hand, my free skating (jumping and spinning) left something to be desired, and I wound up finishing third. Many years later I enjoyed some light moments with my parents when I accused them of putting me in the wrong sport. I was five foot seven with the legs of someone five foot ten, exactly the wrong body type to get any leverage for jumping. "I should have been a tennis player," I told them. They reminded me that it was I who'd wanted to be a figure skater

That summer competition was the only one in which I ever

placed. I was simply not a very good skater. I couldn't bend my knees, leading one judge to remark, "It's amazing you can do a jump. You never actually leave the ice." But I was lucky to have wonderful coaches, including Wally Sahlin, who would always tell me to keep my chin up. "You'll get 'em next time," he would say after one of my many mishaps. In any case, I loved the challenge, and the sport taught me discipline and perseverance. I have often said that skating taught me more about character than the piano did. It's really difficult to work hard, fail at the moment of truth, and have to get up and work at it the next day. But that is precisely what skating taught me to do. It may be why my parents continued to pour money into my obviously limited potential on the ice. And why, until I was finally sixteen, my father got up every morning and took me to the rink before dawn.

I'd settled into a very nice life and didn't think much of it when my parents said one day after school that they wanted to talk about college. I assumed they meant that it was time to think about applying to universities, since I was entering my senior year. But they had something else in mind.

We sat in the living room, my mother on the sofa, Daddy in the pink chair, and I on the piano bench. This put us in a semicircle so that our eyes met very directly. Daddy seemed quite hesitant. He started the conversation by noting that I had almost completed the requirements for graduation at St. Mary's. This was true, but I was planning to take a set of Advanced Placement courses and work extra hard on my piano the next year. I had my eye on entering and finishing conservatory and then going to study in Europe.

Daddy said that he'd been talking to people at the university and that it might be possible for me to skip my senior year and

My great-grandfather was illiterate, but my great-grandmother, Julia Head, was a favored household slave who had learned to read as a young girl.

The son of sharecroppers, Granddaddy Rice received a scholarship to study at Stillman College after agreeing to become a Presbyterian minister. He was an "educational evangelist," establishing local schools and impressing upon his students the importance of attending college.

My father at three years old and his sister, Theresa, at five, shown here with my grandparents. Daddy was an easygoing personality and a superb athlete. Theresa was reclusive but brilliant.

My mother, Angelena (right), at three, and her sister, Mattie, at five. The cute little darlings were featured here as "calendar" girls for the local barbershop.

My maternal grandmother, Mattie Lula Parrom, had rich-brown skin and very high cheekbones, attesting to an ill-defined American Indian heritage. She is pictured here at her graduation from St. Mark's Academy, a "finishing" school for well-to-do young black women. RIGHT: After running away from home, my maternal grandfather, Albert Ray III, found himself alone in a train station one evening with just one token in his pocket. "Old Man Wheeler," the patriarch of a white family, brought him home and raised him with his sons.

Mother (far right), her brother, Alto, and her sister, Gee (far left), were often reminded by their parents to maintain their dignity despite the degrading circumstances of segregated Birmingham. They and their cousin, Kate, are pictured here with my grandfather's truck.

Daddy completed college and seminary at Johnson C. Smith University in North Carolina. Like his father, he would become an educational evangelist and mentor students in Birmingham, Tuscaloosa, Denver, and Palo Alto.

Courtesy of Johnson C. Smith University, 1946 Yearbook

JOHN WESLEY RICE
Alpha Phi Alpha Fraternity
A.B. Major in Religious Education
Birmingham, Alabama
"Our thoughts and conducts are our own."
Activities: Stillman Institute 1, 2; Y. M.C.A. 3, 4.

LEFT: My mother's students remembered her as an extraordinary beauty but also as a demanding teacher whom they obeyed despite her diminutive stature.

BELOW: Here I am sitting in Mother's lap, my little foot poking out from underneath the blanket. Had I been born a boy, my father would have named me John. But Mother got her way—a girl named Condoleezza, meaning "with sweetness."

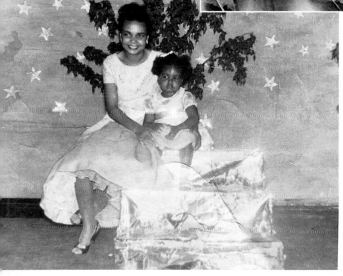

Mother believed passionately in the importance of the arts and organized student-led performances wherever she taught. Here, the two of us pose for the cameras after one of her productions. It was late, and I was clearly ready to go home.

I started to play the piano at three. The little organ pictured here didn't have enough keys in the bass, so after I learned "What a Friend We Have in Jesus," my parents found the money one day to rent a real piano. I began to play at recitals throughout the city. Here I am playing for the new teacher's conference. I still don't understand my mother's decision to have me wear that fuzzy white hat.

LEFT: I spent the first three years of my life living with my parents in a small apartment in the back of Westminster Presbyterian, my father's church.

RIGHT: Mother and me, dressed in our swimsuits. I did not learn proper swimming techniques until I was twenty-five because Eugene "Bull" Connor closed Birmingham's recreational facilities after the courts ordered him to integrate them.

Here I am eyeing Santa Claus suspiciously. A few years later when we went to see Saint Nick, a racial incident almost broke out when my father noticed that the Santa in question was treating black and white children differently. Daddy was prepared to "pull all that stuff off him and expose him as just another cracker." Fortunately, Santa got the body language and treated me very well.

Mother filled our home with beautiful, well-preserved mahogany furniture. The sofa on which my mother and I are sitting resides in my home today. *Courtesy of Chris McNair.* RIGHT: I liked but didn't love school. I got good grades despite a tendency toward procrastination. Clearly art (notice the string of Cs) was not my strong suit.

Pupil *Rice, Condolezza*							
Meaning of Marks A—Excellent B—Good C—Fair D—Poor (barely passing) F—Failure	1st Period 6 Weeks	2nd Period 6 Weeks	3rd Period 6 Weeks	4th Period 6 Weeks	5th Period 6 Weeks	6th Period 6 Weeks	Average
Days Present	29	26	32	29	26	24	164
Days Absent	8	4	1	1	5	2	13
Times Tardy	0	0	0	0	0	0	0
Conduct	A	A	A	A	A	A	A
Arithmetic	A	A	A	A	A	A	A
Art	C	B	C	C	C	C	C
Auditorium	B	A	B	A	B	A	A
Geography	A	A	A	A	A	A	A
Health	C	C	B	A	A	A	A
History	C	A	A	A	A	A	A
Home Economics							
Language	A	A	A	A	A	A	A
Library	A	A	A	A	A	A	A
Literature	B	A	A	B	A	A	A
Manual Training							
Music	C	C	C	B	B	B	B
Physical Education	A	A	A	A	A	A	A
Reading	A	A	A	A	A	A	A
Safety	C	C	C	C	C	C	C
Science	B	A	A	A	A	A	A
Spelling	A	A	A	A	A	A	A
Writing	B	B	B	A	A	A	A
Sunday School Credit	0	A	A	A	A	A	A

Here I am standing outside the White House during a family trip to D.C. My father said that I proclaimed, "I will work in there some day." I don't remember saying that, but my parents did have me convinced that even if I couldn't have a hamburger at Woolworth's lunch counter, I could grow up to be President of the United States.

Daddy established a kindergarten program at his church. Here, at a "graduation" ceremony for his students, he is handing a diploma to Denise McNair, one of the four little girls who were killed in the Sixteenth Street Baptist Church bombing in 1963.

Courtesy of Chris McNair

Daddy's youth programs were renowned throughout the city. Here I am standing with members of Westminster's children's choir in the back row, second from the left.

December 11, 1961

Hon. Bull Connor
City Hall
B'ham, Ala.

Honorable Bull Connor:

I want to congratulate you for your actions in closing the city parks. I feel you acted in the best interest of all citizens of Ala., especially of Birmingham and Jefferson County.

Segregation is one of our most prized possessions, and we should maintain our prized possessions no matter what the price maybe.

Your decision in closing the city parks will go down in history.

I believe, your decision, will be praised by all white and most negroes of the South.

James W. Hartley

James W Hartley

It was in 1961 that Eugene "Bull" Connor decided to close Birmingham's recreational facilities rather than integrate them. He received wide support from whites, like the author of this letter.

Eugene "Bull" Connor Papers, Birmingham, Alabama, Public Library Archives, Cat. #268.8.12.

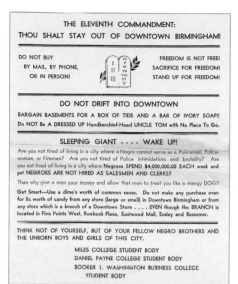

Local civil rights leaders urged black customers to boycott white merchants who did not treat them equally. I was disappointed that we had to forgo our annual Christmas shopping but was old enough to understand the larger issues at stake.

Birmingham Civil Rights Institute

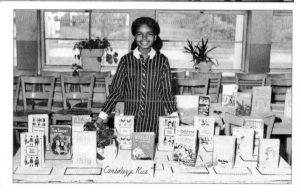

While the civil rights movement is remembered for nonviolent civil disobedience, that was not always the case. A full-scale riot erupted on May 11, 1963, with black protesters setting fire to police cars and confronting an armored personnel carrier rumored to contain Bull Connor himself. My parents and I went to survey the damage that next morning.

Associated Press

My school was selected to participate in the city's first integrated book fair at the Tutwiler Hotel. Here I am displaying my reading project. Mrs. Green, our teacher, was very proud to say that our presentations were far superior to the "shabby" ones of the white kids.

TOP LEFT: I took up figure skating while my parents pursued graduate work at the University of Denver. I was simply not very good. "It's amazing you can do a jump," one judge remarked. "You never actually leave the ice."

TOP RIGHT: The rigorous academics at St. Mary's Academy prepared me well for college. Life also revolved around trying to attract the boys at our brother schools, Mullen Prep and Regis High. Plaid skirts, bobby socks, and saddle shoes were part of the uniform.

Courtesy of St. Mary's Academy, 1969–1970 Yearbook

RIGHT: During my senior year at St. Mary's, Daddy "presented" me (top middle) at the Owl Club cotillion, a debutante ball for accomplished black high school girls. I felt totally out of place, since I had already transitioned to being a college student, taking classes at the University of Denver.

Courtesy of the Denver Public Library, Western History Collection; photo by Burnis McCloud

My father said that I couldn't live in the dorm because "he knew what went on in there." So I pledged Alpha Chi Omega. Here I am (back, right), pictured with my sisters.

Courtesy of the Archives and Special Collections, Penrose Library, University of Denver

RIGHT: As an assistant dean at the University of Denver, Daddy was the liaison to students during the raucous Vietnam War demonstrations, such as this one on Denver's Carnegie Field in 1971.

Courtesy of the Archives and Special Collections, Penrose Library, University of Denver

BELOW: I thought I'd found the man I wanted to marry, Rick Upchurch (center), a wide receiver for the Denver Broncos. He is pictured here with Rubin Carter, the Broncos' nose tackle, and my father, who is holding two-year-old Brian, the son of wide receiver Haven Moses and my good friend Joyce.

After deciding to abandon my dream of being a concert pianist, I wandered into a course in international politics taught by Josef Korbel (center). In one of those odd coincidences, the man who opened up the world of Soviet studies to me was the father of Madeleine Albright. Here I am (leaning forward) in Dr. Korbel's "Comparative Communism" class.

Courtesy of the Archives and Special Collections, Penrose Library, University of Denver

I received my PhD in
August 1981 with a job offer
from Stanford in hand.
That morning, Daddy gave
me a set of classic books
that Granddaddy Rice had
purchased during the Great
Depression, despite his
modest means. It remains
one of the proudest
moments of my life.

Stokely Carmichael
(seated) was a regular
speaker in my father's
courses and even at an
adult education seminar
at virtually all-white
Montview Boulevard
Presbyterian Church in
Denver. This radical
black activist was a good
friend of the family.

*Courtesy of the Archives and
Special Collections, Penrose
Library, University of Denver*

At Stanford, I developed
a close circle of friends,
including Randy Bean
(center), Chip Blacker
(left), and Louis Olave
(right). My father loved
Chip and Louis's dinners,
followed by music played
on Louis's amped-up
stereo.

*Courtesy of Chip Blacker and
Louis Olave*

Jendayi Frazer was a sophomore in one of my first classes at Stanford and, later, my first PhD student. She would go on to become the Africa specialist at the NSC, ambassador to South Africa, and the assistant secretary for African affairs at the State Department

I first flew aboard Air Force One while working for President George H.W. Bush. Here is my maiden voyage in April 1989 on the way to the President's historic speech in Hamtramck, Michigan, welcoming revolutionary events in Poland.

George Bush Presidential Library and Museum

I first met Gen. Colin Powell while I was working for the Joint Chiefs of Staff at the Pentagon. He was serving as deputy national security advisor for President Reagan, and this first meeting gave rise to a friendship that I value to this day. *Office of the Joint Chiefs of Staff*

During one of our nightly phone conversations long after my mother's death, Daddy told me he planned to remarry. His intended bride was Clara Bailey, a principal in the Ravenswood School District. I couldn't have been happier for him, and I was thrilled to have the chance to travel back to California for the wedding.

When we scheduled the Malta Summit for December 1989, we didn't account for the weather. Here I am trying to hold on aboard the *Maxim Gorky*, a Soviet cruise ship.

Rice Personal Collection

BELOW: Here I am greeting Soviet leader Mikhail Gorbachev during the 1990 Washington Summit. Gorbachev was losing control of the revolution he had unleashed; the Soviet Union would cease to exist less than eighteen months after this picture was taken.

George Bush Presidential Library and Museum

A close mentor and friend, Gen. Brent Scowcroft (right) invited me to work at the National Security Council, where he served as national security advisor to President George H. W. Bush. Here we are toward the end of my service, standing with Brent's deputy, Bob Gates, who would later serve as secretary of defense.

George Bush Presidential Library and Museum

After returning to Stanford, I provided on-air commentary for ABC News about Soviet affairs. I was pleased to learn that the President, pictured here at Kennebunkport, was still interested in my advice.

George Bush Presidential Library and Museum

President Bush successfully led the United States and its allies through the uncharted territory of ending the Cold War. He and Mrs. Barbara Bush have been wonderful mentors and friends. Here we enjoy a common love of tennis while vacationing at his summer home in Maine.

Rice Personal Collection

Daddy was so proud to see his daughter working for the President of the United States. Here we stand with President Bush and First Lady Barbara Bush in 1992.
George Bush Presidential Library and Museum

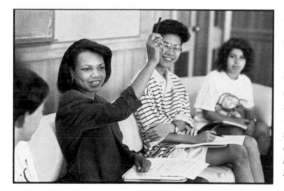

While I was Stanford's provost, President Gerhard Casper and I led efforts to reform undergraduate education, establishing freshman and sophomore seminars. I loved teaching these small classes, such as this one on the Soviet Union.
Copyright © Linda A. Cicero/ Stanford News Service

When budget cuts forced me to make difficult decisions, Chicano students set up a tent city on the Quad and staged a hunger strike. Here, Gerhard (left) and I face the students in front of our offices.
Copyright © Linda A. Cicero/ Stanford News Service

Daddy served on the Board of Governors of the California Community Colleges. Today, annual fellowships are given in his honor, a fitting tribute to his life's work in education.

Courtesy of the Chancellor's Office, California Community Colleges; photo by Sam Wood

ABOVE: Gene Washington, best known as a former NFL wide receiver, remains one of my closest friends to this day.

LEFT: I have been blessed with a wonderful extended family, including (from left to right) Will Alston, my uncle Alto, my aunt Connie, my cousin Lativia, Aunt Gee, my stepbrother, Greg, and my stepmother, Clara.

In 1992, Susan Ford Dorsey and I tapped several other community leaders and launched an after-school enrichment program for disadvantaged children in nearby East Palo Alto. We called it the Center for a New Generation, and it thrives today as a part of the Boys and Girls Clubs of America.

Courtesy of the Boys and Girls Club of the Peninsula

begin my college curriculum there. This would allow me more time for piano as well. He knew that I wanted to apply to a music conservatory, perhaps Juilliard in New York or the Curtis Institute of Music in Philadelphia. But, he said, this was risky, since once I was in a conservatory I wouldn't be able to change my mind and major in something else. Moreover, I had a lot of interests, and Daddy and my mother thought that I would be unhappy in a conservatory.

I protested that I really wanted to be a musician and that they knew that. Was this just a way to keep me in Denver? This retort came out rather bluntly, but I'd long suspected that my parents did not want me to leave home. It was true that I was pretty young. I believed that they just couldn't imagine sending me off to college and breaking up our tight-knit threesome. For the first time in my life I felt that this was more about them than about me, and I resented it.

Mother said nothing when I leveled this charge. Daddy remained calm and explained that I could always transfer after one year at Denver if I really wanted to but that they felt strongly that I should forgo my senior year at St. Mary's. I could go to Denver practically tuition free thanks to a deep discount for the children of faculty. I said I'd think about it, but I didn't like the idea.

Several days later I came back with a counterproposal. This time they sat on the sofa and I stood the entire time. I told them that I'd thought about it and had come up with a good idea. Why not finish my senior year in high school and start my freshman year in college at the same time? I wanted to finish with my high school class but was attracted to getting a jump on college. I'd talked to my piano teacher, Mr. Lichtmann, who was thrilled at the prospect of my early entry into the rigors of the performance major.

My parents explained that St. Mary's cost a lot of money. I selfishly said that I knew that but wasn't prepared to give up my senior year. I remember this as one of the most unpleasant conversations I ever had with my parents. They stood their ground and I stood mine. It was late and we went to bed. I know that I was angry, and I suspect that they were too.

The next day we talked again and after some back-and-forth they agreed to my idea. We set about designing a hybrid path. Each day I would skate and go to DU until eleven o'clock. Then I'd head over to St. Mary's, where I'd take only a couple of required courses and practice the piano. After that I'd go home to study, skate, and practice the piano some more before bedtime. When I started this gauntlet I was only fifteen, too young to drive to college.

This worked for exactly one quarter. I am disciplined, but I am not a grind, and I've always needed more in my life than success at work. I quickly found that I didn't belong socially to either St. Mary's or the university. The final year is supposed to be a bonding year for seniors, but I was rarely around for any of the activities and largely excluded from various committees and class offices. Some of my teachers resented my attending the university, taking it as an affront to the quality of their teaching. When I proudly showed my first college English paper, for which I'd received an A, to a teacher at St. Mary's, she grumpily dismissed it as not very good or worthy of an A in her Advanced Placement course. St. Mary's made it quite clear that my college grades wouldn't be counted toward my academic standing. There was no chance that I would be valedictorian.

I knew that something had to give, but I was bound and determined not to admit to my parents that they'd been right—especially given the high tuition they were paying. So I decided that I'd complete the hybrid year but that I was going to have to find footing in one world or the other. It would be easier to go forward than to go back, I reasoned. That meant really becoming a college student.

First I had to free up some time. I was tired of getting up every morning at four-thirty, never being able to go out with my new college friends for pizza or a burger. So I quit competitive skating that spring, continuing to skate but at a greatly reduced level. Second, I started spending what free time I had at the university, going to St. Mary's only for my classes. Since I had turned sixteen and could now drive, traveling back and forth was much easier. My life began to revolve around the university and my new friends—many of them hockey players, in whom I had more than a passing interest as potential boyfriends.

St. Mary's receded more and more into the background. I'd been fifteen at the time of my junior prom and not yet dating. My father had arranged for his secretary's brother to take me to the dance. He was a nice young man, but I decided that night that I was never again going to a big dance with someone my father had chosen. When senior prom rolled around, I asked one of the hockey players. He went with me, but the poor guy—a college boy—was so uncomfortable at a high school prom that we left early.

The social strains of being so young and so advanced in school had finally caught up with me. I was now barely sixteen and a freshman in college. My parents were concerned too. They worried that I was suddenly hanging out with a crowd much older and far more mature than I was. Nineteen seventy-one was a time of sex, drugs, and rock and roll. When I announced that I wanted to move to campus for my sophomore year, they came unglued. My father said that I'd never live in the dorms because as a university administrator he knew "what went on in there."

My mother added her two cents: "You are just too young to be hanging out with these people. What could they possibly want from you except to take advantage of you?"

I hit the roof. "This early college enrollment was *your* idea," I said. "Now you're going to have to live with the consequences and trust that I'm smarter than you think I am."

This was the biggest fight my parents and I had ever had. Looking back on it, I see that they had set in motion events that challenged me to grow up very fast. I think they believed that I could advance in school and remain their little girl socially. But I was not one of those prodigies who had no social skills and no social life. I loved to have friends, and for better or worse, my friends were now college kids.

In response to my father's retort about the dorms, I asked him what he thought of the sorority houses. I don't think he saw what was coming and said that the Greek houses were a lot better. "Okay, then I'll join a sorority," I told them, and I did. I pledged Alpha Chi Omega. I loved the house and spent much of my free time there, learning to play bridge, planning social functions, and becoming a little sister of the fraternity Lambda Chi Alpha.

In time my folks settled down and suppressed whatever continuing misgivings they had about my new life. I felt no connection to high school any longer. When I was selected for the Owl Club cotillion, a debutante ball for accomplished black high school girls, I did not want to participate. I was in college, for goodness' sake! I eventually did allow my father to "present" me, so as not to embarrass my parents in front of their friends.

It wasn't until many years later that I admitted to them that they'd been absolutely right about St. Mary's. It had been a fine place for me to go to school, but by the winter of 1971 I was done there. One of the truly anticlimactic days of my life was high school graduation. The school didn't even spell my name correctly on my diploma. My mother, who sixteen years before had put so much work into creating that name, sent the diploma back so that "Condoleezza" would be spelled properly, with two z's. The diploma was never returned until some members of the State Department press corps, having heard the story, petitioned St. Mary's for a replacement as a departure gift when I stepped down as secretary of state in 2009.

CHAPTER EIGHTEEN

College Years

As it turned out, I didn't move immediately into the sorority house. It did finally begin to dawn on me how much money my parents had been and were still investing in me. Time was running out on our lease in university housing, which expired after two years. I knew that my parents couldn't afford new housing *and* room and board for me on campus. So I relented and joined them in hunting for a house for us. I learned many years later that Vice Chancellor Blackburn had tried to get my father to buy a house. Daddy told him that they couldn't afford to because "Condoleezza is our house." My parents' investment in me meant that they had no choice but to adopt the itinerant lifestyle of my paternal grandparents rather than the landowning lifestyle of my mother's family. They would occupy four different rental properties before finally buying a house in 1979, ten years after moving to Denver. The fact is, my parents probably never made more than $60,000 a year between them. In retrospect, I wish I'd been smart enough to understand that at the time and found a way to relieve some of the financial pressure.

So, needing to move out of university housing, we began looking with some urgency for a new place to live. One of my father's friends had seen a house for rent in a neighborhood not too far from the university. It sounded perfect: three bedrooms and a large living room to accommodate my grand piano. When you own a grand piano it's like having a child or a pet. You have to have the right place for it, and this was always a major consideration in house hunting.

When we met the landlady at the door, I could tell that she was anxious and acting strangely. After showing the house, she said that she had some other people who were likely to rent it. That would have been an acceptable explanation, but she went on to say that she couldn't rent it in any case to someone who owned a piano because it might disturb the neighborhood. It was a dead giveaway. She was finding an excuse not to rent to us because we were black. Somehow when you grow up in Alabama you can spot racism at a hundred paces. My parents and I knew immediately what was happening.

My father challenged her. The house had been available only a day before when his friend had seen it. It didn't make sense to rule out pianos. Didn't any of the neighbors have stereos? Maybe some even had pianos? "You don't want to rent to us because we're black," he told her. "And now nothing that you do can convince us to rent this house. But I hope you'll enjoy dealing with the equal housing suit that we are about to file."

The woman almost fell over backward. No, no, she had just

heard complaints in the neighborhood about music, she explained. We were such a nice family. Our piano would be no problem. My parents and I left and we didn't file suit. My father said that the threat had accomplished its purpose because she'd never discriminate again. He would explain to Dr. Blackburn what had happened, and he was sure that Blackburn would extend our lease in university housing. Daddy went on to say that racism was clearly alive and well in Denver in 1972 and that he preferred the blatant racism of Alabama, for in the South "at least you knew where you stood."

I understood that sentiment because I'd experienced this implicit racism firsthand. There was, of course, the incident with my guidance counselor, in which she advised me to try junior college. And then in my freshman Introduction to Government course, the professor, Robert Eckelberry, had given a lecture on theories of racial superiority professed by social scientists such as William Shockley. Shockley had posited that blacks had lower IQs because of nature, not nurture. Eckelberry had given the lecture under the guise of simply introducing us to the literature, but I sensed that he bought into some of the theory. I was the youngest person in the class but I challenged him. "I speak French, I play Bach, I'm better in your culture than you are," I said. "That shows that these things can be taught!" He was angry and said the next day that I had tried to silence him. I thought that this was a ridiculous exchange between a senior professor and a college freshman. But I persisted.

Finally I went to the dean and complained, mostly to create a record should Eckelberry decide to retaliate. After a few days the professor asked to see me and then went on to compound the problem. He drew a little graph. Black IQs were charted along the bottom, with those of whites above them. "But sometimes there are people like you," he said. He then showed my IQ line positioned above both, saying that I was special. Clearly, he didn't get the point. I left determined to ace his exam, which I did. He told me that he'd be glad to be a reference for me at any time. I'd made my point but obviously never asked for his help.

In this way, Denver was an odd departure from Alabama. On the surface everything was just fine, fully integrated. But underneath—in the occasional college class, or when we looked for housing, or in my high school guidance counselor's reaction to my low standardized test scores—there was racism, perhaps unconscious and certainly unacknowledged. We hadn't left racism behind in Alabama. And in some ways this less explicit form of prejudice was more insidious and harder to confront.

Many years later, when I was asked about my decision to become a Republican, I first explained quite honestly that the choice reflected my disgust with Jimmy Carter's foreign policy and my attraction to Ronald Reagan's worldview. But, pressed about the domestic agenda of the two parties, I gave an answer that came directly from my experience with the many forms racism can take. "I would rather be ignored than patronized," I said, pointing to the tendency of the Democratic Party to talk about "women, minorities, and the poor." I hated identity politics and the self-satisfied people who assumed that they were free of prejudice when, in fact, they too could not see beyond color to the individual.

The fact is, race is a constant factor in American life. Yet reacting to every incident, real or imagined, is crippling, tiring, and ultimately counterproductive. I'd grown up in a family that believed you might not control your circumstances but you could control your reaction to them. There was no room for being a victim or depending on "the white man" to take care of you. That self-sufficiency is the ethos passed down by my ancestors on both sides of the family, and I have internalized it thoroughly. Despite the gross inequities my ancestors faced, there *has* been progress, and race is today no longer determinative of how far one can go. That said, America is not color-blind and likely will never be. Race is ever present, like a birth defect that you learn to live with but can never cure.

CHAPTER NINETEEN

A Change of Direction

AFTER THE housing incident we did indeed stay in a university-owned home for another year. Mother was hired by the university as an admissions officer and threw herself into this new opportunity with great enthusiasm. She was good at it too, receiving reams of thank-you letters from prospective candidates and their parents whom she had helped. I was so happy for her because finally she had her professional life back.

Daddy earned accolades for his work at the university as well, becoming at Denver, as he had at Stillman, one of the best-known figures on campus. He was a magnet for students—including David Ayers, soon to become the comedian Sinbad. But many of his students were white and considered Daddy essential to their success. My father's touch with young people easily translated across racial boundaries.

The university administration relied on Daddy for difficult tasks. When the shootings of students protesting the Vietnam War at Kent State took place in 1970, Denver, like virtually every other campus, erupted in protests and sit-ins. My father became the university's liaison to the students, helping to calm the situation. I wasn't particularly caught up in the political fervor but did attend one rally on Carnegie Field where my father proclaimed to the crowd, "It seems to me as if we need a demonstration to end all demonstrations!" Somewhere there is a picture of me sitting with the student demonstrators looking up at him on the stage. Ironically, these were exactly the kinds of campus incidents I dreaded as provost at Stanford.

The truth is that music majors were so busy with practice, rigorous and difficult theory classes, and performance demands that there wasn't much time for anything else. I can remember distinctly sitting in the music building lounge reading about Nixon's invasion of Cambodia. I mentioned it to another student, who apparently was not aware that the events in Cambodia were connected to America's involvement in Vietnam.

I found the insularity of the music school terribly stifling. When I tried to break out by accepting a post as news editor of DU's student newspaper, the *Clarion,* I quickly learned that I simply didn't have enough time for extracurricular activities. I couldn't stay at the paper all night with my colleagues, reading copy and producing the paper. Eventually I quit, or perhaps I was fired. I quite honestly can no longer remember the circumstances.

I constantly clashed with the music faculty, which, rightly, didn't think me singular enough in my devotion to piano. After one fairly poor jury performance (the final exam, in which a student plays for the entire piano faculty), Mr. Lichtmann suggested that I rededicate myself to the piano by going to the Aspen Music Festival School the summer of my sophomore year.

I applied and was accepted, studying with great pedagogues such as Edith Oppens. I knew that I'd become a far better pianist that summer. And I also knew that no matter how much better I became or how hard I worked, I'd never be good enough. The many prodigies studying there, some not yet into their teens, gave me a glimpse of the barriers to a concert career. I left Aspen having experienced a crisis of confidence and returned home to Denver set on finding a new path.

I asked to talk to my parents. We sat in the living room, they on the sofa and I on the piano bench. I told them that I wanted to change my major. I hated the single-minded focus of the piano program and had determined that I'd never be good enough to rise to the top of the profession. "It's not good enough to have a career teaching thirteen-year-olds to murder Beethoven," I told them.

They knew me better than anyone else, but they hadn't seen this coming. At first, my dad suggested that I change my major from the very demanding bachelor of music (the performance degree) to the broader bachelor of arts in music, which meant that I could take a number of courses in other departments. I explained that this wasn't just about the narrowness of the degree. "I've played the piano since I was three," I said. "But I don't love it enough to end up as a music teacher, and that's where I'm headed."

"What are you changing your major to?" Daddy asked.

"I don't know Just not music," I said.

"You're going to end up as a waitress at Howard Johnson's

because you don't know what you want to do with your life," he responded. I don't know why he picked on Howard Johnson's, and after all, he'd once waited tables himself, but this was as powerful a rebuke as he could muster. I was accustomed to my parents supporting me in everything that I did, so my father's response was truly shocking.

"I'd rather be a waitress at Howard Johnson's than teach piano. And after all, it's my life."

"It's our money," Daddy retorted.

Mother intervened. "Come on, Rice, that's not fair." She looked back at me. "What your father is saying is that you're already a junior in college and you don't know what you want to do. You need to find a major or you won't graduate on time," she said calmly.

That evening I asked Mother why she wasn't upset about my decision. More than anyone she'd been responsible for my love of music and my pursuit of a career in it. I would never fulfill that dream. Mother just smiled and said, "Do you remember when I told you that you weren't old enough or good enough to quit." I laughed, recalling that moment. "Now you are old enough *and* good enough. For the rest of your life your piano will always be there for you." When I had the chance many years later as national security advisor to play with Yo-Yo Ma and as secretary of state for the Queen of England, I knew how wise my mother had been.

I did eventually find a major. After false starts in English literature and political science with a focus on state and local government, I was getting pretty desperate by the spring of my junior year. That's when I wandered into an introductory course on international politics taught by a man named Josef Korbel.

Korbel had been a Czech diplomat during World War II and had successfully mediated the 1948 Kashmir crisis for the United Nations before settling in Denver and founding the Graduate School of International Studies. He opened up an entirely new world to me. I loved his stories about the work of diplomats. He was a specialist on the Soviet Union, and I was quickly drawn into his tales of the byzantine intrigue of Josef Stalin. At the end of the quarter I asked to see him and told him that I wanted to be a Soviet specialist and study international politics. He encouraged me to do so, saying that he had a daughter who was studying at Columbia. Her name was Madeleine Albright and perhaps we could meet someday.

When I went home and told my parents that I'd found what I wanted to do, they were really happy. If they had any doubts about the wisdom of a nice black girl from Alabama studying the Soviet Union, they didn't express them, though in retrospect I'm sure they had plenty. "Jump on it with four feet," my father said. And I did. I declared myself a political science major and started studying the Russian language. I had found my passion, or more accurately, it had found me. In any case, I finally knew what I loved, though I didn't know, frankly, where it would lead me. I remember being very conscious of starting down a path that was different from anything in my parents' experience. They had always been there for me and always would be. But I would have to navigate my professional life on my own. That brought an unexpected sense of maturity and newfound freedom.

The remainder of my college time seemed to fly by. I worked in the summer of my junior year and during Christmas break as a temporary secretary at the university. I took a job typing purchasing requisitions, which required six carbon copies. If you made a mistake, you had to start all over again, since there was no way to correct the carbons. As awful as the job was, it allowed me finally to help with the financial demands on the family. Thus, in the fall of my senior year, my parents and I agreed that I could move into the sorority house. I'd live apart from them for the first time in my life. That Saturday in mid-September when we loaded up the car with my clothes, a new bedspread for my room, and several other personal items, it seemed like a huge step—this despite the fact that the sorority house was located about five minutes from where my parents lived.

Of course, the distance seemed much greater. I felt a good deal of personal freedom and exercised it. There were some constraints because Daddy was so well known on campus. Yet I managed to allow tendencies toward procrastination and even a little sloughing off to take full flight. Fortunately, the political science classes were much easier than music and I didn't need to work as hard.

EARLY IN the year, I learned that I needed surgery on my hand to remove a ganglion cyst, which meant that I couldn't study piano for several months. I quit skating altogether and gained thirty pounds due to the lack of exercise and a sudden affinity for the International House of Pancakes. This time, despite the extra pounds, when I needed a date for the sorority formal, I didn't have to rely on my father to find one. Rich Preston, the captain of the hockey team and my first real crush, took me to the dance. The night turned out to be a little tense, though, since the hockey game in which Rich was playing went into overtime while I sat at the sorority house waiting. I was relieved when my father called to say that the game had ended and that Rich was on his way.

I also used my expanded free time to become deeply involved in student government and service activities with the sorority, resulting in my selection that spring as Denver University's Outstanding Senior Woman. A few years before, the award had carried the politically incorrect title of Miss DU.

Throughout this period, my parents and I were developing a new kind of relationship. We still met every Saturday night for dinner followed by the hockey game. And I found it useful to drop in on them during the week, bringing my laundry with me. We also established a pattern that we kept until the end of their lives: we talked on the telephone every night.

That fall, I started to think seriously about the next chapter in my life. My parents and I were in complete agreement that at age nineteen, I was probably too young to do anything but continue in school. In any case, I had come to political science so late that I needed another year of academic training to pursue my interest in the Soviet Union.

I applied to several graduate schools to study politics and economics and was accepted everywhere except Penn State. Denver was on my list as a fallback, but I never intended to stay at the university. I wanted to go to Notre Dame, which offered a very good program in Soviet studies and encouraged a strong concentration in economics as well. We'd visited Father Hesburgh in South Bend when I was a sophomore in college and I'd loved it. My parents wanted me to stay in Denver, but if that was not possible, they said Notre Dame was a great choice. I've always suspected that my father, in particular, thought that Notre Dame was a protected space for his daughter in the raucous decade of the 1970s. Moreover, his friend Father Hesburgh was there and could keep an eye on me.

One afternoon in April, my father drove up in his red Ford as I came out of the sorority house on my way to class. He stopped at the corner and said, "I have something for you." Daddy handed me the letter from Notre Dame graduate school admissions, which had come to my parents' house. I took a deep breath and opened the letter. The news was good. I was in. Daddy started to get out of the car, so excited that he forgot to put it in park. After quickly securing the brake, my father, all six feet two inches and 260 pounds of him, leapt out and hugged me. I think he was prouder of me than I was of myself and to this day that is one of my fondest memories of him.

After I was admitted to Notre Dame, I relaxed and enjoyed the remainder of my senior year. I loved hanging out with my friends, such as Debbie Byrnes, who gave me my first experience as "maid of honor" when she married Rich Griffin. (I had introduced them.)

The spring and summer were dominated by the Watergate scandal and Richard Nixon's subsequent resignation. My friends in the sorority, unlike the music majors I'd left behind, were also riveted by the proceedings. We'd sprint home from class every day to watch the testimony on TV.

One of the jobs that I had taken on at the university was director of the student speakers bureau. We had invited Bob Woodward, the crusading young *Washington Post* reporter, to speak one evening in May. After returning home from class for lunch, I received a call from Woodward. He was very sorry but something had come up in Washington and he could not make the speech that night. I was angry with him but mostly consumed with managing the fallout, including cancelling the event and refunding tickets. Later that day, another student showed me a headline: "President Hands over Transcripts: Initial Reaction on Hill Divided Along Party Lines." For the first time, all 1,254 pages of the Nixon Watergate papers were made public to the Congress and the American people. I subsequently related this story to Woodward and reminded him of the trouble he'd caused in my life (not for the last time) when I was a senior at DU.

Finally it was graduation day and as the Outstanding Senior Woman, a.k.a. Miss DU, I led the processional. My father, who'd been promoted to assistant vice chancellor that year, marched with the faculty not too far behind. After a drawn-out ceremony, my parents and some of their friends took my friends and me out to dinner. The celebration was very nice but not very memorable. There was so much ahead. I was just starting my life. Thinking back, I'm reminded of that wonderful line in the Barbra Streisand and Robert Redford movie *The Way We Were* when Streisand says, "Commencement. What a funny thing to call the end."

CHAPTER TWENTY

"Rally, Sons (and Daughters) of Notre Dame"

Throughout the summer of 1974, my parents and I were consumed with preparations for my impending move to South Bend. As part of that, I went back to skating and ballet to lose the thirty pounds that I'd put on during my senior year. My mother helped by cooking only healthy foods, leading my father to complain that he didn't really like dinners where "green things were the centerpiece of the meal."

I could tell, though, that the prospect of my really leaving home for the first time, perhaps never to return, was starting to trouble my mother. Tensions would rise between us over the smallest things. One such incident still bothers me to this day. I'd gone to a sorority sister's wedding on Father's Day of that year. My parents and I had planned to have dinner together to celebrate the holiday, but the wedding reception ran very long and it was far away in the outskirts of Denver. When I finally returned home, well after dinnertime, my mother was furious, declaring that I was showing a lack of respect for their feelings. I countered that I'd called to say that I would be late and couldn't do anything about my sisters—and hence my ride—wanting to stay until the bridal bouquet was thrown.

My father called me into my bedroom, said that he fully understood what had happened but that this was a new phase for the whole family, and asked if I could be "a little more sensitive" to my mother's feelings. It occurred to me that my mother and father had grown up very differently in this regard. My father had left home at eighteen, never to return. My mother, on the other hand, had lived at home until she married at twenty-nine. She didn't know what it was like to go off to college, and she was having a difficult time watching her daughter break up the family group—even if it was a perfectly natural thing to do.

The day of my departure for Notre Dame finally came. My parents took me to the airport and waved goodbye at the gate. Mother was, as expected, very emotional. Daddy was mostly worried about whether I would be able to navigate the change of planes in Chicago—not a crazy concern given the complications of O'Hare even in that day. He was reassured when I told him that I was planning to meet my college roommates, Chris, Cindy, and their mothers, during the layover and that Mrs. Buschbach and Mrs. Bailey could help me get the plane to South Bend.

When I called the next day, I told my parents that all had gone well. In fact, it hadn't, and I got off to a rocky start. I arrived at the tiny South Bend airport after it had closed down for the night. The plane from Chicago had been late and South Bend wasn't, in those days, a hub of activity. There was no one at the desk and no apparent means of transportation to the university. I was panicked, but then I saw another young woman who looked lost too and asked if she might by any chance be trying to get to Notre Dame. "Yes," she said, obviously relieved to have found a companion. We tracked down the only cab driver still at the airport. He took pity on us despite the fact that he was preparing to go home for the night. He drove us to Notre Dame. There was never a more welcome sight than that of the Golden Dome in the distance.

The next day I went out to find a few things to furnish my room. My parents had given me a new car for graduation, an Oldsmobile Omega, which I'd named Boris, after my favorite Russian opera, *Boris Godunov*. Boris had a tendency to overheat and did so that day in the August heat and humidity of South Bend. I pulled to the side and walked across the street to the service station. The attendant said sharply, "You'll have to bring it over here." I took offense. When I asked even more pointedly why he couldn't go across the street and fix it, he said very meekly, "I thought it might cool off quicker in the shade over here."

I'd reacted in this way because South Bend in particular, but also Indiana, had a reputation for racism. My father had reminded me that the emergence of the modern-day Ku Klux Klan had occurred in Indiana, not Dixie. To avoid problems, a fellow student at Notre Dame had told me to find the biggest Fighting Irish sticker I could and put it on my car's rear window. "They leave Notre Dame students alone," he said. I was conditioned to expect trouble and viewed the gas station attendant's response through that prism. After that incident, however, I decided that I was going to give people in South Bend the benefit of the doubt. And thankfully, I never had another problem with anyone. To this day, I think back on that rush to judgment whenever I am tempted to see racism in a rebuff.

Later that day as I was moving boxes into my room, a nice young man asked if I needed help. I was immediately attracted to Wayne Bullock, the Notre Dame fullback. When I asked what I could do for him, he said he wanted chocolate chip cookies. Some time later, I was standing in the kitchen of Lewis Hall, the convent that doubled as the graduate women's dormitory on campus, trying to make sense of a Toll House cookie recipe, when I encountered a PhD student named Jane Robinett who seemed to know what to do. Jane became my big sister and my best friend at Notre Dame, and we have remained close ever since.

Wayne and I began to see each other though I knew that he had a "hometown honey." He was a bruising fullback with a heart of gold whose greatest desire was to play pro football and start a family so that he could have lots of kids. When my parents came to visit South Bend that fall, my father fell in love with Wayne. He was my dad's kind of running back, tough and relentless. And he was my dad's kind of guy, sweet and solid. It seemed that every time I called home, Daddy asked about Wayne and was sorely disappointed to learn that the relationship wasn't progressing. When my parents came back in the spring, Daddy was disturbed to find that Wayne was no longer on the scene. I'd dated Randy Payne, another nice guy, for a while, but my new love was a six-foot-five middle linebacker who wore a bandanna around his head and an earring in his ear. "He looks like a thug," Daddy said.

Not surprisingly, I took offense, reminding my father that he shouldn't judge people by how they looked. After all, I was experimenting with bell-bottoms and platform shoes. Daddy didn't say much after that, but he clearly hoped that I'd find "a nice boy." It was obvious by then that we didn't share the same criteria for a mate. My mother gently reminded Daddy that the young John Wesley Rice Jr. had been a bit of a rogue too—dancing and playing cards, smoking cigarettes and drinking whiskey. "And you were a *preacher,*" she added.

All in all, Notre Dame turned out to be a terrific fit for me, providing the typical college experience that I never quite captured at Denver. Many of my friends were undergraduates and my peer group finally caught up with me.

Graduate school was challenging enough but not really difficult. The work in the Government Department confirmed my interest in Soviet studies, but I found the classes in economics more exciting. I liked my advisor, George Brinkley, the head of the Government Department, but thought Kremlinology too amorphous and not very rigorous. Many years later I'd take up the study of military affairs because it was more concrete. Militaries have weapons that you can see, budgets that you can quantify, and doctrine that you can read. Studying the politics of the Soviet Union meant trying to divine what Leonid Brezhnev might have said to Alexei Kosygin from little clues in Russian newspapers. It was not for me.

Fortunately, Roger Skurski took me under his wing in the Economics Department and helped me understand the power (and limitations) of quantitative methods in the study of political and economic phenomena. I was pretty good at math and found econometrics and statistics useful. It was akin to doing the complicated theory problems that I'd encountered in music. I received all A's at Notre Dame but despite the faculty's encouragement, I decided not to pursue a PhD in economics. I thoroughly enjoyed South Bend but wanted to return to Denver. I thought that I should, for the first time in my life, *get a job!*

CHAPTER TWENTY-ONE

A New Start

I RETURNED TO Denver late in the summer of 1975, full of expectations that my new master's degree would help me land an interesting job. As you would expect, my parents were delighted to have me back home. I accepted their invitation to redecorate my room and did so in the style of the mid-1970s, complete with a gauzy red and pink Indian print bedspread and lots of candles purchased from Pier 1 Imports. Nonetheless, I told my folks that I intended to stay for only a year or so until I could afford my own place.

A friend from Notre Dame, Michelle James, called to say that her boyfriend, Eric Penick, who'd been drafted by the Denver Broncos, was planning to go out after the Broncos' first exhibition game with some of his friends. He wondered if I'd be willing to come along. Clearly, Michelle was trying to round up some girls, and I was a little worried because Eric had a reputation as a "bad boy." But I agreed to go.

After the Broncos game, we met up with several of Eric's rookie friends. The night was a disaster. The players that Eric assembled were a bit loud for my taste—and cheap. We went dancing at a bar, but they ran out of money, leaving the girls to pay for the third and fourth round of drinks. Michelle did note that they seemed to find money for a stop at McDonald's on the way home, however. The evening seemed to go on forever, and I was really glad to finally get home well after two in the morning.

The next day Michelle called to say that Eric had another friend who'd seen me the evening before and wanted to meet me. "Michelle," I said, "you and Eric are lucky that I'm speaking to you." She persisted, saying that Rick Upchurch hadn't been among the offending group and was really nice. I agreed to give Eric another chance. The four of us went out, and I found myself very attracted to the fourth-round draft choice from the University of Minnesota. The next day I ran to the grocery store to look up his name in Street & Smith's pro football guide. Frankly, I wanted to see if he was likely to make the team and stick around for a while.

As I was returning home from the grocery store, Rick drove up in his new blue and white Chevy. He entered the house and met my parents, who were very impressed with his politeness. We started seeing each other regularly, almost every day.

Soon I was leading the life of a football "wife." On Sundays I would go to church and sing in the Montview Boulevard Presbyterian Church choir. If the Broncos were away, I would join other "wives" to watch the game on TV. When the team was playing at home, my parents would drop me off at the football game. I'd sit in the wives' section with women who would become, and still are, some of my best friends: Vicki Wright, Diana Carter, and Joyce Moses. The section was always tense with the ever-present possibility of career-ending and even life-threatening injury. It was tense also because every woman there was attentive to any signal that her husband was "stepping out." Whenever there was an unidentified girl in the section, someone endeavored to find out who she was and who had given her the ticket. Strangers were not welcome. The spectacle of visiting players meeting up with women who were not their wives after the game reminded all of us that there was indeed something to worry about. I'd always been a very confident person. But I found myself incredibly insecure when it came to the women who always seemed to be around after the game.

Rick was a good guy and I thought for the first time that I'd found the man I wanted to marry. We were so in sync and he loved my parents. I came home one evening to find Rick in the basement playing pool with my father. It wasn't uncommon for Rick to visit my dad even when I was not there. My personal life was very satisfying, but I couldn't find a job. The economy was in recession in 1975, and I quickly learned that my Soviet studies expertise wasn't very much in demand in Denver. I considered moving to Washington, D.C., but I didn't want to leave Rick and my very happy life in Denver. There was a near miss with Honeywell, which reorganized before I could grab what had seemed to be a promising opportunity. The university purchasing department offered me my old clerical job, but that seemed a huge step backward. I decided to teach piano, the one thing for which there was demand. The irony was not lost on me, or my parents, that the very thing I'd feared had come to pass: I was a piano teacher.

One evening my father came into my room where I was listening to sad songs and feeling very much the failure. He told me that he was sure the setback was temporary but wondered if I'd acquired enough education to do what I wanted to do. He knew that I'd applied to law school and been accepted at several, including Denver. "Do you want to be a lawyer?" he asked. I answered no but I was sure that a law degree would mean something in the workplace. I certainly didn't want to chase a PhD. I could have added, *And end up like Aunt Theresa, reading the same book twenty-five times.* "Well," Daddy said, "your mother and I are ready to help you in whatever you decide to do." He didn't have to say it, but I was glad that he did.

Then, one day shortly before Christmas, I went by to say hello to Dr. Korbel. I hadn't done so since returning from Notre Dame. The afternoon was snowy and cold, and Dr. Korbel was sitting in his corner office in his cardigan sweater, smoking the pipe that he almost always seemed to have with him. He asked what I was doing, and in an instant I poured out everything to him. I wanted to be a Soviet specialist, but I didn't want to take on PhD work. Maybe I would go to law school, but I didn't want to be a lawyer. "Frankly," I told him. "I don't know what I want to do."

Over the years I've seen so many of my students go through this crisis of confidence. It's helped me to be a better advisor to have been through it myself. And I have told countless students what both my father and Dr. Korbel told me. "If you don't want to be a lawyer, don't go to law school."

So I didn't. Dr. Korbel helpfully suggested that I just take a few courses starting that winter quarter. I wouldn't have to commit to a PhD program but could see if I still liked the idea of more graduate work. I learned that there was a master's degree in public administration, which sounded practical, and I thought I might enter that program in the spring. I started classes and was so happy to be back in school.

That winter Aunt Theresa came to visit. We were sitting in the living room just before dusk, waiting for my parents to return home. She asked if I was happy doing graduate work, adding that I seemed to be even if it wasn't leading anywhere. We weren't particularly close and I resented her tone as well as her recounting of her trials, tribulations, and triumphs in achieving her doctorate at Wisconsin. She related the ups and downs of her journey, including her experience as an exchange professor at the University of Liberia in 1961. It started to occur to me that she had indeed had an interesting career. And then something that she said had a lasting impact on me: "Condoleezza, if you don't do the PhD you'll always wonder how far you could have gone."

I thought hard about it, consulted Dr. Korbel again, and before the spring quarter ended was admitted to the PhD program at the Graduate School of International Studies at Denver. And oh yes, I continued to teach piano, but with a new purpose: it helped pay my graduate school bills.

RICK UPCHURCH went back to the University of Minnesota to finish college after the football season. He was therefore away when I resumed my academic career. When he returned for training camp in the summer it was clear that things had changed. We started dating again, still speaking of commitment to each other. But Rick had complications in his life—certain obligations that he needed to take care of. He was and still is one of the best human beings I've ever known, but as a friend of ours put it, he had "too many irons in the fire." Our relationship ended gently and we remained friends.

In fact, I continued to socialize with the Broncos and their wives, as did my parents. My father befriended several players, counseling them and acting as a surrogate father for these young men, many of whom had never experienced that kind of relationship. John Rice's appeal to young people never ceased to amaze me.

Throughout the next year, I threw myself into the curriculum at Denver and thoroughly enjoyed my new colleagues. Denver's student body was very international, and many of my classmates went on to important careers in international politics. One of my best friends there was a young man who was in exile from Pinochet's Chile. Heraldo Muñoz and I would reconnect many years later when as the Chilean ambassador to the United Nations he helped me, as national security advisor, to keep relations between Santiago and Washington calm in the early months of the Iraq War.

My best friend was Cristann Gibson, who'd also gone to Denver as an undergraduate. She'd come early to the study of the Soviet Union, was already fluent in Russian, and was working with Dr. Korbel. Cris was a character—an only child like me—but with platinum-blond hair and four-inch fingernails. We often laughed that it was a good thing we had not known each other as undergraduates because we would have hated each other. Cris was given to torn blue jeans and turquoise jewelry and she managed rock bands. I liked Pappagallo shoes, pearls, and matching skirts and sweaters. We did share a love of hard, acid rock bands such as Led Zeppelin. But as graduate students, we found that we had a lot more in common and she became my best buddy.

In the fall of 1976, Ambassador Horace Dawson, one of the highest-ranking blacks in the Foreign Service, asked my father to serve on an external review of the United States Information Agency. We decided that this would provide me with good exposure to Washington. So my mother and I accompanied my father for the six-week assignment. Since Denver didn't start until late September, I missed only two weeks of school. It was worth it because Horace Dawson became a mentor and friend and remains so to this day. He insisted that I apply for an internship at the State Department for the coming summer. I did and would soon receive my first paying job in international relations.

In general, things could not have been better at Denver. I began to prepare for doctoral qualifying exams, and to satisfy the requirement of a thesis-length research paper, I wrote on politics and music in the Soviet Union, exploring the impact of the totalitarian policies of Josef Stalin on composers such as Prokofiev and Shostakovich. I had finally found a way to unite my interests in music and politics.

Then, early in the spring quarter of 1977, Dr. Korbel asked to see me. He looked awful, and I noticed that his usually ruddy complexion had an undeniably yellow cast. Dr. Korbel said that he would be going into the hospital that afternoon and wondered if I'd take over his undergraduate course. The quarter had just begun, and I told him that of course I would take the class until he could return. He said that he didn't know when that would be. The conversation really unnerved me. As it turned out, the class was a lot of work and I didn't really love the teaching. But I did a creditable job and was pleased to have the experience on my resume.

Soon after, I left for my internship at the State Department.

It was so exciting to move into my first apartment, a little studio in Michelle Towers, a building on 21st and F not far from the Department that has since been torn down for new George Washington University housing. I realize now that it was pretty dumpy, but it was my first apartment and I loved it. Many young Foreign Service officers who were on temporary duty in Washington lived there and I befriended several. One woman, a secretary named Elizabeth, had been in the U.S. embassy during the fall of Saigon in 1975. She had amazing stories of burning classified documents and then escaping on one of the last helicopters as Vietnamese citizens hung from the doors during liftoff. Four years later I was watching television coverage of the attack on the U.S. embassy in Tehran during the Iranian revolution. There was Elizabeth, fleeing the building with the other women who had been allowed to leave by the Revolutionary Guard. I made a mental note to avoid any embassy where Elizabeth was working: she clearly had bad karma.

The internship itself was pretty boring. I was assigned to the Bureau of Educational and Cultural Affairs, working on a project examining Soviet cultural programs in the Third World. The concept seems rather quaint today, but there was great concern that Moscow was making strides with young people throughout Africa and Latin America by sending the Bolshoi Ballet and the Moscow Symphony to these countries to perform. Toward the end I worked on the somewhat more pressing issue of the education of Cuban soldiers in the Soviet Union.

On balance, the internship was a good experience largely because the people for whom I worked took an interest in me and exposed me to the life of diplomats. I liked Washington and would go every Saturday morning to the Watergate bakery for a sweet roll and coffee. It was about all I could afford at the Watergate. But it's funny how those memories imprint. I could almost smell those sticky buns years later when, as national security advisor and secretary of state, I lived at the Watergate for eight years.

Although I became convinced during those months I was interning that I did not want to join the Foreign Service, I appreciated the mentoring. I was especially impressed that Warren Christopher, then the deputy secretary of state, came to speak to us. As secretary of state, I always made a point to engage the interns. "I tell people to be good to their interns," I would say to them. "You never know where they might end up."

With only a few weeks to go in my internship, I received a call from Cris. Dr. Korbel was gravely ill and likely would not last through the night. I was stunned. I thought that he had been diagnosed with hepatitis, but apparently that was the secondary condition. He had liver disease and it had progressed very rapidly. His daughter, Madeleine, called to see if I could come home for the funeral. I declined, explaining that I had a big end-of-the-summer presentation to make to the assistant secretary. Madeleine said that she understood. I sent flowers but felt incredibly guilty for not having made the trip back to Denver. I still do.

CHAPTER TWENTY-TWO

A Lost Year

RETURNING TO Denver without Dr. Korbel to guide me was disorienting. I'd served on the search committee for the new dean of the school and had gotten to know Michael Fry well. He took an interest in my academic work and was immensely helpful, guiding me through my doctoral qualifying exams in the spring of 1978. Back on campus I reconnected with Professor Charles "Mike" Beall, whose courses on Soviet affairs I'd enjoyed as an undergraduate. The university had also hired Catherine Kelleher, a highly regarded specialist in international security affairs from the University of Maryland. I took a tutorial with her and began to gravitate toward military affairs. In addition, Jonathan Adelman, a young Soviet specialist, had come onto the faculty and would eventually become an important mentor.

But there was no one like Dr. Korbel, and in the immediate

aftermath of his death, I lost focus for the better part of a year. I made little progress toward choosing a dissertation topic, let alone working on it. My dedication to my academic work diminished significantly. Cris and I were feeling the same loss of Dr. Korbel and found comfort in each other's company. Almost every day, after a few—very few—hours at the library we'd go to a long lunch, which would soon roll right into dinner.

When I wasn't goofing off with Cris, I found time to play my new sport, tennis. I had finally decided that figure skating was not a sport for adults—after all, you couldn't really invite someone to go skating with you and then whirl away while the other person struggled to find some sort of balance on the ice. I joined a fancy tennis club, which I could barely afford, but I loved playing club and league tennis with my doubles partners Linda Tinney and Charlene Reynolds. We won our share of matches due to big serves and power games. Once in a while we met up with opponents who just kept the ball in play. We usually lost those matches since we weren't the most patient players.

Nonetheless, I loved playing competitively and realized that tennis should have been my sport. I'd always struggled with jumping leverage in skating, but in tennis, my height was an asset. When I asked my father why he'd not introduced me earlier to this wonderful game, which he himself had played, he reminded me that he'd tried. When I was eight we'd gone out on the red clay courts of Alabama in the 98 percent humidity and ninety-degree heat. I'd lasted about fifteen minutes and, with my little socks caked with clay, begged to go home. Tennis was more fun in the cool, dry climate of Colorado.

Life was full of interesting diversions, but I was twenty-four, living at home, still teaching piano, and making little progress toward getting out of school. Every time I went to register for a new quarter, the longtime registrar, who'd known me since my freshman days, would say, "Are you still here?"

Adding to my vague frustration was the difficulty I faced in being an adult child in my parents' house. For example, there was the expectation that I should account for my whereabouts. One evening I stayed out late—really late—with Cris and some friends. When I got home, my parents were worried and furious. "Why didn't you at least call?" I responded that I was an adult and didn't have to call. But a few weeks later when my parents went to an anniversary party and didn't call me, not returning home until one in the morning, I understood their point. After that, we agreed to keep each other informed so that no one worried.

By the beginning of 1979, I was increasingly frustrated and so were my parents. My father asked pointedly when I planned to finish. But, as was typical of my parents, rather than criticize me, they asked if there was anything holding me back. I explained that I needed to find a way to improve my Russian and wanted to study in Moscow. The problem was that in the 1970s most of the exchange programs would not take students who were studying modern Soviet politics. I was a budding Soviet specialist who had never been to the Soviet Union. Somehow my parents came up with the money themselves to send me to the Soviet Union in July of that year. The idea was for me to attend a major political science conference and then work on my Russian at Moscow State University.

My first exposure to Moscow had an enduring impact on me. The first time I saw Red Square and the Kremlin I somehow knew that I had made the right decision in choosing to study the

Soviet Union. While life was not easy—fresh food was hard to find and the rooms were basic at best—I learned so much. I loved riding the elaborate subways, exploring Moscow and Leningrad, and spending time with Russian students. My linguistic skills improved considerably as I moved from using the language in the classroom to using it in real life.

One incident illustrated the point. When Cris, Lisa, and I first arrived, we found to our horror that our rooms were infested with roaches. I was deputized to go and tell our hall lady about the problem. She was a strict elderly woman who never smiled. I approached her gingerly and said in my best Russian, *"Y nas y'est klopi,"* or "We have bugs." At least that is what I thought I had said. But the word for "roach" is actually *tarakan.* I had unwittingly told the woman that we had lice. She recoiled, undoubtedly thinking that this was exactly what she expected of Americans. After consulting my dictionary and realizing my mistake, I corrected myself. It didn't matter. She did nothing about the roaches, which we learned to kill when we could and live with when we could not.

I came back from Moscow in the fall refreshed and ready to sprint to the finish line. My mother had begun teaching in the Denver public schools and came home one day with a story about one of her students. She explained that the little girl had come to class with a note that said, *I don't speak English.* Mother had asked the school principal, "What language *does* she speak?" Russian, she was told. Mother asked if I might be able to help Alla and her family at the upcoming parents' night event. I went to the school and befriended the family, offering to help with medical appointments and basic necessities such as grocery shopping. In time, I took a part-time job helping the Jewish Community Center, which had sponsored Alla's family, to take care of Russian Jewish immigrants who'd relocated in Denver. It was a wonderful experience and my Russian improved immeasurably, though most of my vocabulary concerned various medical and dental ailments.

I was finally making progress on my dissertation as well, having decided to study civil-military relations in Eastern Europe. I chose to work on the case of Czechoslovakia. The Russian professor at Denver, Libor Brom, was Czech, and I convinced him to start a class in the language. I talked five other students into joining me, though to this day I am puzzled as to why they agreed. Nonetheless, I learned Czech well enough to conduct research in it.

That fall I also applied for and received a coveted internship for the summer of 1980 at the RAND Corporation in Santa Monica, California, where I worked on projects related to my interest in the Soviet Union's military alliance, the Warsaw Pact. The research opportunity at RAND propelled me toward the completion of my dissertation.

When I returned from RAND, I felt that I'd broken through. Denver wasn't among the first rank of schools of international relations in those days. The Kennedy School at Harvard and the Woodrow Wilson School at Princeton were the incubators for those who would eventually populate the foreign policy elite. But I was beginning to collect experiences that would get me past the gatekeepers to the next level. RAND introduced me to some of the best-known security specialists in the country, such as A. Ross Johnson. And while in Moscow I'd met Alexander George, a giant in the field of political science who was teaching at Stanford.

Throughout my life, however, something has always come

along to shake things up just when I am feeling settled. Maybe this is the fate of a striver, someone always trying to be "twice as good," so that just good is never enough. The RAND internship had come on the heels of an even more fundamental turning point in my life.

At the start of the 1980s, everyone was worried about the security environment and growing tensions between the United States and the Soviet Union. The Soviet invasion of Afghanistan in December of 1979 had put an end to hopes for prolonged détente between the superpowers. I myself had been deeply affected. I'd registered as a Democrat and voted for President Carter in my first presidential election in 1976. I had this narrative in my head about reconciliation of the North and South; he was going to be the first southern president. Now I watched him say that he had learned more about the Soviet Union from this Afghanistan invasion than he had ever known. "Whom did you think you were dealing with?" I asked the television set. When Carter decided that the best response to the invasion was to boycott the Olympics, he lost me. I voted for Ronald Reagan in 1980, and a few years later I joined the Republican Party.

The security situation convinced the Ford Foundation that there was a need for people who were expert both in Soviet affairs and in hard-core, bombs-and-bullets security policy. Catherine Kelleher insisted that Cris and I apply for the inelegantly named Dual Expertise Fellowship in Soviet Studies and International Security.

Just a few weeks before leaving for RAND, I received the news that I'd won the fellowship. I can remember getting out of the car with my letter in hand. Cris was getting out of her car waving her letter too. I looked at her and we had the same reaction: if we deep-sixed these letters, would anyone ever know that we'd received them? We knew that the fellowships meant the end of our comfortable lives as big fish in Denver's small pond. Cris would go to MIT. There were four other choices: Harvard, UCLA, Columbia, and Stanford.

I eliminated UCLA. I'd liked RAND but didn't really want to return to southern California. I sent inquiries to the other three. Harvard didn't answer my letter. My colleagues there dispute this now, but trust me, I didn't get an answer. My father eliminated Columbia, saying that he didn't want me to live in such a dangerous neighborhood in New York. Fortunately, Stanford answered. I received a lovely letter from the assistant director of the Arms Control and Disarmament Program, Coit "Chip" Blacker. Stanford would be delighted to have me as a postdoctoral fellow. Chip added that Alexander George had told him more than a year before to keep an eye out for me.

CHAPTER TWENTY-THREE

Senator Stanford's Farm

THE NEWS that I would be accepting the fellowship and leaving for Stanford in the fall of 1980 was greeted with a mixture of pride and sadness by my parents. Several months before leaving for RAND, I had also been offered a part-time job at Science Applications Incorporated (SAIC) when I returned. SAIC had a small unit in Denver working on game-theoretic approaches to understanding Soviet military policy. John Battilega, the chief of the unit, liked my academic work and wanted to hire me full-time when I finished my degree.

When I told Daddy about SAIC, he said that he had been waiting for that moment for as long as he could remember. My parents had finally bought and settled into a very nice house about a year earlier. The two of us sat in the den making plans for me to find my own place to live. "You're welcome to stay,"

Daddy said, "but you are probably tired of living with us." We both laughed and agreed to tell my mother together. Those plans would now be placed on hold since I was off to California. Despite the fact that the Stanford fellowship was for only one year, Daddy sensed that I would never return to Denver, and that made him very sad.

In fact, my father's life had taken a turn for the worse, and my departure was coming at a bad time. Daddy was increasingly active and well regarded as a community leader. He was asked, for instance, by Mayor Bill McNichols to serve on the very important Denver Urban Renewal Authority. That body oversaw the successful remaking of downtown Denver, and Daddy was heavily involved. A plaque at the Tabor Center commemorating the project even bears my father's name.

But things were changing at the university. Chancellor Mitchell, who'd been Daddy's strong mentor and friend, had retired in the spring of 1978. John Blackburn, Daddy's good and faithful friend, competed for the chancellorship but wasn't selected. He decided to leave the university and returned to Alabama. Ross Pritchard, the new chancellor, saw my father as "Mitch's guy." It didn't help their relationship when one of my father's former students, now an administrator at the university, passed on to the new chancellor an offhand comment my father had made about Pritchard's "lack of vision." For the first time in my memory, Daddy felt professionally vulnerable. He told me that he was living on borrowed time at the university because under Pritchard the finances of the school were worsening. Daddy knew that without tenure he was vulnerable. He sought out other employment opportunities. But though he knew a lot of people in

Denver and was well regarded, no one wanted to hire a man in his late fifties.

Daddy's health was also a growing concern. Like many former athletes, my father had very bad knees, and as he got older he stopped exercising and gained weight. At the age of fifty-four he was diagnosed with both high blood pressure and diabetes. His father had died of a heart attack. Yet Daddy simply couldn't muster the willpower to lose weight. The two of us clashed regularly about his eating habits, but he just couldn't give up the fried food—pork chops, in particular—of his southern upbringing.

Nonetheless, we both knew that I couldn't pass up an opportunity to go to Stanford. I decided to defer until the winter quarter. I took the part-time job at SAIC in order to make a little more money before I left for the fellowship, which didn't pay as well. I also wanted to give my parents—and, frankly, myself—a little more time to get used to the idea of a departure that might be permanent.

I called Stanford to tell the director of the arms control program, John Lewis, that I would come in January. John said that it would be no problem to defer but invited me out to Palo Alto for a November conference so that I could get acquainted with everyone.

When I arrived at Stanford, I was overwhelmed by its beauty and unnerved by its reputation. Stanford's 8,180 acres, set against the foothills of northern California, were once the farm of Senator Leland Stanford and his wife, Jane Lathrop Stanford. In 1885, the Stanfords donated the land for a university that would honor their only child, who'd died of typhoid fever at sixteen. The university is thus colloquially called "the Farm." It was a good

regional university until the mid-1950s, when its reputation sky-
rocketed, particularly in the sciences and engineering. Now, in
1980, it was an elite university whose only real peers resided in
the Ivy League.

That first morning I walked from the Faculty Club, where I
was staying, to Galvez House, where the arms control program
was located. As I made my way along the long colonnade flanked
with sandstone columns, I felt a level of insecurity that I'd never
felt before and have never felt since. I'd been slowly climbing out
of the obscurity of the University of Denver, but I couldn't quite
believe that I was about to become a doctoral fellow at Stanford.
A part of me wondered if the university had made a mistake.

Galvez House was a dumpy one-story sandstone building
that had once been a dormitory for university laborers. The
other fellows, including three women, greeted me. It seems that
the Stanford arms control program had never had a woman fellow before 1980. Now it had four. Janne Nolan was tall, blond,
and fluent in French, and she had already held an important
post in the State Department. Gloria Duffy was tall and swar-
thy with a can-do western spirit that led her, among other feats,
to change the oil in her own car. That same spirit allowed her
some years later after the collapse of the Soviet Union to negotiate the return of all nuclear weapons to Russia from the
newly independent states such as Kazakhstan. The third fellow was Cynthia Roberts, a short, fast-talking New Yorker who
was also a Soviet specialist and a fluent Russian-speaker. We
were an odd bunch—the "fellowettes." There was a subtle com-
petitiveness among us but also a sense of shared sisterhood as
we talked about building careers in the male-dominated field
of national security policy. Together with our "godfather," the

smart, elegant, and really good-looking assistant director, Chip Blacker, we'd form a tight bond. Already that night, after a bottle or two of wine at dinner, I knew that when I returned in the winter, I'd feel right at home.

THE TIME until my departure for Palo Alto went by swiftly. I continued to work on my dissertation, trying to finish as much as I could before departing. There were also a lot of farewells to my friends. But as January approached, I could hardly wait to go.

Two days after the New Year, I came home to find Mother lying on the sofa, clearly in distress. She explained that she was experiencing horrendous stomach pain, and then she went up to bed. In the middle of the night, my father came into my room and said that Mother's temperature had spiked to 103 degrees. He was going to take her to the emergency room. I didn't want to delay them and said that I'd meet him at the hospital.

Sitting in the waiting room, my father and I prayed. My mother was a cancer survivor, and both of us immediately worried that this illness might somehow be related. Those fears were reinforced when my mother's physician, Dr. Hamilton, came out to say that the imaging showed a large unidentifiable mass in her abdomen. "I don't know what it is," he said, "but I'm going to get it out. Now!"

"Dr. Hamilton, could it be related to her cancer?" I asked.

"I just don't know," he replied and rushed off down the hall to prep my mom for surgery.

Waiting rooms outside of surgical units are, to my mind, the most unpleasant places on earth. You sit and read magazines, the substance of which you care nothing about and of which you remember nothing. My father and I sat together watching the hands move glacially on the black-rimmed clock on the wall.

Several times that morning I asked the "pink lady" at the desk if she could call to see how things were going. Each time the poor lady tried but could only get a, "They're still operating." It wasn't her fault but I wanted to yell at her, "Thanks for the penetrating glimpse into the obvious."

Finally Dr. Hamilton came out. I could see the relief on his face immediately. Mother had suffered a burst appendix several days before. He explained that this was causing toxins to spread through her system, setting off a raging infection and thus the high temperature. The appendix had actually broken into two parts, resulting in the weird image that he'd seen on the ultrasound. "She'll be fine, but she is going to be pretty sick for a while," he said.

I was scheduled to leave for Palo Alto a few days later. Mother, still weak and very frail, insisted that I go. When I boarded the plane, she was out of intensive care but still very sick. It wasn't the way that I wanted to start my new life in Palo Alto. But each time I called she sounded better. I was relieved when she was finally home, and I resolved to go back to Denver within a couple of months—just to see for myself.

I SETTLED into a studio apartment in the Alma Village Apartments in Palo Alto. It was about two miles from campus, alongside the Caltrain railroad tracks. The apartment complex overlooked a gas station, which never seemed to have any customers, and a strip mall with a Lucky's grocery store, a cleaners, and a Chinese restaurant whose kung pao chicken was of questionable origin.

My rented furniture was a little classier than the red plastic sofas in Michelle Towers in Washington. And "Moon Palace," as Janne, who also lived there, nicknamed it, had a swimming pool, where at the age of twenty-five, I finally learned to swim.

Unable to afford a new ride, I gratefully accepted my parents' old car, delivered to my door in Palo Alto by one of those drive-away services. Boris, my cute little Oldsmobile Omega of Notre Dame days, had long since become an unreliable ride. So I drove to Stanford each day in a huge green Chevrolet Impala that the fellowettes nicknamed the "football field."

Galvez House was a great place to work and had supportive staff, including our "den mothers," Barbara Johnson, Gerry Bowman, and Nancy Okimoto. I made rapid progress toward finishing my dissertation, an accomplishment that had eluded me in Denver. "Dissertations don't write themselves," I tell my students now. It's a fact that I learned from the discipline of getting up every day and writing a few hours in the morning. I was the only morning person among the fellows and largely had the office to myself until about noon. Once Janne, Gloria, and Cindy arrived I found that my productivity slowed as we engaged in hall conversation about everything from missile defense to movies. We went to dinner together a couple of times a week. And Janne and I would go shopping, one such trip to Saks resulting in the purchase of our first pair of Ferragamo shoes, which neither of us could afford but bought anyway. I also established a lifelong friendship with Chip and his partner, Louis Olave, who often invited us to their house for dinner and dancing to Louis's amped-up stereo. I loved Stanford.

That didn't mean that I'd overcome the insecurity associated with my rapid ascent from Denver to one of the world's best universities. It could be a bit intimidating, learning from prominent national policy makers such as Bill Perry, who had just returned to Stanford after being President Carter's undersecretary of defense, and Sid Drell, a leading scientist and arms control expert who graciously spent time tutoring me in the physics of nuclear weapons.

Though I began to feel comfortable in elite academia, I still had moments of doubt. Every fellow was required to prepare a seminar on his or her dissertation. While the exercise was intended to be a helpful step toward finishing the dissertation, it was actually a fairly nerve-wracking experience. Seated at the head of the table in the overcrowded conference room, I started out slowly, looking for any sign of approval as the presentation went along. About halfway through I saw a Japanese colonel who was visiting that day nodding vigorously in support of what I was saying. This fired me up. If my presentation on civil-military relations was meeting with the approval of this career military officer, I must be doing well. The affirmation fueled me through the rest of the presentation and the question-and-answer session that followed. I finished and walked over to him, hoping to engage him about my topic. It was then that I learned he spoke no English.

A few weeks after my seminar, John Lewis, the program's director, called me into his office. John was one of the world's most eminent China scholars and quite a character. He spoke in staccato sentences that often made him hard to follow. John also had a habit of confusing the fellowettes, calling blond Janne "Gloria" or, even more amazingly, calling me "Janne." But John had an amazing eye for talent and a tremendous capacity for institution building. John was personally responsible for bringing several people to Stanford early in their careers who went on to reach star status at the university. By the time I'd arrived there, he had almost single-handedly built Stanford's international security program into one of the nation's strongest.

John started our conversation with a somewhat disjointed but clearly positive assessment of the seminar I'd given. He said that the Political Science Department had invited me to give a seminar for their faculty the following week. I said that I'd just given the only seminar that I was capable of giving in that time frame. John said that I should give the same seminar because the audience would be different. I agreed to do so.

The next week I repeated the presentation that I'd given at Galvez House for a somewhat smaller but far more skeptical audience in the mahogany-paneled Graham Stuart Lounge in Building 160 on the main quadrangle. Universities have a rigid hierarchy. Interdisciplinary centers such as the Arms Control and Disarmament Program are viewed with suspicion by university departments such as political science, which see them as too policy-focused and insufficiently attentive to the rigors of disciplinary research. At Stanford, only the departments can hire and tenure faculty. And they rarely hire them from places like the University of Denver.

When I'd finished the presentation, the first question came from Heinz Eulau, the chair of the Political Science Department. Heinz was a German Jewish émigré who'd spawned the "behavioral revolution" in political science. Put simply, Heinz believed that the study of politics was a science and any worthwhile project had to be quantifiable in some way. The kind of analytical/descriptive work that I did was not scientific enough for him. And he looked down on "area studies," which posited the uniqueness of, say, Russia, or the importance of the study of culture and language in China.

I knew Heinz's work and braced myself for what I expected to be a hostile question. He took his time, taking one more puff on his pipe before speaking. "How," he asked after what seemed like an eternity, "can any of what you have said be rigorous enough to have any theoretical value? You can't measure anything." I'd anticipated that line of attack. Going back to the work I'd done at Notre Dame, I explained that I could not quantify the relationship between Soviet power and the response of the Czech military but that I could ask rigorously structured questions and examine alternative explanations. I then proceeded to do so. Heinz cocked his head to the side and his eyes twinkled— something that I later learned to read as a signal of approval. The rest of the question-and-answer session went smoothly.

A few days later, John called me in again. The Political Science Department had an opening for a specialist in international political economy, and Heinz wanted me to apply. "But John, I do international security," I protested.

"That's okay. Just apply," he told me.

So I put together my resume and the one article that I had written and sent it forward to the department. The answer came back that they were looking for someone in political economy. Nonetheless, they'd been impressed with my work and wanted to explore a three-year "term appointment," meaning that it could *not* lead to tenure. In addition, I would serve as the assistant director of the Arms Control Center. Chip would be promoted to associate director. I told John that I was interested and wanted to talk to Heinz about it.

I walked across campus that sunny and warm April afternoon

wondering if indeed I was about to join the Stanford faculty. "Could this really be happening?" I asked myself out loud. I walked into Heinz's office on the third floor of Building 160. I looked out the window at the main approach to the university, feeling very much preoccupied with the question that I was asking. Heinz came in and sat down. But he didn't offer the term appointment. "Would you be interested in a tenure-line appointment?" he asked. At first I didn't think I'd heard him correctly. I asked if he meant a regular tenure-line appointment as an assistant professor.

"Well, yes," he said. He then proceeded to explain that the eminent Soviet expert, Alexander Dallin, and several other faculty of the Political Science Department had been very impressed with my seminar and wanted to hire me. They had done an evaluation of my work, consulting specialists in the field of international security and Soviet studies, as well as reading some chapters of my dissertation. This wasn't the kind of national search (widely advertised with many applicants) Stanford usually conducted. "This is the file of someone whom we're about to hire after completing a big search," he said, pointing to a file at least three times as thick as the one that he had for me. Then he got to the point that he was trying to make. "You do understand that there would be nothing special done for you at the time of tenure," he said. "You'll sink or swim just like everyone else. It won't matter how you got here. Only 30 percent of the people who come up for tenure get it. In fact, there is a review after three years, and it is likely that you won't make it through that."

"I see," I said. "That sounds fair. After three years you can see if you like me, and I can decide if I like you."

Heinz smiled. I don't think he had ever encountered anyone

naive enough about faculty hiring at an elite university to say something so dumb.

A few days later, I got a call from Cecilia Burciaga, Stanford's affirmative action officer, asking if we could have lunch. We went to the Faculty Club and talked for a while. At the end of the conversation she said that she wanted to meet me because my case had been unusual. Usually she was in the position of pushing departments to hire minorities. This time the department had come to her. If a department was willing to hire a minority professor, the university would provide the money for half of the position. Even with that incentive, departments were reluctant. "How did this happen?" she asked. I told her the story but I didn't really understand what was going on myself.

Years later, after having been on the other side of faculty hiring, especially as provost of Stanford, I understood exactly what had happened. Stanford, in an effort to diversify its faculty, had made it possible to hire minorities without going through the "normal" processes. The Department of Political Science saw a young black female Soviet specialist and decided to make an affirmative action hire.

Contrary to what has sometimes been written about me, I was and still am a fierce defender of affirmative action of this kind. Why shouldn't universities use every means necessary to diversify their faculty? And frankly, any new assistant professor, no matter how promising, is a risk: some will succeed and some will not. Tenure is a proving ground. A lot happens between hiring and judgment day.

I went home for Easter a few days after receiving the Stanford offer and talked it through with my parents. Sitting in the kitchen, my father and I at the table, my mother preparing dinner at the stove, I asked their advice. While I was thrilled that Stanford wanted me, I still had reservations about an academic career. I had job offers from RAND and Science Applications and was not sure what to do. Sitting in the kitchen, Daddy asked how much each job offered. RAND and SAIC were comparable, about $26,000. Stanford offered $21,000. "Take the $21,000," he said.

I was surprised, not because he wanted me to take the lower salary but because I had assumed that he'd want me to stay in Denver. "Why?" I asked.

"It's Stanford," he answered.

I explained that the "process" had been irregular and asked what he thought of being hired under affirmative action. "Don't worry about it," he said. "Their 'processes' have been excluding us for years. Just go and show them how good you are."

After Easter, I returned to Stanford and made an all-out effort to finish my dissertation, working seven or eight hours every day toward its completion. The reviews from my committee were positive. This was especially true of the evaluation I received from Michael Fry, by far the most difficult critic. He'd left the Denver deanship for the University of Southern California and suggested that I come down to Pasadena to go over his comments. After dinner at his home, he launched into his comments, but it was clear that he thought my work was nearly done. That night, I stayed at the Frys' home. As I lay in bed, a deep sense of satisfaction, almost wonder, came over me. I was indeed about to become a PhD, and I had landed a coveted job at Stanford. I said a little prayer of thanksgiving and drifted off to sleep.

CHAPTER TWENTY-FOUR

My Rookie Season

THE AUGUST commencement at Denver University was really a cause for celebration. Both my high school and my undergraduate graduations had been anticlimactic. Now, with the receipt of my PhD and the job offer at Stanford, my parents and I could acknowledge that all they had tried to do—even that premature stab at early education when I was three—had paid off. The night before the ceremonies, there was a large reception at the Phipps Mansion, a beautiful old white elephant that had been deeded to the university by one of Denver's most important families. At one point, the master of ceremonies read off a list of where the PhD students had been hired. When he read my name and said Stanford, there was an audible reaction of approval and surprise. My parents just beamed.

The ceremony itself wasn't particularly memorable. This time my father did not march with the Denver faculty. He said that he wanted to sit with my mother, but I suspected that he was starting to feel alienated from the university, and that worried me.

Several friends had traveled from out of town to attend commencement and there were many more from Denver. My parents held a big dinner afterward at our favorite restaurant. At the dinner, Daddy choked up when trying to make a toast. It took him a while to regain his composure and to say, "Your mother and I always knew that you were special. You are God's child." My parents had said this before to friends and family, and I always found it embarrassing. I tried to deflect the comment by saying something like "We're all children of God." But that commencement night Daddy wouldn't be deterred, repeating the phrase again and again. Finally, I just changed the subject to make a joke about the gifts that I'd been given. "You all gave me household gifts," I said. It was true. I had gotten fancy candlesticks and linens as well as a beautiful set of silverware. "Maybe you thought this was a bridal shower," I joked.

I returned to Stanford and moved to new housing. Gloria Duffy and I rented a house together not far from the campus. The old house was constantly in need of repair. I came home one rainy evening to find that the water heater had burst. Another night I walked into a frigid house only to find that the ancient radiator had given up the ghost. But at least the house had more room than the little studio I'd rented in Palo Alto when I had first come to Stanford. And when various appliances were not breaking down, it was a pretty nice place to live.

I wasn't required to teach in my first quarter at Stanford. That's not unusual, since the university tries to give new assistant professors a chance to get their feet on the ground before taking on the Stanford student body. But I would be required to teach three courses after the first of the year. And unfortunately, graduate school doesn't really prepare students for teaching responsibilities. At best, an advanced graduate student will act as a teaching assistant to faculty a few times. The whole process of graduate education is geared toward compiling a research record. That is the basis on which elite universities hire assistant professors. In those days, no one even asked whether the job candidate could teach. Frankly, they still don't.

I sat down with Heinz to decide what three courses I would teach. Obviously, it made sense to offer a course on civil-military relations, the topic of my dissertation. I said that I could also offer a course on Soviet policy in the Third World. But I had no earthly idea what else to propose. Heinz asked whether I could teach something called "Elite Politics." I immediately said yes, though I didn't really know what one would do in such a class. Perhaps sensing my discomfort, Heinz said, "Let's co-teach the course in the spring." I felt as if I'd been delivered from certain doom, and readily agreed. I would teach civil-military relations in the winter. In the spring, I would teach Soviet policy in the Third World and co-teach "Elite Politics" with Heinz.

As winter quarter approached, I realized that my proposed course on civil-military relations had not been listed in the course catalogue. The irregular process by which I had been hired had somehow failed to trigger the normal mechanisms. An embarrassed Eulau said that the department would widely "advertise" my course. When January rolled around, six—yes, six—students had signed up. Moreover, because the course was a late addition, all of the classrooms were booked. Thus, the morning of my first class at Stanford, I walked to the other side of campus and met my six students in the old chemistry building. The classroom even had one of those old sliding blackboards and a periodic table of the elements. I hadn't been in a room like that since Mrs. Sutter's chemistry class at St. Mary's Academy. After the major earthquake of 1989, the building would become uninhabitable, and I'd feel just a little pang of nostalgia when, as provost in 1995, I gave an initial order to demolish "Old Chem." But others had fonder memories of the campus relic, and so it remains today, fenced off and boarded up, waiting for the wrecking ball—or for a donor to save it.

I was anxious at the outset of the class that January morning. Stanford students have a well-deserved reputation for showing young faculty who's smarter—and of course the students assume they are. The course met three times a week, and I was struggling, working late into the night to read and reread the material that I had assigned. I was just flat-out exhausted every day.

At my first departmental faculty meeting about two weeks into the quarter, I looked around at all of the giants of the field gathered there—Seymour Martin Lipset, Gabriel Almond, Robert North, Heinz Eulau, and Alexander George, among others. I was having another one of those "they must have made a mistake in hiring me" moments when Marty Lipset looked over at me and smiled. "First-year teaching is hell, isn't it," he said. I laughed, but he was absolutely right.

Over the quarter I grew accustomed to life in the department. It wasn't always easy since there were only two women—Judy Goldstein and me—both of us junior faculty. It didn't help that Heinz often addressed the assembled faculty as "gentlemen." In time, I started to realize that I was a really good teacher. My first students gave me outstanding evaluations, and when I taught the course the next year, its ranks swelled to fifty. By the third year,

"The Role of the Military in Politics" was overenrolled and I cut off admission at 120.

When I taught the course on the Soviet Union and the Third World, I spotted a black woman wearing a red, yellow, black, and green hat, symbolizing African liberation, and eyeing me suspiciously. A few weeks into the class the young sophomore, Jendayi Frazer, came to office hours. "I don't like what you are saying," she said, "but I think you know what you're talking about and you can teach me a lot." Jendayi would go on to complete her PhD under my direction at Stanford. She would eventually become the Africa specialist at the National Security Council, ambassador to South Africa, and assistant secretary for African affairs at the State Department—all during President Bush's eight-year term. She is now a professor at Carnegie Mellon. I began to mentor students with whom I remain close, such as Kori Schake, who went on to work for me at the National Security Council and the State Department as well.

On balance, my first year was satisfying but very hard. In addition to teaching, you're expected to push ahead with your research agenda. With only three years to prove your worth before the crucial review, the pressures are immense on new faculty. It's also not unusual for young faculty to start teaching before conferment of the PhD. I was somewhat ahead of many of my peers since I'd completed my dissertation and could now try to polish and publish it.

I'd planned to spend the year revising my dissertation and sending it out to publishers for review. I asked John Lewis and Alexander George to read the manuscript and give me comments before I started to rework it. They both suggested that I send it out without revision. Though I thought that this was a risky strategy, I followed their advice and sent the manuscript to three university presses.

Much to my surprise, Princeton University Press offered to publish my dissertation as a book. My editor, Sandy Thatcher, told me revisions would be necessary but they were prepared to offer a contract immediately. Princeton was the gold standard for university presses, and publishing a first book with them was a real coup.

During my first year, I made a point of getting to know key leaders at Stanford, asking to visit with the president of the university, Donald Kennedy, and later Provost Jim Rosse. If they thought it odd that an assistant professor had asked out of the blue for an appointment, they didn't say so. Both treated me as if I were their most important meeting of the day. Later, I'd advise young faculty to be aggressive in getting to know people in the university and seeking out mentors. My father had taught me how to do that by example. Even in segregated Birmingham, Clay Sheffield had been an important guide and counselor to my dad. Maurice Mitchell and John Blackburn were also keys to his success. I've never subscribed to the idea that you have to have role models who "look like you." If that were the case, there would be no firsts. My friend and former neighbor Sally Ride never would have been an astronaut if she had waited to see a female in that role. Sure, it's good to have female or minority role models. But the important thing is to have mentors who care about you, and they come in all colors. Thus, I made certain years later as provost that I always made time to see junior faculty who asked. And many did—including lots of white males.

My work at the arms control center was also progressing well. I liked administrative work and found it a nice break from teaching and research. My social life revolved around the people at

Galvez House, a somewhat odd collection of American experts on international security and visiting fellows from Asia. There were also colonels from the Japan Self-Defense Forces who became good friends and allowed me to gain remarkably good access to the Japanese military, an institution that was at the time very closed.

But it was the fellows from the People's Republic of China who were the most unusual and provided some of the most memorable moments at Galvez. Among them was an engineer who'd been involved in nuclear cooperation with the Soviet Union before the Sino-Soviet split. He loved to unnerve Russian visitors with his tales of working inside the Soviet military establishment, delivered in perfect Russian.

Then there was Madam Zhou, who came to the center every day in her blue Mao jacket. We knew that she was really the party "commissar," sent to keep tabs on the other Chinese fellows. She seemed at times to be quite put off by the whole California experience. One day she stopped by my office to say that she'd seen *Gone with the Wind,* which, she opined, was obviously about the oppression of black people by the capitalist classes. I didn't counter that most people saw it as a love story between Rhett and Scarlett, asking instead whether she was interested in the history of black people in America. "Not particularly," she answered as she walked away.

There were dinners and parties almost monthly and "sings" at John Lewis' house, where the assembled would croon old favorites such as the Depression-era anthem "Hallelujah, I'm a Bum." As odd as the social outings were, the people were really genuine and gave me a tight-knit community to which I could belong. I made new friends easily, taking in concerts at the university and in San Francisco with Wendy Frieman, a young Asia specialist whom I had also met at Galvez.

Stanford sports provided yet another touchstone. I bought season football tickets with Randy Bean, a journalism fellow at the university. Randy, like me, is a preacher's kid, and her father, like mine, had raised her to be a rabid sports fan. We enjoyed afternoons at the Stanford stadium, where John Elway was then in his senior season. Season tickets for basketball followed. Randy would become one of my closest friends. I found time to play sports too, befriending Nancy Hubbell, a recent Stanford grad and fellow Soviet specialist, whose family had a tennis court. And I met a young assistant director in the Athletic Department, Gene Washington. Gene was a handsome former all-pro wide receiver who'd played at Stanford. One day he asked if I wanted to play tennis. I've told him and others that I let him win because I wanted him to ask me to dinner. He was a good tennis player and probably won outright. But he did ask me to dinner, and we dated for a while before becoming the fast friends that we remain to this day.

I also reconnected with church life, though initially through the Baptists, not the Presbyterians. Frankly, with all the upheaval of the move I'd fallen away from the discipline of weekly church attendance. One Sunday morning (when I should have been in church) I was grocery shopping at Lucky's. A black man named Dale Hamel walked up to me in the spice aisle and began to talk. There just aren't that many black people in Palo Alto, so I was surprised to learn that he was buying food for a church picnic at Jerusalem Baptist Church, a long-standing black congregation. We chatted for a while and then he asked, "Do you play the piano? We need someone to play the piano." I answered yes and within about a week began to play for the choir. Despite my marginal talent for gospel music, I served as the pianist at Jerusalem for about six months. But since the long arm of the Lord had reached all the way into the spice aisle at Lucky's, I resolved to find a good Presbyterian church and get back to weekly attendance. I soon joined Menlo Park Presbyterian Church, which has been my church home ever since. Stanford and California were turning out to be very good for me.

There were troubles back in Denver, however. Ironically, my mother, for whom Denver had never really been a comfortable fit, was doing quite well. Mother was teaching at Gove Middle School and was about to complete a master's degree at the University of Denver's Graduate School of International Studies, where I had done my PhD. The degree, through the Center for Teaching International Relations, prepared high school teachers to teach international subject matter. She loved the program, and the work brought her closer to my world. Her work was so good that her advisor, my former classmate Steve Lamy, encouraged her and her team to publish the curricular materials they had developed. It was fun to see her blossoming professionally. I went back to Denver for her graduation ceremony in the summer of 1982.

For Daddy, though, life was turning sour. Sitting at my desk at Galvez House one fall morning in 1982, I received a call from him. He was obviously upset, saying that he'd been told that the university no longer had a job for him. When Ross Pritchard became chancellor, Daddy had tried to find a place in the new administration by accepting the role of director of religious life. The truth was that Denver was not a particularly religious campus and there was little for him to do. He tried to organize the loose association of campus ministers and occasionally conducted church services during special events such as Parents' Weekend. But Daddy was clearly being marginalized at Denver and this latest news didn't really come as a surprise. Ross Pritchard had not even bothered to deliver the news himself, relying instead on the head of Human Resources to do so.

"How long do you have?" I asked Daddy. He answered that he'd be terminated at the end of the school year, in about six months. He was particularly worried about the imminent loss of health insurance. Mother had health insurance through the Denver Public Schools, but it was expensive to add my father because of his significant preexisting conditions. I suggested that he ask to retire from the university, thereby retaining health coverage and his pension. We hired a lawyer who worked out a decent settlement, and though Daddy did not have enough years in service to retire, the university called it retirement rather than termination even though he had to pay for his health benefits.

I was furious with the university. Many years had to pass and Ross Pritchard had to step down before I would again acknowledge my association with the University of Denver. When I was asked to accept the Evans Award for outstanding alumni, I did so only on the condition that my father be acknowledged too. Even to this day I'm a major supporter of the Graduate School of International Studies, which was renamed in honor of my advisor Dr. Korbel, but I don't feel close ties to the broader university.

Daddy's situation threw everything into a tailspin. The house that my parents had bought in 1979 had been a stretch for them financially on two salaries. Now they simply couldn't afford the mortgage. My father was too proud to call their banker, and so I did. He found a buyer for the house. That spring I went back to Denver and helped Mother and Daddy find a small but very nice condo not far from where they'd lived. It broke my heart to see their furniture, particularly the grand piano, jammed into the small living room. Mother had always wanted a house of her own and had finally gotten it, only to have to sell it a few years later. We all pretended that it was better since I was no longer at home and they didn't really need the space. It was true that the old house was a lot to maintain, and Daddy was glad not to have to cope with the flight of stairs that made his knees ache. But losing the house was a bitter pill for Mother and a source of deep embarrassment for my dad. For me it was more evidence that my parents' investment in me—skating, piano, St. Mary's Academy—had cost them dearly in terms of their own financial security.

Eventually, my parents adjusted to their new life. Mother continued to teach, carrying most of the financial burden. My father was able to piece together consulting work and became very active with a nonprofit that counseled troubled young men and helped them find work. He loved Colorado UpLift, but it paid him almost nothing. Daddy kept looking for new employment, but nothing materialized. Yet he maintained his dignity and sense of humor, saying that he was finally using the advice that he'd given so many unemployed people over the years. "They must have wanted to tell me to shut up," he said. "Now I understand that."

I tried to help my parents financially when I could. They visited me in California each Thanksgiving between 1982 and 1984. I paid their way, calling it their early Christmas present so as not to embarrass them. Occasionally, if I received a little extra income from a speech or an honorarium for an article, I'd just pay a bill for them without saying so.

But I too was under some financial strain since I'd decided to buy my first house in the fall of 1982. With my Princeton book contract in hand, I was pretty sure that I would make it through the three-year review and be reappointed to the faculty. I decided to take the home-ownership plunge. Stanford offered very generous assistance to young professors who wanted to buy in the insane housing market of northern California. When I needed to dip into my grandfather's small trust to help with the down payment, I called Aunt Theresa, who was thrilled that I was doing the responsible thing and buying a house.

"How much does it cost?" she asked.

"A hundred and twenty-four thousand dollars," I answered.

"Don't you think that's a little above your means?" she huffed.

Aunt Theresa was by this time living in Edwardsville, Illinois, and I am sure that her five-bedroom house was worth about half of what the two-bedroom, one-bath, walk-up condo on the Stanford campus was about to cost me. Fortunately, my father convinced her that it was a legitimate purchase, and I bought 74 Pearce Mitchell. I loved my little place, even though I could stand in the living room and see the entire condo. For several months I had to put my toothpaste purchases on my credit card, but in the long run the investment paid off.

THE NEXT few years were certainly easier for me, and I continued to do well at Stanford. My first book, *Uncertain Allegiance: The Soviet Union and the Czechoslovak Army,* was published. I was so happy to be able to give my mother the first advance copy for Christmas in 1984. The reviews of the book were pretty good, but the most important one in the discipline's flagship journal, the *American Political Science Review,* was really good. That was the one that mattered most in the upcoming three-year evaluation.

I was also receiving national recognition, including an invitation to attend the New Faces Conference in Bellagio, Italy. This was a real plum, in part because it was a one-week meeting at a spectacular villa overlooking Lake Como. I made sure to go into Milan, where I bought my mother a stunning Ferragamo purse. She said that she'd never been given anything so beautiful, and carried it everywhere. I was happy to be able to do something really special for her.

Then, sitting at my desk as the end of the school year approached, I received a call from the president's office. The assistant to the president, Jean Fetter, wanted me to know that I would receive the Gores Award for Excellence in Teaching, the university's highest honor. The award would be bestowed at commencement. She asked to know if my parents wanted to come at the university's expense. I waited until I knew they would both be home and called with the news. Though I couldn't see them, I knew that they were both crying. It was a thrilling moment for the three of us. Weeks later they attended the commencement ceremony held under bright blue skies at the Stanford baseball stadium. It was one of our happiest days together.

After commencement I received many congratulatory comments from my colleagues, who seemed genuinely happy for me. But there's always one sour apple. A senior professor, who shall remain nameless, said, "Congratulations on the Gores. Now you'll never get tenure since you're branded as just a good teacher." I was a little stunned, then thought, *What a stupid thing to say.* I knew what he meant, however. The situation has changed somewhat over the years, but great research universities tenure their faculty first and foremost on their research prowess. When I was an assistant professor, good teaching was interpreted by some as a sign that you were not sufficiently devoted to research. A junior faculty member couldn't *possibly* be good at both.

Nonetheless, I wasn't going to let this sourpuss rain on my parade. "Oh yes," I said. "I expect the book contract from Princeton University Press will help on that score." He didn't say anything in response.

CHAPTER TWENTY-FIVE

The Darkest Moment
of My Life

I STARTED 1985 with growing confidence in the direction of my career. Many young faculty are still trying to find a publisher for their initial book at the time of the third-year review. I was ahead of the game, having already published my first book and being well on the way to designing a second research project. I was granted a sabbatical and applied for and received a prestigious National Fellowship from the Hoover Institution. I was particularly pleased that I could take my sabbatical just a few paces across campus and did not have to move. Feeling quite comfortable, professionally and even—thanks to a couple of raises—financially, I bought a car with my own money: a little rocket ship of a Buick that I named Misha, the Russian nickname for Mikhail Gorbachev. I thought I deserved a little break, and for the first time in three years, I decided to go home for Easter.

A day or so into my visit, I was watching television in the den when my mother came in with obvious bruises on her arm and leg.

"What happened?" I asked.

"I fell down the basement stairs on the way to do the laundry," she answered. "I'm getting clumsy in my old age. This is the second time this month!"

I didn't think much about it, assuming that she had just been careless. She also had a penchant for wearing high heels even when doing chores around the house. Maybe that was the explanation. I returned to Palo Alto after a lovely Easter and finished the quarter, planning to visit again sometime in the summer.

A few days before the Fourth of July, though, my father called. His usually deep booming voice was shaking. "I think I need to take your mother to the doctor," he said. "She keeps falling and she seems really forgetful. The other day she asked our neighbor about a friend of ours from Alabama who's been dead for ten years."

July 5 was one of the darkest days of my life. Daddy called to say that Dr. Hamilton had taken an X-ray and there was a large mass on Mother's brain. The doctors were sure that it was inoperable and cancerous. Ever since Mother's breast cancer diagnosis, I'd feared this moment. Mother had lived long past the five-year point at which she was considered cured, and had done remarkably well. True, there had been a scare the year before when she'd required surgery to remove a small tumor on her lung. But she'd undergone follow-up chemotherapy during the summer of 1984 and had tolerated it well. She'd returned to work in the fall, and though I worried that the cancer, having returned once, might do so again, I buried that thought deep in my subconscious. Now I was faced with the worst possible news.

Mother got on the phone. "I've got this little thing in my head," she said. "It's not in such a bad place."

"Yes, Mother, but I want to come home for a little while," I said.

"Okay, but don't hurry," she replied.

When I got to Denver, my father picked me up at the airport. We went directly to the hospital where Mother was undergoing more tests. The room was pretty dimly lit, but Mother was remarkably upbeat. We talked for a while, and I didn't notice any of the mental deterioration of which my father had spoken. But the conversation with Dr. Hamilton couldn't have been clearer. When I asked how long she had, he said, "I've seen some people make it a year. But it won't be longer than that. I'm so sorry."

The doctors prescribed a treatment regimen for her. They were certain that surgery wasn't an option but believed tumor-shrinking radiation and medication could prolong her life.

Every day I'd accompany Mother to the hospital where she would undergo treatment. The effects were pretty devastating. Her once beautiful hair began to fall out. She'd also lost some of her hair during the previous treatments in 1984, and we had actually had a little fun finding a wig that she loved wearing. But this was different. This time she was left with almost no hair. I was absolutely crushed when I saw her sitting on the bed holding a large clump of her hair in her hand and crying.

The four weeks in Denver were the hardest of my life. Mother's mental capacity was clearly diminished. One day I saw her sitting at the piano. She couldn't remember how to play. Yet when I sat down next to her on the bench and began to move her hands toward certain keys, she started to play—a few notes at first, then miraculously a song, and then another and another. "I can play," she proclaimed. When she started to play "The Lord Knows How Much You Can Bear," I said to myself, *Mommy, I hope so,* and left the room in tears.

Daddy and I didn't really talk very much about what was happening. Life revolved around trying to make Mother comfortable. We went about the daily routine, even going out to brunch for her sixty-first birthday on July 21. As Daddy tried to raise his glass and say "Many happy returns," he finally broke down. Mother looked confused, not sad. It suggested to me that she didn't fully comprehend that she was dying.

I returned to Palo Alto at the end of July when my mother's sisters, Gee and Mattie, came out to be with her. I told my father that I needed to go back home for a few weeks. I planned to teach my scheduled two-week alumni summer school session, go to a conference at Cornell, and then return to Denver in the middle of August.

Though I knew that she was gravely ill, I realize now that I just didn't let myself believe that I was losing my mother. Somehow I kept expecting a miracle, or perhaps I was just putting the awful truth out of my mind. I called Sarah Donaldson, a friend and radiologist on the Stanford Medical School faculty, and asked whether I should bring Mother to Palo Alto for a second opinion. She offered to call Dr. Hamilton, and after talking to him said that she thought it best that she finish her treatment in Denver. We could then think about whether it made sense to have her come to Palo Alto. I suspect that she knew that there was little point in doing so, but I clung to the idea that Stanford might have an answer. Then one day I was sitting at my desk at Galvez House when Herb Abrams stopped by. He was a world-renowned radiologist who was working at the center studying the potential effects of nuclear war. Herb had heard about Mother and wanted to offer his support. I think he was taken aback by my optimistic assessment of my mother's chances.

"They say it's not the worst kind of brain tumor," I told him.

"Well, you make sure to spend time at home with her now. Don't wait," he replied.

THE LAST session of the summer course I taught at Stanford was on Saturday, August 18. I had planned to leave the next day and stop in Denver overnight on my way to Cornell just to check on Mother. After the two-day conference in Ithaca where I would give a paper, I intended to return to Denver and stay for several weeks. There would be no pressure to return to Stanford early in the fall, since I was beginning the Hoover sabbatical. And I was pleased that the summer teaching and the conference paper were yielding additional income. I intended to use the money to help my parents, since my mother would no longer be able to teach.

Mother had not been doing very well that weekend. I had talked to her several times Saturday and she seemed weak, unable to finish a full sentence without running out of breath.

"Why don't you take her to the hospital?" I asked my father.

"She doesn't want to go," he said.

I called Saturday night before going to bed.

"She's a bit better," Daddy said.

Hours later the phone rang, jerking me out of a very deep sleep.

"Ann isn't breathing," Daddy said.

"What?" I asked, still not fully awake.

"I've called the ambulance because your mother isn't breathing," he said, clearly frightened but relatively calm.

"Call me when you get to the hospital," I said.

I just lay in the dark and prayed. Over and over, I asked God not to take my mother.

Daddy called back less than an hour later. "She's gone," he said.

"I'll be there first thing in the morning," I told him.

"No need to hurry. She belongs to the ages now," he replied.

After hanging up the phone, it occurred to me that Daddy must have been alone at the hospital. I called Beverly Phillips, my mother's friend with whom she'd taught school. She agreed to meet my father at the hospital. I didn't want to be alone either, so I called my dearest friend, Chip Blacker. When he answered the phone, I simply said, "Mother's dead, Chip. Can you come over?" He did so, sleeping on the sofa while I tried to go back to sleep for a few hours. I already had reservations to Denver the next morning. Chip drove me to the airport, and I boarded the United Airlines plane for what seemed like the longest flight of my life. Going to my seat, I ran into a former student.

"Hi, are you going home to Denver for a visit?" she asked, knowing nothing of my mother's death.

"My mother died last night," I said. Then, to reinforce the point more for myself than for her, I said, "My mother's gone."

Beverly picked me up at the airport. My father greeted me at the door and we hugged each other, tears flowing gently. His first words surprised me. "She was such a fighter. She fought to stay with us. She fought so hard," he said. He was right. Ever since her first bout with cancer Mother had refused to let her own circumstances intrude on our family's life. Because she'd been so tough and unyielding to her disease, sometimes even making light of it, we had been able to get on with our lives.

Daddy continued pouring out his thoughts, saying that he already missed her but that he had thanked God for answering his prayer.

"What prayer?" I said, somewhat puzzled.

"The one that asked him not to leave me alone with a fifteen-year-old girl," he replied. I was hurting then more than I ever had, but I too felt just a touch of gratitude that my mother had died when I was thirty, not fifteen. She'd seen me grow into a successful adult. I was so grateful that she'd held my first book, attended the Gores teaching awards ceremony, and shared with my father a glimpse of how well I would do at Stanford.

Still, I was so incredibly sad. I went into my parents' bedroom and sat on the side of the bed. There I looked around a room filled with my mother's belongings: her jewelry box, family photos, and the heavy mahogany furniture that had been her pride and joy since I was a child. And then something happened. I felt my mother's spirit release, breaking its bonds with earth. There was the unmistakable sensation of someone or something leaving the room. I had not made it home before she died. Had she in some sense waited? This was a mystical moment that I have never been able to adequately describe. Yet I suddenly felt at peace. The Apostle Paul had called it "the peace that passeth all understanding." I got down on my knees and prayed that God would take care of Mother's eternal soul.

Daddy and I planned a very small funeral, not making a newspaper announcement of her death until the day after the services.

My mother did not have many close friends outside of her family, and a public funeral just seemed wrong. About fifty friends and family—her brothers and sisters and my cousins—gathered at Montview Boulevard Presbyterian Church and then at the cemetery. We laid her to rest elegantly dressed in a gray and black dress and very high black heels. Even after all that she had been through, she still looked very beautiful. It wasn't too hard to picture the long-ago image of the pretty young teacher. The thought crossed my mind briefly that I should have dressed her in red.

CHAPTER TWENTY-SIX

"The Moving Van Is Here"

I<small>T IS</small> often said that the hardest days after the loss of a loved one are when all of the mourners leave and you're truly alone. Mother was buried on a Wednesday, and the last family member, my cousin Denise, left that Sunday. My father and I went back to the apartment and there was truly nothing to do. We tried watching television but finally decided to go out to dinner. The two of us had never been at a loss for words, but now we were. Daddy kept ordering vodka. I snapped at him that he had had enough. "I need you to be with me," I blurted out. He didn't drink any more. We sat in silence.

The next day we took care of a number of business matters, primarily insurance and financial tasks. Daddy said that he'd like to visit his mother and sister in Illinois. My eighty-eight-year-old grandmother was pretty frail, and Daddy had discouraged her from attending the funeral. The trip to Illinois turned out to be good for him, but I worried about returning to Stanford and leaving him alone. I suggested that we go directly from Illinois to Palo Alto, where he could spend a couple of weeks with me. My friend Randy picked us up at the airport. Years later she'd tell me that she was worried for Daddy's survival when she saw him. "He was as broken as any person I had ever seen," she said.

Many people—doctors, ministers, and colleagues—had told Daddy what people always tell widowers: "Don't make any decisions for at least a year." But my gregarious and popular father somehow felt isolated after my mother died. I sensed that there was nothing to keep him in Denver any longer. We had thus agreed that he should look around Palo Alto to see if he might want to move to California in the next year or so.

One evening during Daddy's stay, I arranged a little dinner at my house. Harold Boyd, a black colleague from Stanford, invited a few people closer to my dad's age. Daddy had a great time that evening and in his subsequent meetings at the university, befriending Catherine Milton, the director of the Public Service Center. The Center's mandate was to connect Stanford students to public service opportunities. Catherine and my dad really hit it off, and my father came back brimming with ideas about what Stanford could do in the broader community.

After a couple of weeks, Daddy said that it was time for him to return to Denver. He told me he really liked Palo Alto and might consider moving, but he wanted to think about it. I encouraged him to do so, telling him that we only had each other and should be together. I didn't push, figuring he needed time to decide. So I put him on the plane in early September and worried constantly about him. A couple of times when I called, I could tell that he'd been drinking. I worried less about any kind of addiction than about what it signaled regarding his state of mind—and, I had to assume, his health. My concern deepened when one of his former students called to say that he seemed to be cutting people off. As much as people tried, they couldn't get him to leave the house.

I was physically in Palo Alto, but my heart was in Denver with my dad. And I was having a rough time too. I threw myself into my work at Hoover, but the sadness was sometimes overwhelming. I had many friends and found plenty to do, but I felt incredibly empty. Deep despair could be triggered by seemingly innocuous events. One evening in the checkout line at the grocery store I saw a woman of about seventy. She was wearing comfortable, old-lady shoes. *My mother will never grow old,* I thought. I left my groceries on the counter and ran to my car, where I sobbed uncontrollably until the feeling passed.

The first weekend in October, Randy suggested that we take a football trip. Perhaps it would help me to get away. I was by this time a rabid fan of the Cincinnati Bengals (the Browns had folded for a time), and Randy loved the New York Giants. The two teams were playing in Cincinnati, where she had family and a place to stay, so we decided to make the trip. I got up that Sunday morning in Cincinnati and called my dad to check on him. I noticed that he sounded more cheerful than he had in many weeks.

"Daddy, what are you doing?" I asked him.

"I'm packing up," he said. "The movers will be here tomorrow. I'll be in Palo Alto on Wednesday."

Daddy had arranged a visiting fellowship through Catherine Milton and rented an apartment at Alma Village (aka "Moon Palace"). I later learned that he was already in touch with Harold Boyd, from the dinner, and new friends Lois Powell and Betty Allen. Harold was a little surprised to find that my father hadn't told me he was moving. So was I, but I couldn't have been happier. I wanted to be with my dad. I was really pleased that he wanted to be with me too.

Within a few weeks, Daddy had settled in. In addition to diving into his work at the Public Service Center, he once again befriended and began to counsel student athletes. My father was making friends as rapidly as he always had. His little apartment, stuffed with the family furniture, became a gathering place for all kinds of people—especially middle-aged ladies who brought him food. Daddy would, in turn, invite them out to dinner or buy them Valentine's Day candy. After about six months he asked me, "Do you think I'm dating?" It was so cute. I answered that yes, I thought he was, and that I was very happy about it. He beamed and continued to ask the ladies out—several of them. Yet he kept a crocheted plaque above the refrigerator that said "Angelena's Kitchen."

We still had our moments of great sadness, the most wrenching coming the first Christmas Day after Mother's death. The holiday season had been tolerable. We engaged in many of the Christmas traditions we always had, decorating both my house and his and shopping for family presents. But on Christmas morning when we lit the last Advent candle the emptiness was overwhelming. We'd received an invitation from my senior faculty colleague Jan Triska to join his family for dinner. I'd declined, thinking that Daddy and I would want to be alone. But as we sat in silence after dinner, I decided that we had to get out of the house. I called Jan and we went to his home for dessert. I have been forever grateful to the Triska family for the kindness of that invitation and the respite it provided on that difficult day.

Ultimately, I decided that Daddy was adjusting very well, so I

felt freer to travel and accepted a three-week visiting professorship at the National Defense Academy of Japan in Yokosuka. I
had never been to Japan and I have to admit that it was a somewhat hard place to be under the circumstances. The Academy,
their West Point, had never had a woman teach there. In fact,
I don't think they had ever had a woman on the school grounds
before I came. One clue was the absence of a ladies' room. The
school solved the problem by making one of the men's rooms
off-limits to everyone else but me. I never knew exactly what the
huge sign on the door said, but it had a few too many characters to simply say "Do Not Enter." I was pleased to learn that the
Academy admitted its first female cadet in 1992.

I also had a hard time adjusting to the rigid hierarchy. All military academies are hierarchical, but in Japan this is exacerbated by
cultural customs. Somehow I could never learn to bow at exactly
the right level. One day my host professor told me that I was bowing too low, requiring the cadets to try to go lower. The next day I
wasn't bowing low enough. The language, which is also hierarchical, made it difficult to find an appropriate greeting in a case where
a female of higher status addresses a male of lower standing. When
one of my host professors invited me to his home for dinner and
his wife served us but ate in the kitchen, I was just appalled.

In general, I found the whole experience stultifying and
looked forward to returning to my tiny hotel room every day.
I've always said that I love sports so much that I'll watch anything with a score at the end. In Japan that meant watching the
Grand Sumo Wrestling Tournament. I actually came to like it,
giving the wrestlers nicknames such as "Fred" and "Toby" since I
couldn't understand what was being said. To this day, I still like
to watch sumo wrestling.

At the end of my trip, one of the professors told me that I'd been extremely successful in my teaching. "More important," he said in heavily accented English, "it shows the Japanese that not all black people are stupid." I knew that he meant it as a compliment and thanked him for his kindness. Fortunately, I've since made many subsequent trips to an evolving Japan that have wiped away some of those early negative memories. I am happy to say that I'm now quite fond of the country, which has changed a lot in twenty-five years.

Not long after returning to Palo Alto, I left again—this time for Harvard to take up a six-week visiting position at Sam Huntington's research center, the Center for International Affairs. Huntington was the godfather of the study of civil-military relations. His epic book *The Soldier and the State,* though published in 1957, was still the most important work in the literature. I wanted to get to know him and to seek his advice. I also understood that developing this relationship was a key to my future. At the time of tenure decisions, universities send out letters asking the most eminent senior faculty to rank tenure candidates against others in their field. A junior faculty member who doesn't rank number one or two is unlikely to get tenure. The worst thing that can happen is for a senior evaluator to say something like "I am not really familiar with her work." I was determined that Sam Huntington would be familiar with my work.

Alexander George agreed to contact Sam for me, and I sent along my proposal for a new book comparing civil-military relations in the Soviet Union to those in the United States. I explained in the proposal how my theory of institutional development related to the work that Huntington had done and how it would both corroborate and challenge some of his propositions.

He couldn't have been nicer, responding quickly and inviting me to Harvard to spend some time with him.

The time at Harvard was really important to my professional development. I lectured in several classes and found that the Harvard students responded equally well to my teaching. Occasionally I'd be reminded that I fit better at Stanford, which was definitely less formal. I couldn't get over the fact that questions in faculty seminars were asked in a strict pecking order: senior faculty, then junior faculty, then graduate students, and finally, if time permitted, a stray undergraduate or two.

I enjoyed living with my old friend Cristann, who had married Steve Meyer, a political science professor at MIT. They lived in Sudbury, and every day I'd somehow make my way to Cambridge despite the fact that the Boston drivers terrified me. Sudbury was one of those quaint New England communities incredibly proud of its role in the Revolutionary War. Several of the town's homes had been owned by patriots, but apparently none by loyalists. According to Steve, the latter had been renters back in 1776.

One day I came home a little early and accidentally set off the alarm. As I waited for the police to arrive, I thought about how I'd explain what had happened. *I'm just going to tell them I'm the maid,* I thought. I was thankful when Cris' neighbor came over to vouch for me. The fact is, the Boston area was really quite segregated when it came to housing. When a year later I was recruited by MIT, a faculty member took me on a tour of the area. "This is the Jewish neighborhood," he said. "And this is the Italian neighborhood." He continued in that fashion until I finally interjected, "Where is the black neighborhood so I'll know where I'm going to live?" To be fair, a lot has changed, but I always felt that Boston was racially charged in a pretty overt way.

CHAPTER TWENTY-SEVEN

Inside the Pentagon

IN 1985 I had applied for the Hoover fellowship and a fellowship from the Council on Foreign Relations. I was awarded both but asked the Council if I could defer for a year. The Council on Foreign Relations is an organization and think tank that includes among its members all major American figures in international politics. Founded in 1921 and located in New York, it is arguably the most prestigious organization in the field.

The Council's International Affairs Fellowship is thus, not surprisingly, highly coveted. Young faculty and other midcareer professionals are awarded the fellowship and given a year-long appointment working for the federal government. I was offered positions in the National Security Council, the State Department, and the Pentagon. Specifically, I wanted to work for the Joint Chiefs of Staff, reasoning that I might have other opportunities to work in civilian agencies but would find it difficult to land on a military staff again. Thanks in part to my Stanford colleague Scott Sagan's successful tenure with the Joint Chiefs the year before, the military agreed to take me on. I told Scott that they had gotten used to having a civilian around thanks to him; now we would see whether they would be ready for a civilian black woman.

Stanford readily granted me a second year of sabbatical, though a few faculty friends wondered if leaving during the year when I would be considered for tenure was really wise. "Out of sight," one said, "out of mind."

For my part, I was more concerned about leaving my father yet again. He had lived in Palo Alto for ten months, and I'd been gone for three of them. I asked him to meet me for dinner at a local restaurant and started to talk about why it was so important for me to work for the Joint Chiefs. Then I just stopped and said, "Do you mind if I move to Washington for a year?"

"No," he replied, and began to ask if I could afford it financially. It was clear from his demeanor that he really didn't mind. He wanted me to go.

As it turned out, my year with the Joint Chiefs of Staff was one of the best of my life. I worked for the Nuclear and Chemical Division, which analyzed situations in which the United States would use its nuclear forces. As a Soviet specialist, I helped to develop guidance for the type of war that everyone thought unthinkable. As difficult as it was to contemplate such a scenario, this particular unit had to plan for it anyway. This led to black humor like the bottle of champagne that the division chief stashed in his drawer in the event of pending nuclear annihilation. When the missiles were on their way to Moscow and Moscow's were on their way to Washington, the plan was to pop the cork and kiss your "expletive" goodbye.

I loved working with these officers, who all held the rank of lieutenant colonel or naval commander. They were dedicated, smart, and relegated temporarily to office duty in the Pentagon. It's absolutely true that there are so many generals in the Pentagon that officers who would otherwise be in command of a base are forced to do tasks that could easily be carried out by a second lieutenant. All of my colleagues looked forward anxiously to the day when they could leave Washington and go command a ship or an air wing.

Truthfully, my officemates didn't know quite what to make of me when I arrived in the summer of 1986. On the first day, they informed me that it was the responsibility of the rookie to make the coffee. They probably thought I'd make a fuss or maybe even claim gender discrimination. I just made the coffee—really, really strong. I was never asked to make coffee again. It helped too that I won the first football pool of the year. Sports provided an instant bond. All in all, it was a great experience. My respect for the American officer corps deepened, and I made very good friends, one of whom was an air force lieutenant colonel named Michael Hayden. Years later we would serve together in the administration of George W. Bush—me as national security advisor and then secretary of state, and Mike as director of the National Security Agency and later as head of the Central Intelligence Agency.

It was also during this time that I first met Colin Powell. One day I got a call from the office of my boss, the director of the Joint Staff for strategic plans and policy, a gruff (but kind to me) army lieutenant general named Dale Vesser. When I arrived in

Vesser's office, he told me that the deputy national security advisor, General Colin Powell, had invited me to visit him at the White House. Colin was already legendary in the Pentagon, and I could tell that Vesser thought it a little odd that this important man wanted to see me. I immediately called Powell's office, and within a few weeks I met with him in his corner office in the West Wing. That was the start of our friendship. Colin had sent an important message throughout Washington that I was someone to keep an eye on. I never forgot that act of mentorship and kindness.

MY TIME in Washington was interrupted in the fall by a health crisis of my own. One evening, while riding the Metro from the Pentagon to my Van Ness Street apartment, I started to experience excruciating stomach pains. At first I chalked it up to stomach flu, but it simply got worse as the week went on. Fearing appendicitis, I took the next day off from work and went to a doctor. After a few questions and an exam, he told me it was likely that I had uterine fibroids—a nasty condition that can afflict as many as 70–80 percent of women. He arranged a consult with an obstetrician-gynecologist, who recommended that I have a hysterectomy.

This was terrible news. In the back of my mind I had always assumed that I would get married and have kids. I wanted to find that special man because I had been inspired by the wonderful example my parents had provided through their marriage. I was not at all concerned that marriage might hold me back professionally. Again, both my parents had managed careers and family life quite well. But as I told (and still tell) my friends, you don't

get married in the abstract; you have to want to marry a particular person. And frankly I'd always hoped to marry within my
race. If the right man does not come along, it is better to enjoy a
fulfilling and happy life as a single person. But in 1986, at the age
of thirty-one, the prospect of not even having the *option* to have
kids was devastating.

That night, I called my ob-gyn back in Palo Alto and asked
whether there were other approaches. She suggested that I come
back and see a young doctor who was doing pioneering work in
alternatives for women with my condition. I called the physician,
who said that he couldn't be certain until he examined me, but
he was having great success with myomectomies, which removed
the fibroids and left the uterus intact. I immediately felt better
and more in control of the situation. The next day, I informed
my division chief that I needed to go home for a few weeks. It
was just after Thanksgiving. I told him that I would likely return
in January.

My father met me at the airport two days later. At his apartment I calmly went through the diagnosis that I had been given.

"Are they ever malignant?" Daddy asked.

"Only in about 1 percent of the cases," I said, relating what I
had been told.

"I'm sure you will be all right," he said.

I thought that he was correct, but I was nonetheless very
apprehensive: 1 percent seems a lot bigger when you are the
daughter of a breast cancer victim. But a couple of nights before the surgery, I had a dream about my mother in which she
affirmed that everything would indeed be all right. I'd never
before had a premonition and have never since.

Several days later I had the surgery, which took more than seven hours. When I woke up in my room, I heard the doctor say that everything had gone fine. I looked around and saw my father and one or two friends, including John Lewis, who was smiling broadly. In my semidrugged state he looked a bit like one of those distorted faces in a horror movie. I closed my eyes and went back to sleep. Though the surgery had been successful, the recovery was difficult. My digestive system shut down, which required that I undergo an extremely uncomfortable procedure to insert a tube through my nose and down my throat. After enduring two days of this, I called for my doctor. "If you don't remove this thing, I'm going to die," I told him. Fortunately, I got better, and he decided to remove the tube—a little prematurely. He told me he was worried that I was so strong-willed I might die just to spite him.

All of this medical drama had been extremely wearing on my father. He practically lived at the hospital for that entire week. Finally, on Friday, seven days after I'd had the surgery, I told him to go home and get some rest. I was to be discharged on Saturday and was feeling just fine. Shortly after Daddy left, the doctor came in and said that I could go home that night instead. Because I had rented my Stanford condo to another faculty member when I left for Washington, I went back to Daddy's apartment to recuperate.

At about three in the morning Daddy came in and woke me up. "Something isn't right with me," he said. "I've called 911." Still groggy from pain medication, I got up and went into the living room, where Daddy had been sleeping on the pullout sofa. He had thrown up, and he told me he was experiencing pain in his chest. An ambulance arrived moments later and rushed him to the hospital. I got dressed and called a friend, who took me there about thirty minutes after that.

A young resident met me in the emergency room when I arrived at the Stanford Medical Center. He said that Daddy was undergoing some tests and that he'd get back to me when he knew what had happened. After what seemed like an eternity, the doctor emerged to say that Daddy had indeed suffered what he described as a major heart attack. "The next twenty-four hours are crucial," he said.

I called my friend Randy, who came over immediately and sat with me for the rest of the night. Finally they let me see Daddy, who was weak but in surprisingly good spirits. "This is a wake-up call," he said. "I've been tempting fate for a long time." I was relieved to see him talking and upbeat, but I was still very worried that I was going to lose him. I told Randy that I couldn't bear to lose my father just over a year after Mother's death.

Daddy had lost considerable heart function and would from then on suffer from congestive heart failure. Given that he also had diabetes and high blood pressure, his long-term prospects were not very good. But at least he was alive. He'd tempted fate, but at least for the time being, he'd won.

AFTER THE first of the year, I returned to Washington and resumed working for the Joint Chiefs. I felt more and more integrated into the daily life of the office, taking on my share of assignments, ranging from exciting ones to the more routine. One highlight was the opportunity to do a presentation in "the Tank" assessing President Reagan's idea of a world without ballistic missiles for the chairman and the Joint Chiefs. Although it's little more than a large conference room, the Tank carries a certain mystique in the military since it's the place where all-important decisions are made. I was so excited that I quite literally forgot to be nervous until the presentation was over. Frankly, it's not unusual for me to put the consequences of failure out of my mind until an event has finished. After my presentation in the Tank, I woke up in the middle of the night. *It was risky for you to come here and work for the military,* I thought to myself. *This could have really backfired.* Then I went back to sleep.

A few days after the presentation, I received a phone call from the chair of the Political Science Department back at Stanford. "The department has voted to recommend you for tenure," Steve Krasner told me.

"Oh. I thought the vote was next week," I said clumsily and without a sense of how ungrateful that must have sounded. Fortunately, Steve is an easygoing guy. "No, it was this week," he said, chuckling slightly.

Stanford's dean of the School of Humanities and Sciences, the university provost, and the Advisory Board (an elected body of seven senior faculty) still had to approve the department's recommendation, but I knew that they rarely overturned such decisions. I was pretty sure that I was about to receive tenure at Stanford. I called my father and my friend Chip. The truth is that I had been so busy preparing for my opportunity in the Tank that I'd forgotten all about the departmental vote. For that I was grateful; it turns out that it's far better to be out of sight during that awkward time when your colleagues are deciding whether you live or die.

The remainder of my time in Washington seemed to fly by.

In addition to my work at the Pentagon, I was tapped in the spring of 1987 to do national television commentary for the first time. Out of the blue one day, the office secretary passed through a call from ABC News anchor Peter Jennings. I was a little stunned when this famous newsman said he'd like to meet for lunch. They were looking for "fresh faces," he said, and Bob Legvold, a professor of Soviet studies at Columbia and an ABC News consultant, had recommended me. Peter and I met, and after getting permission from General Vesser, I agreed to do some on-air commentary concerning U.S.-Soviet relations. This gave me my first national exposure and invaluable media experience. It also gave me a lifelong and dear friend in the late Peter Jennings.

CHAPTER TWENTY-EIGHT

Back to Stanford

I RETURNED TO Palo Alto in September 1987 and took up the duties of a tenured associate professor. I started new research activities that drew upon my experiences in Washington and began training new graduate students such as Amy Zegart, who is now a professor at UCLA. I also took on some administrative duties such as overseeing the graduate admissions process for the Political Science Department. I even served on the search committee to select a new football coach for Stanford. It was great fun, and I especially enjoyed surprising the candidates with detailed questions about what kind of offense they'd run. Even the candidate who called me "sweetie" during the interview process was impressed that I knew Stanford was not an option offense team. (By the way, he didn't get the job.)

There's no doubt that people treat tenured faculty differently.

There is still a lot of pressure to publish, but one feels far more secure. The closest analogy is making partner in a law firm. After years of uncertainty about your fate, the university finally gives you lifetime employment. It is virtually impossible to lose your job as a tenured professor. In fact, it has happened only once in the last century at Stanford, when H. Bruce Franklin was fired for inciting students to storm the university's Computation Center during a Vietnam War protest.

I know that tenure is controversial. Many believe that it allows faculty to be lazy if not irresponsible for the rest of their careers. Since tenure is generally awarded when a faculty member is in his or her thirties, the university has bought into that person for decades to come. But I'm a fan of tenure, and not just because I have it. The system was originally conceived to prevent faculty from being pressured politically. In fact, one of the most widely cited cases by advocates of tenure actually happened at Stanford, where founder Jane Lathrop Stanford essentially forced Edward A. Ross to resign in 1900 because of his political views. The so-called Ross Affair has been credited with raising the question of academic freedom at universities, but that's rarely a concern in today's academy. It's true that university faculty since the 1960s have been overwhelmingly liberal. I strongly believe that students would be better served by a wider range of views and an environment that challenges the liberal orthodoxy that is so pervasive in universities today. Yet I don't believe that conservative faculty members fear retribution for their opinions, though I've heard conservative colleagues say that they simply censor themselves in political debates. I have never felt the need to do so.

The real reason for tenure, it seems to me, is that it's impossible to evaluate academic achievement every year or even every five years. The ebb and flow of intellectual activity may mean that a faculty member produces great work at thirty and not again until sixty. Junior faculty must prove themselves within the known confines of their disciplines. They must "color inside the lines," if you will. Tenure provides the freedom to pursue ideas— no matter how untested and controversial—that sometimes lead to important intellectual breakthroughs. As long as faculty members aren't allowed to skirt teaching duties once tenured (and it does happen all too frequently), I believe that both the university and those who are tenured benefit from the system.

I WAS pleased to see that Daddy had done very well in Palo Alto during my time in Washington. He'd made many friends and was active with the university's Public Service Center and with the Stanford Department of Athletics. We settled into a nice pattern of getting together two or three times a week. Though we spoke by phone every day, we led separate and fulfilling lives.

By the start of 1988, the presidential campaign was, of course, heating up. George Herbert Walker Bush, the sitting vice president under Ronald Reagan, was the front-runner to become the Republican standard-bearer. I hadn't met Vice President Bush, but I did know his principal foreign policy advisor, General Brent Scowcroft. Brent was one of the wise men of the foreign policy establishment, having served Gerald Ford as national security advisor.

I'd come to know Brent when he visited Stanford in the spring of 1983. At the time he was chairing President Reagan's independent Commission on Strategic Forces. There had been outrage when the President declared his intention to launch the

Strategic Defense Initiative (SDI), a ballistic missile defense system that pundits derisively dubbed "Star Wars." The Soviet Union, America's European allies, and most of the American national security establishment opposed SDI as unworkable and dangerous. Brent's commission was largely a bipartisan attempt to bridge the differences between the administration, Congress, and foreign policy elites.

During the question-and-answer session, I suggested that the Commission was just a cover under which the President intended to do whatever he wanted to do. "It's an abdication of executive and congressional responsibility," I said. Brent was somewhat taken aback by the sharpness of my comment, which even I now see as having been a little rude. But he was nonetheless impressed and came over after the talk to continue the discussion with me. He stayed in touch, appointing me to the Aspen Strategy Group, a bipartisan study group of senior national security experts.

As I attended the weeklong summer sessions at Aspen over the next few years, I got to know Brent very well. When George H. W. Bush won the presidential election, Brent called and asked me to join him at the National Security Council. Jim Baker also invited me to join him at the State Department as deputy director of policy planning, helping oversee the Department's internal think tank on strategic issues in foreign affairs. Then Senator Bill Cohen, whom I had gotten to know during my time with the Joint Chiefs, also called me—during the Super Bowl, no less—on behalf of the designee for defense secretary, John Tower, to offer me a job in the Pentagon. After a brief trip to Washington to check out the prospects, I settled on the job of director of Soviet and East European studies at the National

Security Council. I decided that while the other jobs were interesting, there was nothing like being a member of the White House staff. And I liked the people. Robert Blackwill, a former ambassador and veteran of government service who was said to have a "black belt" in bureaucratic politics, would be my direct supervisor. And I was drawn to Robert M. Gates, the deputy national security advisor, with whom I shared a background in Soviet studies as well as an acerbic sense of humor.

When I told Daddy that I wanted to take the job, he was not surprised. "You're going again!" he exclaimed, smiling broadly to let me know that it was fine with him. Stanford was quite surprised since I would be taking my third leave of absence in four years. Nonetheless, Provost Jim Rosse approved unpaid leave from the university, and I headed to Washington.

CHAPTER TWENTY-NINE

D.C. Again

I QUICKLY LEARNED that work at the National Security Council is hard and not very glamorous. Unlike the layered bureaucracies in the Department of State or the Department of Defense, the NSC staff is small. When I asked how we'd be staffed, I got blank stares. Eventually it dawned on me: I *was* the staff, assisted only by a secretary who was shared with two other people. That meant that I had to do whatever needed to be done—sometimes whispering important facts to the President and sometimes photocopying his papers.

Generally, NSC staffers write memoranda to prepare the President for phone calls and meetings, take notes to create a permanent record, coordinate other government agencies to keep them on track with the administration's priorities, and just take care of whatever the President needs to do his job. They have enormous responsibility and little real authority, since they are neither confirmed by nor accountable to the Senate.

The key, I learned, is to work *through* the agencies, not around them or as a substitute for them. If the NSC staff becomes too operational by trying to execute the nation's foreign policy instead of coordinating it, there's usually trouble—especially for the President. The Iran-Contra affair had been one such case where the NSC devised and carried out controversial policies within the White House. As the facts emerged, it was clear that the plan to divert funds from covert Iranian arms sales to the Nicaraguan resistance (the Contras) had been cooked up secretly within the NSC staff—apparently without the knowledge of even the secretary of state, let alone the Congress. The fallout was disastrous; the affair almost brought down the Reagan presidency.

Brent Scowcroft, former Secretary of State Edmund Muskie and former Senator John Tower had led the commission that made recommendations in light of that scandal. Brent was, therefore, a stickler for keeping the NSC staff in its proper place—as staff to the President, not a rival to the assistant secretaries at the Department of State or Defense.

At the NSC, the hours are long, there is little tolerance for mistakes, and one must pay close attention to details: for instance, making certain that there are no embarrassing photographs of the President in chance encounters with notorious dictators. NSC staffers even approve the guest lists for White House events to prevent international incidents that might arise from omissions of key officials—or, for that matter, invitations to controversial attendees.

Sometimes the work has very little at all to do with serious policy making. My first task, only two days after I arrived in Washington, was to deal with a minor crisis involving the Soviet Union. It seems that a bakery cooperative somewhere in the USSR had sent a huge, several-hundred-pound cake congratulating President Bush on his election. By the time the cake arrived, it had crumbled into pieces, and a number of vermin had had their way with it. The Secret Service called Brent, who called Bob Gates, who called me. I went down to inspect the gift and suggested that we dispose of it—but only after taking a picture of the cake in a part of the White House that would be easily recognizable. We could then send the picture to the wonderful Soviet citizens who'd been so thoughtful.

I settled into my new job and life in Washington, renting an apartment on Connecticut Avenue. Each morning I arrived at the White House at six-thirty and rarely left the office before nine at night. I found the work demanding, and I sometimes wondered if I'd make the cut. The NSC was known as a place where the weeding-out process was pretty severe: it wasn't uncommon to have a colleague with whom you were working on Monday disappear by Friday. No one ever asked what happened, but it was assumed that he or she had made an unforgivable mistake that embarrassed the White House or, even more unforgivably, the President.

Slowly I found my footing and realized that Brent had great confidence in me. I adored him. Nonetheless, I had to be careful to balance our close relationship with the fact that I reported through Bob Blackwill. Bob and I had good rapport, but he was hierarchical and sometimes prickly if it appeared that Brent had gone around him to me directly. I wanted Bob to trust me and to know that I wouldn't use my close relationship with Brent against him. On balance Bob and I managed well, becoming good colleagues and friends, but there was a tension there that always bore watching.

I also knew that Brent preferred the NSC staff to remain relatively anonymous and out of the spotlight. He set the standard as the most important man in Washington whom few Americans could identify in a photo lineup. But there was great media interest in me. When the *Washington Post* wanted to do a profile on the new Soviet specialist, a black woman professor from Stanford, I asked permission from Brent, who agreed I should do it. The morning the profile appeared, I was stunned to see a long, eye-catching article with a gigantic picture of me reading *Pravda,* a Soviet newspaper. It wasn't exactly the anonymity that was expected of the President's staff. I was relieved when Brent called to say that he thought the article was terrific, but I was appalled to see that there was no reference to my boss Bob Blackwill.

Not long after the article appeared, Vernon Jordan, the civil rights leader and venerable Washington lawyer, called and invited me to lunch, saying that he was going to tell me "how to survive in this town." He gave me a lot of advice, including an admonition to remember that Washington loved to create celebrities and then tear them down. Vernon and his wife, Anne, became wonderful friends to me in what can be a very lonely town. I resolved not to let celebrity status undermine my effectiveness in Washington. I don't know why I worried—I never had time to attend the cocktail parties and dinners that came with a high profile anyway.

Office and Beltway politics aside, there were certain moments that reminded me why I had chosen the White House over other, more senior jobs in the administration. The first such experience came when Brent called late on a wintry Friday afternoon in February. The President wanted to invite a group of Soviet specialists to Kennebunkport on Sunday to discuss the unfolding changes in Moscow.

"Could you round up a few experts and bring them to the President's home at Walker's Point?" he asked.

"Yes, sir," I said, and then despaired at having to round up a group of academics so late on a Friday.

I quickly learned, though, that when the White House calls, assistants and spouses manage to find people. So that Sunday I met five other Soviet specialists at the airport in Portland, Maine. We made our way along the icy roads to Walker's Point, where we briefed the President in the bedroom—the only room at the time that had heat.

My first face-to-face encounter with the President was wonderful. He was kind and thanked me profusely for everything that I'd done. "You're so good to agree to leave California and help me out," he said. *Is he kidding?* I thought. *He's the President.* But I learned that day, and would see throughout my time with him, that this wasn't false modesty: George H. W. Bush is simply one of the nicest and most self-effacing people that I've ever met. He taught me so much about leading people. Countless times he would send a congratulatory note to a foreign leader for a seemingly innocuous achievement. I came to understand that he was building a relationship, which would serve him well when he needed to ask that leader to do something hard. Even I frequently received a thank-you note from the President for a job well done, and this propensity for kindness and courtesy made it a joy to work with him. Most important, his natural geniality served American diplomacy well when he was faced with revolutionary changes in world politics.

Because so much was unfolding in the Soviet Union and Eastern Europe, I began to see the President quite often. Just a few
days after Kennebunkport, Jack Matlock, the able U.S. ambassador to the Soviet Union, came back to report to the President,
and I was asked to join them. I will never forget my first time in
the Oval Office: I was overjoyed—and overwhelmed—by simply
being there. As I sat in the pale yellow room with the sun streaming through the French doors, I suddenly realized that we were
two-thirds of the way through the meeting and I hadn't taken a
single note. This snapped me out of my Condi-in-Wonderland
moment. I went back to my office, tried to re-create a record
from memory, and vowed to remember that I was there to work,
not for the ride.

Yet it turned out to be a wild ride indeed. When I arrived in
Washington in January 1989, there was simply no way to predict
the historic events that I'd witness and help shape. At the beginning of the decade, Ronald Reagan had come to office determined to challenge Soviet power and had done so successfully.
In 1985, Mikhail Gorbachev rose to power as General Secretary
of the Communist Party of the Soviet Union. Facing rapid internal decay, Gorbachev began to loosen the reins of communist
authority at home and to pursue a more conciliatory course
abroad. The Russian terms that Gorbachev adopted for his re-
forms, *perestroika* and *glasnost,* meant "to reconstruct" (or make
anew) and "to make clear" (or transparent). It was a course that
overturned decades of hostile Soviet policy toward the West and
rapidly reshaped the foreign policy landscape.

By 1988, prodded by then–Secretary of State George Shultz,
Reagan had decided that Mikhail Gorbachev was indeed a different Soviet leader. A tremendous thaw in U.S.-Soviet relations

followed. Some, including Brent Scowcroft and Bob Gates, believed that Reagan had gone a bit soft on Moscow. They—and I—were skeptical of how authentic the shift in Soviet policy really was, and we wanted to slow the pace of the rapprochement to get a better feel for the changes that were taking place in the Soviet Union and Eastern Europe.

When policy makers want to slow things down, they order policy reviews. This is what Brent did in March 1989, entrusting me with the two that would examine U.S.-Soviet relations and American relations with Eastern Europe. I called together an interagency group to conduct the reviews, and we began to plow through the various aspects of U.S. policy, meeting two or three times a week.

While we were meeting, though, history was sprinting ahead. In April, the Communist Party of Poland was losing control of the country and called a "Round Table" negotiation session with Lech Walesa's underground Solidarity trade union. The talks would, it seemed, end in a power-sharing arrangement that heavily advantaged the Solidarity workers and committed the Polish government to hold free parliamentary elections. There was an internal debate in Washington about how to respond. The State Department urged caution and recommended taking only tiny steps toward the emerging democratic forces. But the outcome of the Round Table negotiations would, I thought, be a turning point. Working quietly with Daniel Fried, the young Foreign Service officer who headed the Polish desk at State, and urged on by Bob Blackwill and Bob Gates, I managed to get the President to take a more aggressive line.

The day that the negotiations were to end, we wrote a statement for Marlin Fitzwater, the President's press secretary. The

United States wouldn't just welcome the agreement but also would be clear about the implications for freedom in Eastern Europe. Marlin read the statement at his morning press availability. Unfortunately, the Round Table negotiators had taken a break for dinner and hadn't yet concluded the agreement. They did shortly thereafter, and fortunately no one noted our mistake. Ultimately, it didn't matter because the President of the United States was now firmly on the right side of the historic changes unfolding in Europe.

Within a few days, President Bush went to Hamtramck, Michigan, to give a speech on Poland. The site was chosen by the domestic side of the White House to honor one of the nation's largest Polish American communities. I accompanied the President, riding for the first time on Air Force One. When I got home, I called Daddy and gave him a thorough account of the day, including the lunch on the second floor of a miserably hot Polish American restaurant. I didn't tell him that the President had mispronounced the phrase "Polish people," calling them instead the "polish people"—as in furniture wax. At that slip, Brent had turned to me and barked, "Did you forget to capitalize the *P*?" I was mortified and took responsibility, though in fact the *P had* been capitalized. It was my first experience with the maxim that I would later pass on to NSC staffers: "It's the President's triumph and the NSC staffer's fault."

Over the next two months we finished our policy reviews, and the President delivered a couple of speeches loosely based on them. The effort to define a new course for U.S.-Soviet relations—called moving "beyond containment," a phrase that I coined—laid out a series of benchmarks that the Soviets would have to meet in order to show their seriousness about change. We had to keep revising the speech because they kept leapfrogging our "tests." From then on, even the most cautious among us knew that the changes were real. Now it was just a question of how far the Soviets were willing to go. Or more correctly, it was a question of whether Gorbachev was any longer in a position to stop the cascade of events that he had now unleashed.

I'D BEEN stretched thin by events since arriving at the White House. I continued my long-standing practice of talking to my father on the phone every night, and I could tell that his life was increasingly intertwined with that of Clara Bailey, a principal in the Ravenswood school district where Daddy was volunteering. Coincidentally, Clara had been born in Birmingham too. An attractive, quiet, church-going Baptist lady, Clara was divorced with one grown son, Greg. I'd gotten to know her before leaving for Washington and noticed that Daddy seemed to favor her over the many other ladies who sought his attention.

One night when I called him, Daddy's voice was halting. "I'd hoped to talk to you about this in person," he said, "but you're so busy, I don't know when you're coming home. Clara and I want to get married." Then he abruptly stopped talking, waiting a second or so for me to respond. But before I could say anything he started talking again about how his love for my mother had been so special and nothing would ever replace that. I stopped him. "Daddy, I know that," I said. I told him that I liked Clara and was glad that they'd decided to get married. Frankly, it never occurred to me to question his decision.

The formal wedding was set for July 1, 1989, at Clara's house in Palo Alto. Greg and I were the witnesses, and I arranged to host the reception at the Stanford Faculty Club. At the reception, I realized that Daddy had made many new friends since my departure for Washington, and that was gratifying. Clara was clearly very good for him: compassionate and kind, she gave him a new lease on life. To this day she and I remain close. I must admit, though, that I felt a tinge of remorse at the wedding. I was glad that Daddy had found a companion, but his marriage opened the wound again of my mother's untimely death at the too-young age of sixty-one.

CHAPTER THIRTY

"I Don't Think This Is What Karl Marx Had in Mind"

I STAYED IN Palo Alto for just two days. With the quickening pace of international events, I simply couldn't afford any more time off. President Bush had decided to visit Eastern Europe in order to signal American support for what was unfolding there. Any doubts about the momentous nature of the changes were wiped away when we arrived in Poland on July 9 and in Hungary two days later.

Hungary had been a center of reform, managing even in the depths of the Cold War to gain some modicum of independence from Moscow. But now the Hungarians were challenging Soviet power directly and moving toward multiparty elections. More astonishingly, Hungary had decided to dismantle the barbed wire demarcating its border with Austria. In fact, during our time in

Budapest, Hungarian Prime Minister Miklós Németh gave President Bush a piece of that twisted metal fence. He proudly and rightly told the President that his country had been the first to breach the Iron Curtain.

It was in Poland, though, that the Cold War had begun in 1945, and it was now clear that it was in Poland where it could end. Air Force One landed on a muggy, hot evening in Warsaw. Wojciech Jaruzelski, the communist general who'd imposed martial law in 1981 and was now the president of Poland, greeted President Bush. A goose-stepping military band paraded in front of us and played the national anthems of the two countries. I flashed back to the last time I'd been at this airport. Returning from the Soviet Union in 1979, I'd had to make an unscheduled stop in Warsaw, where we were told to get off the plane and leave all of our belongings. Cris, Lisa, and I had sat nervously in the lounge wondering if we were going to be detained by the communist authorities. After a while the passengers were permitted to reboard the Air France flight. The whole plane erupted in cheers as we ascended into the air and out of harm's way.

But now communism in Poland had lost its ferocity. That night at the state dinner, held in a tacky, faded dining hall, the room suddenly went dark due to a power surge caused by the hot television lights. It was a metaphor for the Communist Party's coming fate.

It was clear that the party's demise was sealed the next day when we went to Gdańsk, the home of Solidarity. In contrast to the stultifying arrival ceremony, President Bush was greeted in the town square by hundreds of thousands of cheering Polish workers. "Bush, Bush, Bush!" they chanted, waving American flags. "Freedom! Freedom! Freedom!" I turned to Bob Blackwill and said, "I don't think this is what Karl Marx had in mind when he said, 'Workers of the world, unite.'"

BY THE end of August 1989, it was clear that the cascade of events would not stop in Poland and Hungary but would roll back into Germany—the epicenter of the Cold War—and sweep away the line that had divided East from West for more than forty years.

At the time, the division of Germany into two parts was one of those givens of international politics. Each year West German leaders would mechanically repeat platitudes about the coming day when all Germany would be united. But nobody actually believed it. After 1971, a workable *modus vivendi* was put in place so that the divided city of Berlin could function more efficiently. By September 1973, East and West Germany had become separate members of the United Nations and competed in the Olympics as separate countries (the East Germans as a sports superpower).

Although the two countries had learned to live next to each other, their continued division hardly bred stability; the best troops of NATO and the best troops of the Warsaw Pact stood stationed on high alert at the border between East and West. War between the Soviet Union and the United States seemed unlikely, but if it were to start, the most plausible scenarios always involved these frontline troops, facing each other across the Fulda Gap.

Even with the collapse of communism in Poland and Hungary, few believed that the Soviet Union was ready to contemplate the unification of Germany. Moscow still wore the victory over Germany in "The Great Patriotic War" as a talisman against decline at home. And for the Kremlin, East Germany was a source of pride. Widely believed to be the most successful state in the Eastern Bloc—more efficient and advanced than even the Soviet Union itself—Berlin was proof that communism could work.

By the fall of 1989, the impact of Gorbachev's policies was becoming evident. Erich Honecker, the hard-line leader of East Germany, had been forced from power, ironically because he was unwilling to pursue Moscow's liberalizing policies at home. Now, because of the refusal of other Warsaw Pact states, particularly Hungary, to enforce the border controls between their countries, hundreds fled East Germany without fear of being returned to the German Democratic Republic—the official name of a country that was anything but democratic. As the Hungarians put it, East European states stopped being "Honecker's border guards." The flow quickened until it was a veritable flood. One news cartoon, captioned "Germany Unifies," depicted West Germany full of people and East Germany empty. That wasn't far from reality.

The GDR was dying and, increasingly, Germans were speaking about what had only months before seemed impossible. I attended a meeting in Germany at the end of October. Usually these transatlantic conferences were filled with talk of arms control and relations between the Warsaw Pact and NATO. This time, however, Germans wanted to talk to each other across the political divides of socialist and conservative, East and West. As an American, I felt like a bystander. On the plane ride home, I penned a memo for the President reporting that German unification was suddenly on the agenda. But before I could send it, the unthinkable happened: the Berlin Wall fell.

It turns out that the most momentous event in forty years

of international history occurred thanks to a gigantic bureau-cratic screw-up in the GDR. To stem the exodus of its citizens, the East German government decided to develop new, liberal-ized travel policies that would give East Germans the ability to leave the country. The hope was that in making it easier to travel back and forth, people would visit other nations but ultimately return home. Interior Ministry officials intended to have these relaxed restrictions apply to the border between East and West Germany, but *not* in Berlin, which had a different status as an occupied city. That point, however, was somehow left out of the draft regulations.

The new policies were written on November 9, 1989, but the internal security forces didn't yet have clear instructions on how to implement them. That night the party press secretary spot-ted the draft policies on a table as he headed to the podium for what had become a daily press conference to try to calm the wa-ters. He read the regulations to the astonished press and almost immediately realized that he couldn't explain what they meant. But it was too late. People began to flock to the Berlin Wall, the symbol and reality of Europe's division for decades. The Interior Ministry guards didn't know what to do. Faced with the flood of people, the commander made a historic decision: he ordered his troops to withhold fire. The Berlin Wall collapsed in joyous celebration.

At about three that afternoon Washington time, the phone rang in our suite of offices in the Old Executive Office Build-ing, the place within the White House complex where most of the President's staff works. The assistant to Brent's deputy, Bob Gates, was on the phone. "The General"—as we called

Brent—"wants you and Bob Blackwill to come over and talk to the President about what is going on in Berlin," Dianne said.

Unfortunately, we had all been too busy doing other things to know what was happening. "What do you mean?" I asked.

"Turn on CNN," she said. "The Wall has come down."

Bob hastily called his contacts at the CIA, while Philip Zelikow and NSC Eastern Europe Director Bob Hutchings called the State Department and I monitored the news coverage. Within a short time we were in Brent's office, trying to recover from the fact that the crack staff of the NSC had been scooped by CNN. The President was already in the Oval Office with the press. He was careful and guarded in his public reaction to the unfolding events, telling reporters that he was very pleased with the development. "We are saluting those who can move forward with democracy," the President said. "We are encouraging the concept of a Europe whole and free."

Some pundits criticized the President for what they interpreted as a relatively subdued response to a clear victory for freedom. The truth was that the President did not want to alarm the Soviets or get too far ahead of the West Germans in pushing for reunification.

In private conversations within the West Wing, however, his support for unification was unequivocal. The President didn't wait for a careful analysis of the pros and cons of German unification. He reacted based on principle and his gut instincts. Germany should unify as quickly as the Germans themselves desired, he told us. He had faith in German democracy; there was nothing to fear.

This was a momentous decision. George Bush's certainty

meant that it was no longer a question of whether Germany should unify but how to make it happen. America would be resolutely at the side of Helmut Kohl, the West German chancellor. Leader of the conservative Christian Democratic Union party, Kohl was staunchly pro-American and ready to make difficult decisions in order to seize the opportunity to do what no chancellor had ever thought possible. He no longer had to worry about where America stood on reunification.

Nevertheless, when we suggested on that momentous day that President Bush go to Berlin, as Kennedy and Reagan had done, the President demurred. "This is a German moment," he said with characteristic modesty. "What would I do? Dance on the Wall?"

Blackwill and I returned across West Executive Way to our offices. We plopped down in the large wing chairs in his office in front of the fireplace, exhausted and exhilarated at the same time. As we continued to watch the extraordinary pictures from Berlin, Bob said that I should write something for the President. Clearly, everyone would worry about the reaction of the Soviet Union. "You need to write it before you leave tonight," he said.

I sat down at the word processor. "Mr. President," I wrote, "we have now entered the end game of the Cold War." What I really wanted to say was that I couldn't believe our good fortune: we were lucky enough to be charged with making history come out right. We couldn't afford to fail.

The next day, Bob Gates and I received a letter that Gorbachev had sent to the other three "occupying powers"—France, the United Kingdom, and the United States—as well as a copy of the somewhat tougher letter he'd sent to Chancellor Kohl. The Soviet leader suggested that any attempt to unify Germany in light of these events amounted to "political extremism" that could bring about "not only the destabilization of the situation in Central Europe, but also in other parts of the world." It sounded a bit ominous, but we'd come to know Gorbachev as one who didn't threaten. We began to consider how we would manage the unification process. We knew where we stood thanks to the President's clarity. The French and British, however, particularly Margaret Thatcher, weren't so sure that it was a good idea. Whenever she would talk about German unification, Thatcher would bristle, recalling how the Germans had sent her family scurrying into bomb shelters when she was a child. Clearly, alliance management would be a huge task. And what of the Soviet Union? Was Moscow really prepared to see Germany unify, and on what terms? We wanted to be sensitive to Soviet interests. After all, with about thirty-five thousand nuclear weapons and nearly five million men under arms, the Soviet Union was a weakening but still formidable force. The United States would need to be Germany's anchor and advocate. But we would also need to make sure that U.S. interests were protected. We couldn't allow Germany to make a deal that gave us half a loaf—for instance, we would not want them to take the unified state out of NATO. American power needed to be preserved in Europe even as the Soviet Union retreated. The Cold War was almost won after forty years. We didn't want to make a fatal mistake at the very end.

President Bush decided that he needed to sit down with Gorbachev. Events were unfolding very rapidly, and the President wanted to take the temperature of the Soviet leader in a face-to-face encounter. Perhaps naively, we hoped to arrange a low-key meeting between the two and worked with the Soviets to hold talks in the island country of Malta on December 2–3, 1989. The arrangements were to be kept secret until the last minute to prevent too much buildup.

Unfortunately, we didn't anticipate two problems. First, we could not keep a meeting between the two world leaders quiet, and when it leaked, the expectations for the summit were even greater, since the secrecy itself fueled speculation about what would happen.

Second, Malta is a beautiful place—but not in December. When we told our secretaries of the upcoming summit, one of them who had served there said, "Are you crazy? Have you ever seen the weather in Malta in December?" She was right. Storms and gale-force winds forced the cancellation of the first session and the summit dinner since they were to be held at sea aboard an American destroyer.

When we did finally meet for the second session aboard the Soviet cruise ship *Maxim Gorky*, it was clear the President's instincts had been right. He and Gorbachev started to develop a relationship of trust, which served them well through the coming metaphorical storms at the end of the Cold War. It was also aboard the *Maxim Gorky* that I met Gorbachev for the first time. "She tells me everything I need to know about the Soviet Union," the President said as he introduced me to the Soviet leader. "I certainly hope she knows a lot," Gorbachev quipped.

AFTER THE first of the year, Jim Baker's State Department struck a deal to set up a negotiating forum for German unification called the Two-Plus-Four process; the two Germanys would be represented alongside the four Allied powers from World War II. There was some grousing among the NSC staff that we had not been properly consulted. But there wasn't much time for bureaucratic politics. History was moving too fast.

Brent called me into his office the afternoon of the announcement of the Two-Plus-Four negotiations. "I want you to be the White House representative on the negotiating delegation," he said.

"But this is about Germany," I replied. "I'm your Soviet specialist."

"I know," Brent insisted. "For us, German unification is a Soviet problem."

He was right, and I joined Bob Zoellick, Baker's State Department counselor, and Raymond Seitz, the assistant secretary for European and Canadian affairs, on the team that would negotiate the unification of Germany.

From that point on, we faced a daily cascade of events toward the Cold War's end. It was, frankly, exhausting. The delegation traveled to Germany several times between March and September, arriving early in the morning, meeting all day, enduring heavy German cuisine at dinner, and then returning home the next morning. When we asked whether we might have longer but fewer sessions given how far we had to come, the French delegate replied, "Rather puts to rest that notion of America as a European power." We ignored the dig and suffered silently through the brutal schedule.

At the end of May 1990, Gorbachev came to Washington for a full-scale summit, his popularity in the West growing even as it declined at home. We wanted to make the visit special to shore up the Soviet president, whom we now saw as essential to ending the Cold War peacefully. There was a grand ceremony to sign an arms control treaty in the East Room, a magnificent state dinner, and a trip to Camp David, all underscoring the importance of the man and his excellent relationship with President Bush.

It is not unusual that foreign leaders travel to other parts of the country during a trip to the United States. George Shultz, who had returned to California, invited Gorbachev to visit the West Coast and give a speech at Stanford. President Bush called me to the Oval Office a few days before Gorbachev's arrival in Washington. "Stanford is your home," he said. "I want you to accompany Gorbachev to Palo Alto." As I sat on the South Lawn of the White House waiting with Gorbachev and his wife, Raisa, to take off in the presidential helicopter, Marine One, a thought crossed my mind: *I'm awfully glad I changed my major.*

Gorbachev seemed to enjoy his time in California. "They ought to make you pay to live here," he told George Shultz.

"They do," George replied, referencing the high cost of living in northern California.

The trip was one of the highlights of my career and a remarkable moment for my father, who attended Gorbachev's speech in Stanford's Memorial Auditorium. He was so proud to see his daughter sitting next to the leader of the Soviet Union, representing the President of the United States. Unfortunately, this moment was followed by a well-publicized tussle with an overly aggressive Secret Service agent who tried to prevent me from going onto the San Francisco airport tarmac to say goodbye to Gorbachev. I wasn't sure if he just didn't have me on the list or if he couldn't believe that the President's Soviet advisor was a black woman. Whatever his motivation, the incident didn't sit well with the President or with his chief of staff, John Sununu. I was assured that the offending agent had been dealt with appropriately.

Across the Atlantic, our work was paying off. On October 3, 1990, Germany unified fully within NATO. It was an acquisition, not a merger, with the Federal Republic of Germany emerging as the legal successor to the German state that had been defeated in 1945. In short, the GDR was abolished, and with it Soviet power in Europe. Ironically, the agreement granting the unified Germany full sovereignty and ending the occupation was finalized on September 12 in Moscow. Standing behind Jim Baker as he signed the document, I caught a glimpse of Gorbachev, who was tucked away behind a number of midlevel Soviet officials. *What must he be thinking?* I wondered. And then another thought flashed across my mind: *How long can he possibly last?*

WITH EASTERN Europe liberated and Germany unified, I began to think about returning to Stanford. Most universities have a "two-year rule," meaning that a faculty member can take only two consecutive years of leave without forfeiting tenure. Stanford had been very flexible in my case, and I felt that I needed to get back to my academic career. I was also dead tired.

I went to see Brent in September 1990 and told him that I needed to leave at the first of the year. He asked me to stay, saying that he wanted to restructure the staff in light of international events. He would promote me to special assistant to the President and break up the current directorate that included Europe to create a separate entity for the Soviet Union. Moreover, Saddam Hussein had invaded Kuwait that August, and the United

States had rallied an international coalition against him. It was likely that there would be war in the Middle East. Brent would need to turn increasingly to that problem and wanted someone that he trusted to deal with the Soviet Union.

I told him that I'd stay a little while longer to help manage Soviet affairs in light of the coming Gulf War. The next big challenge was dealing with a wounded—perhaps fatally wounded—Soviet Union. Moscow was confronting grave difficulty in managing the republics, particularly the Baltic states, which were suddenly restive, having seen the collapse of Soviet power in Europe. "Brent," I said, "the Soviet Union may break up, and I don't think I have the energy for it."

I did stay until April 1991. During the first part of that year, the Soviet Union's decline accelerated precipitously. I worked together with my new deputy, Nick Burns, who'd come to join me from Baker's staff at the State Department, to adjust our policies accordingly. Previously, in September 1989, Bob Gates had asked me to convene a small and very secret group to consider contingencies for the breakup of the Soviet Union and the overthrow of Gorbachev by hard-line Communist Party leaders. It was time to dust off that work. But we had to be careful to avoid leaks and met privately, allowing no mention of the sessions on our calendars.

We also decided that the President needed to meet Soviet leaders other than Gorbachev. The Soviet president was now wedged uncomfortably between the backlash of alarmed conservatives, who struggled to halt or even reverse the flow of events, and the rise of radical figures, who wanted to move faster even if it meant the end of the Soviet Union,

Boris Yeltsin was one of those radical leaders. He was making a claim—outlandish at the time—that Russia needed to be liberated from the Soviet Union. Yeltsin was Gorbachev's bitter rival, and when he requested a meeting with President Bush in September 1989, there was some reluctance to see him. The President had enormous respect and sympathy for Gorbachev and was determined to do nothing to embarrass the Soviet leader. We settled on a tried-and-true remedy for such a problem: a meeting with the national security advisor during which the President would make an unannounced drop-by. Yeltsin was told only that he would meet Brent.

That afternoon I met Boris Yeltsin at the West Wing basement door. He got out of the car and turned to his aide. "This isn't the door you go in to see the President," he said in Russian. Obviously he'd expected to be received at the columned formal entrance to the White House where the Marine guards stand vigil.

Before the translator could say anything, I replied in Russian that Mr. Yeltsin's meeting was with General Scowcroft.

"Who is this man Scowcroft?" Yeltsin barked. "Is he even important enough to meet with me?" Yeltsin, a big man—more than six feet tall and at least 250 pounds—stood there with his arms folded, red-faced and scowling.

I was furious. "Mr. Yeltsin," I said, this time in English, "General Scowcroft is a busy man. If you don't want to keep your appointment, let me know and I'll cancel it and you can go back to your hotel."

He muttered to himself for a few moments, then huffed and said sharply, "Where is he?" Instinctively, I took him by the arm and almost dragged him up to Brent's office.

Brent, knowing none of this, greeted him warmly. Yeltsin

sat down and launched into a soliloquy on his plans for Russia. Brent, who always worked too hard for his own good, fell asleep. Yeltsin didn't notice, completely absorbed in his own presentation. About thirty minutes into the meeting, the President flung open the door. Yeltsin smiled broadly, jumped up, and embraced the startled leader of the free world in a bear hug. Then he continued his monologue. After about thirty minutes more he was done. The President left, and I escorted a self-satisfied Yeltsin out to his car.

My first impressions of the man were obviously not very good. But more than a year later Yeltsin stood bravely atop a tank on a Moscow street and faced down the army and the security services of the Soviet Union. Boris Yeltsin would become the historic if somewhat flawed figure who brought down the Soviet Union and launched democracy in Russia. I was very glad that we had arranged that early meeting—bizarre as it was—with the President of the United States.

As EXPECTED, January 1991 brought the outbreak of war with Saddam Hussein. This event dominated the news and the attention of the President and Brent. But I was consumed with simultaneous crises in the Baltic states. Suddenly faced with the prospect of Baltic independence, Gorbachev belatedly tried to crack down. Thirteen people were killed and more than a hundred were wounded when Soviet-backed Lithuanian security forces fired on and drove tanks over protesters at the TV tower in Vilnius, the capital city.

I went to Brent to discuss the events and what to do. I told him that the President had to make a strong response. Moscow couldn't be allowed to think that the United States was condoning the Kremlin's brutality. Each day Marlin had read a statement urging restraint on all sides. We were starting to sound as if we thought there was no difference between the innocent protesters and the goons of the Interior Ministry who were beating them up. I was concerned too that Moscow might decide to launch a full-scale military assault against Lithuania or Latvia.

Bob Gates agreed with me, and we argued for a statement that would condemn Soviet actions and say that further violence would harm U.S.-Soviet relations. Brent was opposed, worrying about our dependence on Moscow to keep the coalition against Saddam Hussein together. It is often the case that policy makers are faced with competing priorities. Of the two crises, I knew that the impending war against Saddam was the more pressing.

Nonetheless, we went to the President with two versions of the statement. Standing there in the Oval Office beside the President's desk, I could see how tired he was. He was about to send American forces into battle. It is the loneliest decision that a President has to make, and it was clearly weighing on this veteran of World War II. The President decided to issue the strong version. "We condemn these acts," the President told the press, saying that the events "could not help but affect our relationship" with Moscow.

I had told the President that I did not think the statement would garner much attention and that Moscow had to expect it by now. I was wrong. That night Peter Jennings, Dan Rather, and Tom Brokaw all led the news with the U.S.-Soviet "confrontation," even as we were preparing to confront Saddam Hussein. Brent was furious, but it was the right thing to do.

Violence in the Baltics continued to escalate. The next week five people, including a young schoolboy, were killed by members of a Soviet special-forces unit in Latvia. One of the victims, a journalist, was shot in the face outside a Latvian hotel as our consular office described the unfolding chaos to me on the telephone. The carnage took place as more than a hundred thousand people marched outside the Kremlin in opposition to the Soviet crackdowns. In spite of this upheaval, the Soviet Union did not launch a full-scale military invasion of Lithuania and Latvia. I can't be sure, but I have always thought that the President's clarity helped to remind Moscow of the costs of doing so. After the events that January, it was increasingly clear that the Baltic states would become independent and that Gorbachev's days were numbered.

Fortunately, our pressure on Moscow did not disrupt the Gulf War coalition, which, led by American military power, successfully expelled Saddam Hussein's forces from Kuwait. But the war left the Iraqi dictator in power, able to threaten his neighbors and oppress his people. That would be a problem for another day.

WITH THE war concluded, I decided that I had discharged my duties and could return home. The President sent me a lovely letter recounting the role that I had played. "While the fate of the Soviet Union is still not decided," he wrote, "you have set us on a course to realize the historic dream of a Europe whole, free and at peace." I was sad to leave but felt a tremendous sense of completion and accomplishment.

The day before my departure, First Lady Barbara Bush invited me to join her for tea in the residence. "You are such a good friend of the Bushes," she said. "This won't be the last that we see of you."

CHAPTER THIRTY-ONE

Back in California

I RETURNED TO Stanford tired but content. The university was again generous, telling me that I would not be required to teach until the fall quarter. That allowed me time to design my next research project—the one that I would use to make my case for promotion to full professor during the next academic year.

On the personal side, I decided that I had outgrown my place at 74 Pearce Mitchell, and looked to find a new home. Fortunately, the young couple renting the condo wanted to buy it. Daddy and Clara offered to have me stay with them until I found a new home and renovated it. The transition took a bit longer than I had planned, and I lived with them for five months. I insisted on paying rent because I did not want to take Clara's generosity for granted. I had a good deal of free time in the months immediately after my return and enjoyed long lunches with Daddy, just catching up and spending time together. I also had the opportunity to become closer to my stepmother, whom I hadn't known very well when she and Daddy married.

I didn't miss Washington or the work in the White House. Even when the coup against Gorbachev took place in August 1991, leading to the eventual collapse of the Soviet Union in December, I didn't regret my decision to leave. Throughout the spring and summer, I worked again for ABC News as an expert analyst but largely kept my distance from the policy world. I'd done my part and had no desire to try to influence events from afar.

In fact, new horizons were opening up for me. A few weeks after returning home, I received a call from George Shultz. I had gotten to know George shortly before he went to Washington to become secretary of state in 1982. He had taken an interest in my career and stayed in touch during my time in Washington. George was a director of the Chevron Corporation and wondered if I might be interested in joining the board. Chevron had just acquired a stake in the Tengiz oil field in Kazakhstan, at the time a part of the Soviet Union, and George felt that my expertise would be useful to them. After a day with the CEO, Ken Derr, and his team, I signed on enthusiastically. In retrospect, it was a stretch for the company to appoint a thirty-six-year-old associate professor to a board largely populated by corporate titans. At the time, Chevron named oil tankers for its directors, so in 1993 my entire family and I traveled to Brazil to christen the *Condoleezza Rice*. Several years later, when I was national security advisor, the company and I agreed that it was not wise to have my name floating into ports around the world, and the tanker was renamed. After the terrorist attacks of September 11, I was awfully glad we had made the change.

I quickly learned that once you join one corporate board, other opportunities emerge. A month or so later, Frank Herringer, the CEO of Transamerica, invited me to join the board of the insurance and financial services company, headquartered in San Francisco. Then one day my secretary said that David Packard wanted to come and see me. I'd gotten to know David in Republican politics, but he was a giant figure, a founding father of Silicon Valley and one of Stanford's greatest benefactors. I could not imagine him coming to see me. "Tell Mr. Packard that I'll come to see him," I said to Yvonne.

She returned a few minutes later. "No, he insists on coming to see you."

"How are you, Dave?" I asked to break the ice when he entered my office.

"It's no fun getting old," he said. "But as they say, it's better than the alternative." I laughed, but he went right to the point. "Hewlett-Packard is a good company. You're a good person. I want you to be a director of HP. Call me when you decide." Then he got up and left.

Dave had a reputation for directness, even abruptness, but this was a remarkable encounter. Usually a prospective director meets with the management and other directors. There is a kind of two-way courtship. Not with Dave. So I called him the next day and said yes.

Holding down three corporate board positions, I was quickly becoming busier than I had planned to be. Yet when Governor Pete Wilson called to ask if I would serve on a statewide commission to redistrict California, I couldn't refuse. The commission met every Thursday and Friday in Sacramento. We took testimony from around the state on how to redraw the electoral lines. It was a great experience, and through it, I got to know the state of California intimately.

Pete's appointment of me to the commission was the second time we'd encountered each other. We'd first met back in Washington when he was the junior senator from California. He'd been elected governor in November 1990 and had to appoint a successor to serve the remainder of his term in the Senate. President Bush and his chief of staff, John Sununu, urged Pete to appoint me. Many of the northern California power brokers got behind the idea. David Packard told Pete that he'd personally raise the money for my campaign.

I met Pete in a hotel a few days after his election. Even though I had been careful to avoid press attention, the story of our meeting leaked that morning. I immediately liked the new governor, and we have remained friends over the years. That day we talked about political life, and he asked me if I had the "fire in the belly" to run for office. His successor, he explained, would have to raise money and begin campaigning for 1992 right away. I talked about the issues, particularly education and immigration, but didn't answer him directly. He asked if I was pro-choice. I said that I did not favor overturning *Roe v. Wade* but thought some restrictions were wholly appropriate. Our meeting ended amiably but inconclusively.

Several days later, I read in the *Washington Post* that Pete had chosen John Seymour, the former mayor of Anaheim and a California state senator, to succeed him. John, Pete believed, could raise money and would be able to mobilize the exceedingly important southern California constituencies. Frankly, I was relieved, if a little annoyed, to have found out in the newspaper. I probably would have accepted the job had he offered. But the truth is, I wasn't at all sure of the answer to Pete's question. Over the years I have realized that the answer is no. I don't have the fire in the belly needed to run for elective office. Nonetheless, many in the party have never let me forget the events of that fall. John Seymour was soundly defeated in the 1992 election by Dianne Feinstein.

CHAPTER THIRTY-TWO

Learning Compassion

ONE OF my surprises upon returning to Palo Alto was just how much my father had established a new life and reputation of his own. Daddy was always a magnet for people, and he'd become a powerful one in Palo Alto. Not only was he active with Stanford's Public Service Center and Department of Athletics, transforming what was once just a study hall for freshman football players into an academic resource and tutoring center for all Stanford athletes, but he had also become a well-regarded figure in East Palo Alto.

Not long after I returned home, one of Daddy's new friends—Charlie Mae Knight, the superintendent of the Ravenswood schools in East Palo Alto—asked if I would deliver the district-wide commencement address. Ravenswood is an elementary and middle school district with no high school. Yet as I sat on the stage, it occurred to me that with extended families having come from all over the Bay Area and beyond to attend the ceremonies, the commencement exercises felt more like a high school graduation.

"This is an awfully elaborate commencement for eighth graders," I said to Charlie.

"Well," she said, "that's because 70 percent of these kids will never finish high school. This is their last commencement."

I was stunned and realized that I knew very little of the poverty and lack of opportunity just a few blocks from my house. I'd served on committees such as the Mid-Peninsula Urban Renewal Authority, but frankly, like most residents of Palo Alto, I avoided any real contact with East Palo Alto and its high crime rate. When I first moved to Palo Alto, I'd occasionally take the wrong exit off Highway 101, deceptively labeled University Avenue. After a few encounters with East Palo Alto's "Whiskey Gulch," with its four liquor stores on the corners and a reputation for drive-by shootings, I learned to find the right exit a minute or so down the road.

That evening, I asked my father to tell me about the challenges for the school district, feeling a little embarrassed that I'd lived in the area for ten years and knew nothing, while my father, who'd moved to Palo Alto only recently, was actively trying to help. He told me about some of his efforts, including refurbishing an athletic field for the district. It seems that it was a constant struggle against the gophers, but he felt he was winning and the kids would soon have a nice place to play. Daddy also told me about what Charlie Mae wanted to do. Ravenswood had had eleven superintendents in ten years and the odds were long, but he was impressed with her toughness and commitment. He was going to be a partner to her and mobilize resources from Stanford to help. "Stanford has been running its own programs and its own agenda in East Palo Alto," he said. "It's about time that someone ask the people there what they need."

My father was just doing what he'd done all of his life: following in his father's footsteps of educational evangelism. I resolved right then to get involved too and asked Charlie Mae to lunch a few days later. She talked about the need for extended-day learning activities, saying that children had nothing wholesome to do after school. Most extracurricular activities such as music and art had been cut because of budgetary pressures. We laughed about our experiences as children—Charlie's in Valdosta, Georgia, and mine in Birmingham—learning to perform in endless variety shows, concerts, and debate-team competitions. I flashed back to my horrible tap dancing routine in elementary school but reflected on how lucky I'd been to have so many opportunities. Charlie and I agreed that I'd pull together a group of people who might be interested in helping.

My first call was to Tom and Susan Ford. Tom was one of the founding fathers of Silicon Valley. A real estate lawyer at Stanford in the early 1960s, Tom had developed a low-rise, environmentally sensitive set of office buildings at 3000 Sand Hill Road in Menlo Park, not far from Stanford. But he couldn't get lawyers and accountants to move to the location, considered at the time to be too far from San Francisco. So he made a deal with a new and emerging industry called venture capital, offering reduced rent for a small percentage of their profits. In that way, Sand Hill Road became synonymous with those who funded the information revolution and birthed Silicon Valley. And Tom became very wealthy—and exceedingly generous and compassionate.

Tom had recently remarried, and his new wife, Susan, and I had become friends. They immediately signed on to help. Susan and I brought together other community leaders from Palo Alto, among them Steve Player, a Palo Alto lawyer, and Charla Rolland, the black school superintendent of Los Lomitas, one of the wealthiest districts in California. We enlisted Larry Tripplett, a former school principal who owned the McDonald's franchise in East Palo Alto, and Erma Moore, a well-regarded beauty shop owner. Randy Bean put together our application for 501(c)3 status as a nonprofit. A recent Stanford graduate, Mia Jackson, wrote proposals, and we lined up core donors from local foundations and corporations. The board members all agreed to make individual contributions according to their means. Everything was in place, and so together with Charlie Knight, my father, and my stepmother, Clara, this group planned to launch the Center for a New Generation (CNG).

We had no idea how hard it would be. There was a political power structure in East Palo Alto that was suspicious of outsiders and determined to keep control. It didn't help that I was from Stanford, which, as my father had noted, had a well-deserved reputation for misguided noblesse oblige. There were also a number of nonprofits in East Palo Alto run by residents of the city that were little more than jobs programs for the staffs of the organizations. Money had flowed to these programs from corporations and foundations with little demand for accountability. In this way, Palo Alto had eased its conscience, but it was hard to argue that kids were being helped by what my dad called "guilt money." Some of the directors of these programs, who were often powerful people in the city, saw CNG as a threat to their funding sources.

To break through, we had to work very hard. We held community meetings, including a ridiculously expensive lunch for all of the power brokers, and also scheduled numerous meetings with the Board of Education. We brought the chair of the school board, Myrtle Walker, into the effort, which helped immensely. And we addressed the city council. I finally lost my cool when one of the members asked what was in it for me. I was floored and shot back, "Nothing. But there is something in it for your kids. Why are you so hard to help?"

The experience taught me many tough lessons about the difficulties of community organizing and the power of entrenched interests. I also learned that nonprofit management could be an oxymoron; several of the staff members possessed good hearts but little management skill. But by the summer of 1992 we were able to launch the program for children grades five to eight. Each summer 250 kids were exposed to hands-on math and science instruction, language arts, instrumental music, dance, and art. The curriculum was repeated as an after-school program for 150 kids. We hired the best teachers from the school district and paid them very well, hoping they'd take the innovative curriculum back into their regular classrooms. College students, including many athletes from Stanford, acted as mentors for the kids. The students were chosen on the basis of teacher recommendations, but we were determined that the program not be just for the "talented tenth" or for remedial education. Instead, it was conceived of as an enrichment program. I remember, in particular, one ten-year-old named Oscar. He was not recommended but came to CNG every day. When the teacher told him that he was not a registered Center student, his reply warmed our hearts. "I wasn't recommended because I am what they call a behavior problem," he said. "But I wouldn't be a behavior problem in CNG because it's fun." Needless to say, Oscar was admitted the next day.

The crown jewels of CNG were the instrumental bands: beginning, intermediate, and advanced. The advanced band was very good indeed and became known for its signature song, "When the Saints Go Marching In." After one particularly stirring performance, we found a donor to subsidize all instruments and uniforms. I was in tears, remembering how important bands were to my black heritage in the segregated South. By the way, Oscar turned out to be a terrific trombone player.

Today there are five Centers for a New Generation spread across East Palo Alto, East Menlo Park, and now heavily Hispanic Redwood City. In 1997, under the leadership of Jackie Glaster, the Centers became programs of the Boys and Girls Clubs of America, a strategic partnership that has continued to expand. Whatever our struggles in founding CNG, it was one of the most joyous times of my life. I particularly enjoyed working with Daddy to bring it into being, and I am sure my grandfather John Wesley Rice Sr. noted and approved of the way the experience sparked my own determination to be an educational evangelist. The work was rewarding and exhausting. I once said to Susan that I hoped when we got to St. Peter's gate, he would look at the ledger and see that we had worked in East Palo Alto in the turbulent 1990s. "Go to the head of the line, my children," I would expect him to say.

CHAPTER THIRTY-THREE

Finding a New President
for Stanford

WITH MY academic research, corporate boards, preparation for teaching, and the activities with the Center, I was very busy. I was increasingly sought out by graduate students from around the country, including Kiron Skinner, a Harvard PhD student who is now a tenured professor at Carnegie Mellon University and a close colleague. I also made four trips to Russia, enjoying my freedom to visit the country as a faculty member rather than a government official. These were important visits, as I saw firsthand the disorientation and humiliation of the Russian population after the collapse of the Soviet Union. Years later, that extended time in Russia helped me to understand the appeal of Vladimir Putin, who promised Russians order, prosperity, and respect.

Like most at Stanford, I was following with some interest the impending change in leadership at the university. The school had gotten into a dispute with the federal government about payments for costs associated with government contracts. It was a headline-grabbing scandal, with charges that Stanford had over-billed the government to the tune of $200 million. Don Kennedy, who for ten years had been the highly successful leader of the university and to whom I had been quite close, decided to step down. The *Stanford Report* announced that the Board of Trustees had accepted his resignation and would appoint a committee to select the next president.

I didn't expect to be appointed to the committee. After all, I'd been away from Stanford three out of the last four years. But one day in September I received a call from Jim Gaither, the chairman of the board. "We need you to help find a new president," Gaither said. "This is going to be a tough process because the university is really hurting and a lot of people don't like the direction it has been going in. And I hate to tell you this, but it will take a lot of time. Will you serve?" I readily accepted. The committee of six faculty members, one student, six trustees, an alumni representative, and one senior administrator was announced a few weeks later.

John Lillie, representing the Board of Trustees, and Jim Sheehan, a professor of history, served the committee as chair and vice chair. We agreed to meet every week but often met more frequently than that. I hadn't known how many difficulties Stanford was facing. There had been massive budgetary cuts and layoffs as the federal government slashed payments to the university amid the dispute. Also, the Loma Prieta earthquake of 1989 had left the campus severely damaged, with the four corners of the main quadrangle, the museum, and several other buildings still unusable. The main entrance to the campus, Palm Drive, was one big pothole.

Moreover, there was a serious rift between conservative alumni and the school. Conservative faculty were also disaffected, feeling that the university was compromising academic excellence in the service of political correctness.

One of the precipitating events occurred in 1988, when the university had ended the core humanities curriculum, called Western Civilization. Western Civilization had been deemed to be about "dead white men" and therefore unacceptable for a multiethnic, multiracial, multigendered (yes—multigendered) campus. The course had been replaced with Culture, Ideas and Values, also known as CIV, without the offending "Western" preceding it. CIV's curriculum required race, class, and gender components and at least one book by a "woman of color."

The rifts became chasms when Stanford rejected the request of the family of Ronald Reagan to establish his library on campus. Ostensibly, the excuse was traffic congestion at the site, but everyone knew that it had been the agitation of a small but vocal faculty group that forced the university to turn down the library.

Stanford wasn't exactly falling apart, but it was a very polarized place. There was even a split concerning intercollegiate athletics, with some saying that the university's commitment to Division I sports meant a lowering of academic standards. The new president obviously would have a lot of work to do.

AFTER SEVERAL months, the search committee identified a handful of prospects with the unquestioned academic credentials and administrative experience that would be required of Stanford's president. Then we took to the road to interview the candidates. No sitting university president or provost wants to be identified as a candidate for a job only to fail to be selected. Thus, we always disguised our travel to avoid leaks about who was being considered.

Jim Sheehan; Jim Larimore, a Native American assistant dean in Student Affairs; and I were sent to Chicago to interview Gerhard Casper, the provost of the University of Chicago. Gerhard was an eminent constitutional lawyer who had studied at Yale and served as the dean of the Chicago Law School. A German immigrant whose accent was still evident, Gerhard was an intellectual's intellectual, with refined tastes in architecture and the arts. This was very clear when we walked into his beautifully appointed, early twentieth-century apartment overlooking Lake Shore Drive. I'd never seen so many fine artifacts and books in someone's living room.

After about an hour during which Gerhard quizzed us as much as we did him, he turned to me. "You are representative of the next generation of leadership at Stanford," he said. "What do you think is the greatest challenge?"

I answered that the university had strayed from its core purposes and was trying to do too much. Across-the-board budget cuts threatened academic programs and social activities almost equally. I used an example from my time in the Pentagon grappling with priority setting. "Whenever you ask the Joint Chiefs of Staff a question about what to cut, the answer is one-third of a tank, one-third of an aircraft, and one-third of a ship. That's how the university seems to work too. Everything is equal. No one is prepared to make hard choices."

"Hm. Very interesting," he replied.

As we walked out of Gerhard's apartment and into the frigid Chicago night, I turned to Jim Sheehan. "I could work for him," I said.

The committee deliberated for a few more weeks, but well ahead of schedule we decided that Gerhard Casper was likely the right man to lead Stanford. He came to Los Angeles to meet the committee one last time in secret. There we had a truly open and frank discussion. Gerhard was known as a conservative with very traditional views of the academy. The University of Chicago didn't even have intercollegiate athletics. We worried that there might be some issues with the fit between this distinguished silver-haired German immigrant and northern California's informality. I even asked Gerhard if he believed in affirmative action, citing my own case as one that had worked out pretty well. He said that he did, explaining that he believed diversity and excellence were not enemies. After several hours, we were comfortable with our choice. We believed that Gerhard saw Stanford's unique strengths and that he'd put the university back on course. And he wouldn't try to make our beloved university into something it didn't want to be: Harvard.

CHAPTER THIRTY-FOUR

Provost of the University

GERHARD TOOK the reins in September 1992. Jim Rosse stepped down as provost, and a distinguished member of the engineering faculty, Jerry Lieberman, agreed to serve as interim provost. A committee was appointed to choose a new provost, the second most powerful administrator, responsible for all of the internal operations of the university. I didn't pay much attention to what they were doing. I was busy with my teaching, writing, and corporate boards. And I had submitted my papers to be promoted to full professor.

I was friendly with Gerhard and his wife, Regina, seeing them on occasion. He would consult me from time to time about various university matters. I also took it upon myself to make sure Gerhard became intimately acquainted with Stanford sports. When Stanford played the number-one-ranked University of

Washington, Gerhard asked me to join him in the president's box. The game was at night and, with television time-outs, was going on quite long. But Bill Walsh's Stanford team was somehow still in the game late in the fourth quarter against the heavily favored Huskies. As Stanford took the ball for one last drive for an incomprehensible win, Gerhard turned to me and said, "It's late. I'm going to go home now."

I couldn't believe it. "Gerhard," I said, taking him by the arm, "if you leave now, your presidency is over." He was a little startled but stayed. Stanford went on to win as time ran out, and our new president's reputation for a newfound interest in athletics was preserved.

Because of our relationship, I didn't think much of it when my secretary came in to say that Gerhard wanted me to come to lunch that day. The plan was to eat in his office, not at the Faculty Club, as we'd done a couple of times. I asked for tuna salad and cancelled my other appointments. I walked down the hall and told my colleague Chip Blacker that Gerhard wanted to see me. "I suspect that they've settled on a candidate for provost and he wants to get my opinion," I said.

When I arrived at Building 10, where the president and provost reside, Gerhard and I immediately went into his sunny office and sat across from each other at the round table. After a few pleasantries he said, "I want you to become the provost of the university."

I literally dropped my forkful of tuna back into the bowl. "This is a joke, right?"

His eyes twinkled a bit and he smiled. "No, Condi. I want you to become the provost of the university."

Perhaps to give me a moment to recover, he launched into a

discussion of why he thought I should be provost. "I've decided that it's time to skip a generation in leadership here at Stanford," he said, referring obliquely to the numerous deans and department chairs undoubtedly expecting to be named provost. "After your experience in Washington, and having gotten to know you, I think you're the right person to help me lead Stanford. In fact, I knew it the moment we met in Chicago."

Gerhard then addressed my unspoken concern by saying that he was not making the appointment because I was a black woman, although he was delighted that I'd be the first to hold the job. He added that at thirty-eight, I was also going to be the youngest provost by almost a decade. From his point of view, that would be the real issue, not my race or gender. He could have added that I had never been a department chair, let alone a dean—or he could have mentioned that I'd been promoted to full professor only about a month before.

The provost of Stanford has broad-ranging responsibilities for the academic program, the physical plant, and the budget. The deans report to the provost, along with most other senior officials of the university. Provosts' responsibilities vary from university to university, but the Stanford job is probably the most powerful and broadest in all of academia. And these were not ordinary times. Stanford faced crippling challenges, and the provost would be expected to solve them.

I told Gerhard that I'd think about it overnight and call him the next day. As I made my way back to my office, memories flooded back of walking along the same colonnade as an insecure graduate student going to my first interview so many years before. I knew that I'd say yes and become provost—even though I was still totally stunned to have been asked.

As soon as I got back to the office I told Chip what Gerhard had wanted. He was equally stunned but said, "You'll be great." I made a phone call to my father, who was also flabbergasted but said essentially the same thing, adding a "Wow!" at the end.

The rest of the day I imagined how the news would be received on campus. Not only was I young, black, and female, I was a Republican on a campus where that is rare. I focused on what messages I wanted to send—to the faculty, the students, the alumni, and the trustees. Then I went home to rest. I was exhausted.

The next day I went to see Gerhard and accepted the job. Terry Shepard, the university's vice president for public affairs, and I met to discuss the rollout of the news. Terry echoed Gerhard's view that the biggest challenge would be explaining my lack of experience in university administration. We decided to emphasize my corporate board service and what I'd done in the White House. "After all, you did manage U.S.-Soviet relations at the end of the Cold War," he joked.

"Yes," I said. "But Gorbachev didn't have tenure."

We put together an announcement that underscored the point—Terry's, not mine—and went to press. I made clear that my first priority would be dealing with the university's financial situation. "We cannot live beyond our means," I said. "Unlike the federal government, I can't print money."

The news was received somewhat better than I expected. People were surprised, of course, but with the exception of some grousing by a few faculty members about my being a conservative, there wasn't much negative reaction. I learned later that my name had been one of the six submitted to Gerhard by the committee, so there had been some process around my selection.

I made a point of reaching out to a few senior people who'd most likely been the other candidates for the job—all of whom were generous in their offers of support. Later Gerhard told me that the reaction of Ewart Thomas, then dean of humanities and sciences, probably summed up most people's thinking: "Gerhard," Ewart had said, "you have balls."

In fact, I no longer felt much trepidation about what was to come. I was pretty excited. A couple of days later I found myself driving through campus singing along with the theme from the TV series *The Greatest American Hero:* "Believe it or not, I'm walking on air / I never thought I could feel so free / Flying away on a wing and a prayer / Who could it be? / Believe it or not, it's just me."

I WAS supposed to begin the provost's job at the start of the school year in September. The summer would be a time to get to know the issues better and put together a management structure. Jerry Lieberman, a gentle giant who was a highly regarded academic and university citizen, was suffering from amyotrophic lateral sclerosis, or ALS. Nonetheless, he fully expected to be able to finish his interim term.

Jerry and I decided that the best way to proceed would be to have me shadow him each day, attending his meetings and observing what he did. This worked just fine, since I had no desire to get out ahead on the tough issues until the new school year. One day, though, as Jerry got up from his desk, his feet tangled and he fell with a heavy thud. He got up immediately and turned to me. "It's the ALS," he said. "It's been a little worse lately."

Then, a few days later, Jerry stood up in the middle of a

presentation by the budget director, Tim Warner, and left the room silently. Gerhard came in the next day to say that Jerry could no longer go on and wouldn't return to work. It was the beginning of July. We decided not to make a formal change— Jerry would remain as interim and I would go to his house two or three times a week to consult him. Universities are gentle in that way: there was no need to highlight Jerry's sudden turn for the worse. But in fact, my apprenticeship was over. There had been no time to get ready. I would just have to do the job.

CHAPTER THIRTY-FIVE

Tough Decisions

M Y M O S T important responsibility would be dealing with the university's financial situation. Stanford had an operating budget deficit of about 5 percent. Though the budget at the time was over \$1.2 billion, much of it was restricted to specific uses by the donors of the funds. The university therefore had to operate the physical plant, pay staff and faculty salaries and benefits, and cover the bulk of financial aid costs, among other expenses, on about \$400 million a year. I had to cut \$20 million of those costs. Moreover, the university needed money to rebuild the campus after the earthquake. The low-hanging fruit had already been picked in the previous round of budget cuts. The process had been elaborate with multiple faculty-student committees making recommendations on everything from student housing to university maintenance and academic programs.

The idea had been to ensure buy-in from the entire Stanford community.

There was no way that this process would produce anything but distributive, Pentagon-style decisions of the kind that I had described to Gerhard. I had to be honest about how I would work. So in one of my first Faculty Senate meetings, I explained that we'd have to make significant cuts. "I don't do committees," I said. "I'll consult widely. But someone will have to make decisions, and that will be Gerhard and me."

There was a bit of a rumble through the room, but I don't think the senators really believed me. It didn't matter. I had made a promise to the trustees, particularly the finance committee led by a savvy businessman, Brad Freeman, that I would balance the budget, and I was determined to do it. I required all units of the university to propose 5 and 10 percent cuts in their budgets. That work was presented to a very small advisory committee, including the chief financial officer, my friend and colleague Mariann Byerwalter, the budget director, my closest advisor Tim Warner, Geoff Cox, director of institutional planning, and two faculty members whom I appointed. We met weekly.

Predictably, the pushback came from those who had felt privileged and untouchable for political reasons: groups in Student Affairs where my colleague, the Vice Provost Mary Edmonds, had proposed major cuts. The ethnic centers (Asian American, African American, Chicano, and Native American) were the most offended. The protests heated up, and they called a town-hall-style meeting and asked me to attend. I had a faculty dinner that night, which would make me a bit late, but Chip had gone ahead to assess the situation. As I walked from the Faculty

Club toward Cubberley Hall, where the meeting was being held, Chip met me halfway. "There's a huge and angry crowd," he said.

"Okay. I thought there would be." I took a deep breath and walked in.

The president of Stanford's Black Student Union was serving as moderator. After a few strong words about how marginalized and victimized the ethnic students were feeling, he handed me the microphone. I resisted the temptation to say that I thought *marginalization* was a peculiar term for students who'd been given the chance at a Stanford education. Instead, I plowed into a presentation of the financial situation, saying that I'd asked the Physics Department for the same budget analysis. Everyone had to contribute.

During the question-and-answer session, a young blond woman who was apparently Native American yelled rhetorically, "The problem is, you just don't care enough for the plight of minorities." I waited while the audience erupted in cheers. Then, out of nowhere—not really having thought it through—I said, "You don't have the standing to question my commitment to minorities. I've been black all of my life, and that is far longer than you are old." The buzzing told me that I'd hit a nerve. The young woman sat down. I said a few words more and prepared to leave. But as I was turning away, the moderator decided that he would have the last word. I went back and took the microphone from him. "When you are the provost, you can have the last word," I said. Then I left, feeling that I'd established necessary boundaries.

Those boundaries were tested again when I made the most controversial decision of my tenure as provost. I had to stream-line the staff of Student Affairs and that meant laying off Cecilia

Burciaga, the most senior Latina in the administration. I didn't want to do it because Cecilia had served the university honorably. As the affirmative action officer on campus, she had been involved in my hiring. Nonetheless, I had few options, and I was determined not to cut faculty and the academic program.

The decision sparked a massive protest from the student body. The Chicano students set up a tent city on the quad in front of my office, and four young women started a hunger strike. They demanded that Cecilia be reinstated and that we start a Chicano studies program. I could tell that my decision to visit El Centro Chicano, the Hispanic cultural center, was not going to be viewed as the olive branch I intended. Instead, I sat there in front of what looked like a shrine to Cecilia with the students accusing me of all manner of ill deeds.

As the protest dragged on through the week, the Faculty Senate met that Thursday. Several faculty members took the floor to bemoan the sacrifice the hunger strikers were making. "Don't you feel bad that our children are sleeping on the quad and not eating?" one person asked. I was always struck by how students suddenly became "children" in these circumstances.

"I am sleeping and eating just fine," I said. "They can stay out there until hell freezes over. My decisions stand."

The next day Gerhard and I met with the students. Al Camarillo, a senior faculty member who'd been acting as the mediator, proposed that we form a committee to study the establishment of a Chicano studies program. Gerhard and I agreed and the crisis ended. Eventually this resulted in a popular major called Comparative Studies in Race and Ethnicity and a much more academically sound role for the Chicano studies center.

The end of the crisis was undoubtedly hastened too by an

unusual April rainstorm that dampened the enthusiasm of the students for their tent city. One of the faculty spokesmen told the student newspaper that I'd treated the students as if I were negotiating with the Russians. I laughed out loud when I saw the statement. But it did cause me to think about my interaction with the students. As the year went on, I asked myself whether I was being too rough.

Throughout this period, the headlines about me were brutal and the criticism came almost daily. I talked to Daddy every day, and he brought the perspective of someone who'd been through tough decisions in a university environment. I know that the barrage of criticism directed mostly at me, some of it quite personal, bothered him. I assured Daddy that I wasn't worried about the headlines, but it concerned him nonetheless. His reaction at that time has caused me to wonder how he would have dealt with my encounters with the rough-and-tumble environment of Washington during the George W. Bush administration. I am sure he would have gotten through it, but I could tell that Daddy hated to see his "little girl" demonized.

Nonetheless, Daddy helped me see the student protests in a different light. He believed it important for students to find their political voices while in the university. He reminded me that they were, after all, quite young. Shortly before graduation, the student who had moderated the town hall came to see me and asked how he could be more effective at leadership. I realized that Daddy was right. In the classroom, I was always careful not to put a student down for a comment, no matter how inappropriate. To do so is to freeze the rest of the students, who will fear humiliation. The power relationship is unequal, and students feel it. I decided that I'd try to remember that in my encounters with them as provost. In any case, I had established a pretty tough line. Maybe it was time to back off.

The budget situation took most of my time, but I had to attend to other matters as well. A few games into the football season, Bill Walsh, the legendary coach who had returned to Stanford after extraordinary successes in the NFL, asked to see me for dinner on the Sunday after a home game. He told my secretary that it couldn't wait until Monday. Ted Leland, the athletic director, and I met Bill at the Lake House, a lovely home overlooking Lake Lagunita and the Stanford foothills that, as provost, I used for entertaining and meetings.

Bill was shaking. "I can't go on," he said. "I want to quit now and turn the program over to Terry Shea." (Terry was the assistant head coach.) Bill had found the return to Stanford hard and ultimately unsatisfying. Initially, his team had been very successful, defeating highly ranked Notre Dame at South Bend in the first year. But now, in his third year, Stanford's football fortunes had taken a turn for the worse. The talent was thin and the execution flawed. Bill was in no mood to do what it took to revive the program: spend days and weeks on the road trying to recruit eighteen-year-old studs with good grades to come to Stanford. He was tired.

Gerhard and I had decided that for operational affairs the Athletic Department would report through me. With Stanford's chief academic officer in charge of sports, the right signals would be sent. It helped that I liked sports and enjoyed overseeing the department. Bill's resignation would therefore be my problem.

I told Walsh that I didn't need one of sports' greatest legends quitting five games into the season. I implored him to stay on, saying we'd do a proper search as soon as the season was over. But

Bill persisted in wanting me to appoint Terry as his successor. "I could even stay on for a few years as the assistant head coach," he said.

I shook my head. "Bill, that won't work. I have to do a nationwide search. There are all kinds of reasons, including the fact that I want a chance to look at black coaches." I didn't think much about the statement. It was well known that there are too few African American coaches in college football. I only meant that Stanford needed to pay attention to the issue.

In the end Walsh stayed until the end of the season. We then launched a search for Bill's successor. Tyrone Willingham, who'd been an assistant at Stanford and was now with the Minnesota Vikings, emerged as a top candidate. But Tyrone had not been an offensive or defensive coordinator—the usual stepping-stone to a head coaching position. Even so, Ted Leland; Jerry Porras, the faculty representative to athletics; and I were all in agreement: Ty Willingham should be Stanford's coach.

Gerhard was out of town. I called him to see if he'd be comfortable with the appointment. "We are going to be criticized for his inexperience," I said. "But everyone says he was great when he was here, and we all believe he'll be a fabulous recruiter."

"Do it," Gerhard said. Then he added with a chuckle, "I don't worry too much about being criticized for appointing inexperienced people."

The press conference announcing Ty's appointment was set for the next day. I woke up that morning and went down to get the paper. Glenn Dickey of the *San Francisco Chronicle* had written that Stanford was about to hire an inexperienced coach because I'd insisted on bringing on a black coach. I was furious and called Glenn. "You didn't say that the University of Colorado hired

Rick Neuheisel [who also had not been a coordinator] because he was blond," I told him.

I called Ty, who said that it wasn't the first time he'd been underestimated. Willingham would go on to be one of Stanford's most successful coaches, returning the Cardinal to the Rose Bowl in 2000 for the first time in twenty-eight years. Glenn Dickey later apologized, admitting that he'd been wrong about Willingham.

The truth is, issues of affirmative action are tricky in a university, whether in admissions, in faculty hiring and tenure, or in selecting a football coach. There is probably no single issue on which I've felt more misunderstood. For instance, I have been called an opponent of affirmative action and assumed to hold the same views as some prominent black conservatives.

In fact, I'm a supporter of affirmative action—if done in what I consider to be the right way. No one can doubt that years of racial prejudice produced underrepresentation of minorities and women in all aspects of American life. Corporate boardrooms, management suites, and elite university faculties and student bodies have for our entire history failed to reflect even roughly the ethnic mix of the country. That is not acceptable in America, which is the world's greatest multiethnic democracy.

Yet the question of how to remedy that situation is a delicate one. I've always believed that there are plenty of qualified minorities for these roles—even some who are "twice as good." But the processes of selection, the pools and networks through which people are identified, can very easily be insular and produce the same outcomes over and over. The answer lies in looking outside established networks and patterns of hiring. I consistently told the Stanford community quite openly that affirmative action had figured in my own case. Stanford traditionally found its faculty at peer institutions such as Harvard or Yale or perhaps the University of California—not at the University of Denver. But when, through the Ford Fellowship, I appeared on the radar screen, Stanford took a chance on me as an assistant professor. I always closed by saying that it had worked out just fine for me and for the university.

Unfortunately, very few minorities—particularly blacks, Latinos, and Native Americans—go to graduate school, the pool from which assistant professors are selected. (Law schools are an exception since they sometimes hire practicing attorneys.) Perhaps because many minorities are still first-generation college students, professional school is considered more practical. I had to make this somewhat unpopular point frequently to defend the relatively meager number of minorities we hired onto the faculty in any given year, though those numbers increased during my tenure. When pressed by minority students, I'd ask for a show of hands regarding how many were going on to graduate school. Few hands would go up. I'd then tell them that I couldn't create assistant professors out of whole cloth, and they should consider going to graduate school. And we tried vigorously to recruit good minority students to our graduate programs. Very often, though, we found ourselves competing for the same few black or Latino students who'd been identified by our "peers"—Harvard, Yale, and so on.

It is also true that in student admissions it is necessary to take race into account. I don't know why, but minorities continue to score lower on standardized tests such as the SAT, LSAT (for law school), or GRE (for graduate school). Even when adjusting for socioeconomic status, this disparity holds. But as my own story about the results of my PSAT in high school shows, these tests are not fully predictive of a student's success or failure. Over the years, I have had students with perfect records at entry fail and students who were thought to have been marginal succeed. Yet the idea that minority students are getting a break at the expense of white students is one of the most toxic issues of our time.

While serving in the White House, I'd made this point to President George W. Bush when the administration decided to join the plaintiffs in two cases against the University of Michigan's affirmative action program in 2003. Michigan had established what amounted to a quota system for minority students in undergraduate admissions—a practice to which I objected. Yet the principle that race could be taken into consideration in admissions decisions was worth defending. The President asked for my views. I told him that even if the administration decided to side with the plaintiffs, he should not call for overturning the historic 1978 decision in *Regents of the University of California v. Bakke*—the decision by the Supreme Court that permitted race to be used as a factor in college admissions. Ultimately, the administration did not support overturning *Bakke,* but when someone within the White House leaked, erroneously, that I had urged the President to do so, I was furious. I went to the President and told him that I had to issue a correction. For the first and only time in our eight years together, I drew attention publicly to a key difference between us. I made it clear that I was willing to go further than the President was in supporting race as a factor in admissions. I had no choice. I had advocated for affirmative action as Stanford's provost and still believed that it was the right course.

The key to affirmative action, I believe, is not to lower

standards but to look for good prospects where you would not ordinarily find them. Yet there are pitfalls with the whole concept of affirmative action. There is the stigma that is easily attached to minorities simply because there is a widespread belief that affirmative action figured heavily in every case. This leads to what President Bush called (in the context of K–12 education) the "soft bigotry of low expectations." Having grown up in a community where being "twice as good" was the mantra, I found it appalling that anyone could be so patronizing as to hold lower expectations of minority students.

Many times, well-meaning faculty would say that they were taking extra time with their "remedial students" to help them catch up. A little investigation would typically reveal that these professors equated "remedial" with "minority." When I attended my first Phi Beta Kappa ceremony in 1994, I was surprised to see only two black inductees. I suspected that minority students were internalizing the message of inferiority and living down to the expectations that were being set for them.

I decided to start a program for freshmen called Partners in Academic Excellence. Minority faculty and graduate students agreed to take fifteen or so minority freshmen to dinner once a week. The graduate students also mentored the freshmen—for instance, reading their class papers. My suspicions were confirmed when the black graduate students reported that the freshmen were being given "courtesy" grades, higher than warranted so as not to affect their self-esteem. The problem, of course, was that easier grading early on left the students unprepared for the tougher subject matter that was coming.

Gerhard supported the program but worried that I was setting up a little "segregated" academic system within Stanford.

Ironically, that was *exactly* what I was doing—trying to reproduce elements of my segregated childhood, when teachers did not worry about being called racists for their high expectations and "no victims" approach.

In time, we reworked the program to broaden its participation. We learned that student athletes suffered from the same prejudices, as did women students in math and the sciences. I was reminded again how difficult it is to overcome preconceptions and stereotypes—particularly for people who want so desperately to do the right thing for "those poor minorities and women."

Similarly, there's often misplaced noblesse oblige in dealing with junior minority faculty. The university seemed to accept the canard that life was much tougher for them because it was so difficult to balance the many obligations of minority identity with teaching and research demands. Unfortunately, such coddling encouraged special pleading by junior minority faculty regarding latent racism among colleagues, thereby retarding their growth.

The fact is, life is just not easy for any junior faculty member. As provost, I thought it important not to single out women or minority faculty but rather to deal with their quite real challenges through a more generalized approach. Appointing Bob Weisberg as vice provost for faculty development proved to be very sound. A professor of law with the patience of Job, Bob was able to improve the lives of young faculty immensely and served as a shoulder for them to cry on when things got tough.

Still, all of these efforts didn't convince some that I was sufficiently committed to minority affairs. A decision I made to deny tenure to a woman in the History Department, overruling her dean, sealed the judgment. I made the right decision, but I allowed myself to be baited into a statement that I regretted almost as soon as I said it: "Race and gender should not be considered at the time of tenure." I really meant that they should not be dispositive, turning a failed case into a successful one. I didn't know that my predecessors had actually allowed race and gender to do precisely that—give the "benefit of the doubt" to women and minorities.

The opponents of my policies used the statement to claim that Stanford was in violation of equal opportunity statutes, and the Department of Education launched an investigation. Stanford was eventually found to be in compliance with the statutes well after I had left the provost's office.

THESE TENSIONS aside, the provost's job suited me. My friendship and partnership with Gerhard made the hard work rewarding and—on most days—fun. We undertook efforts to reform undergraduate education, starting and funding freshman and sophomore seminars so that Stanford students would have small-group experiences with faculty members early in their careers. It's all too common in research universities that underclassmen sit through large introductory classes until they declare a major. By that time, many have lost their intellectual curiosity and edge. This program gave students an early introduction to small-group interaction.

We also started Sophomore College. So many students would come to Stanford declaring engineering or pre-med majors, take organic chemistry or multivariable calculus, get their first D's, and suddenly realize they weren't good enough to pursue the career they had chosen. Remembering my disorienting experience of realizing I'd never be a top pianist, I wanted to do something for these kids. We established Sophomore College, a three-week program that allowed selected sophomores to study something topical, in small groups, several hours a day with a faculty member. I taught a seminar on U.S.-Russian relations. The students who applied were usually the ones who were searching, the ones who were trying to find an academic passion and, more important, a faculty mentor.

As the years passed, the hard budget work was done, and thanks to the improved financial situation and prodigious fundraising, we were able to repair the earthquake damage and build an entirely new Science Quad, with buildings named for Bill Gates, Paul Allen, and Gordon Moore. David Packard and Bill Hewlett gave the lead gift. We launched other large-scale academic initiatives, such as reinvigorating the Humanities Center and rebuilding the Music Department, even coaxing a first-class string quartet, the St. Lawrence, into taking up residency at Stanford.

And we reformed the much maligned Culture, Ideas and Values. While there was no chance of returning to Western Civilization and the study of dead white men, we did depoliticize the curriculum. I led a two-year committee (things take a while in universities) to create a new humanities requirement. The turning point was when I asked if the assignment of a book by a woman of color could include my book on German unification. It had never occurred to most faculty members that there was no automatic link between a scholar's color and gender and her subject matter. The reform went through the Faculty Senate without a single dissenting vote.

In short, I loved my years as provost. Blessedly, I didn't travel much, since the provost is really the "inside" presence, paying attention to the daily affairs of the university. This allowed me to take up piano seriously for the first time in two decades. Paul Brest, the Law School dean, had asked me to join a session of his chamber music group one evening. I did so, and began accompanying Paul to a festival in Utah (and later Montana) sponsored by the Muir String Quartet, a fine professional quartet from Boston University. I loved it so much that I decided to study piano again. George Barth, the head of the Piano Department, later told me that when my secretary called to schedule lessons for me, he and others thought there must be some ulterior motive. He couldn't believe that I really just wanted to take lessons.

But I did just want lessons, and every Wednesday afternoon I'd work with George for ninety minutes. My assistant, Marilyn Stanley, knew that only in a really serious crisis should she interrupt. I began performing again, once with the university chorus, and also gave a concert with Yu Ying, a fine professional pianist who had graduated from Stanford, for the fiftieth anniversary of the Music Department. My greatest triumph, though, was playing the incredibly difficult Brahms Piano Quintet in F Minor with the Muir in a house concert in 1994. I worked as hard as I ever had to learn the challenging piece. That night as we began to play, I was suddenly alarmed. Something had gone wrong. It didn't sound right. Then I realized what had happened: the Muir was playing "Happy Birthday," in celebration of my fortieth.

Most important, I loved the regular rhythm of the job, which gave me time to spend with Daddy. We continued to work together on the Center for a New Generation and saw it grow and prosper. I visited him at least twice a week, always going over after church on Sunday to watch sports, as we'd done so many years before. He and Clara and I went to Stanford football and basketball games together, including three Bowl games. Daddy loved my friends and became close to Chip, Louis, and Randy. One day, standing on the practice field while watching spring football together, he turned to me and said, "I'm so glad I came here. Palo Alto is such a nice village. And it is awfully nice to be the father of one of the most important people in the village."

I realized at that moment that Daddy was finally enjoying the comforts of the retirement he deserved. His life had turned around since those dark days in Denver when his professional life crashed around him. It had been hard work rebuilding his life after Mother's death. But he had succeeded beyond my wildest dreams.

Despite struggling with congestive heart failure and arthritic knees, Daddy was active in the community, and I was delighted to see him recognized on several occasions. For close to thirty years, Daddy had been a member of Phi Delta Kappa, the leading professional organization for educators. Then in 1994, for his work on behalf of minority communities in Denver and East Palo Alto, the National Alliance of Black School Educators presented him with their Living Legend award.

Daddy served on the Board of Governors of the California Community Colleges, and in that capacity he became a tireless advocate for accountability and a powerful voice for diversity. In recognition of his contributions, the Community College system still awards John W. Rice Jr. diversity fellowships every year. He'd emerged as a leading citizen in the area. In 1998, the City of Palo Alto honored him with a lifetime achievement award, a fitting capstone to his career. Daddy had blossomed in Palo Alto, and I felt that I had helped. I was sad that I hadn't had time to do the same for my mother and that they couldn't have enjoyed retirement together.

As good as life was for us in the village, I knew that my time as provost had to come to an end. Gerhard had been president for seven years and was starting to think about his successor. During my tenure I'd been asked by many university search committees to consider various university presidencies. I'd always turned them down, saying that the time wasn't right. I began to realize after a while that the time would never be right. I loved being provost but didn't want to be president, even of Stanford, with its emphasis on conducting the external affairs of the university—alumni and government relations and fundraising. Gerhard needed a new provost who could be groomed to succeed him.

I was also beginning to feel that I'd done all that I could do. My tenure had been somewhat controversial, but I don't doubt that the trustees appreciated the six budget surpluses I'd produced, the renewal of undergraduate education that Gerhard and I had championed, and the repair of the physical campus. Even the students had come to like me. When I announced I was stepping down from the post, the *Stanford Daily* ran an editorial entitled "Farewell, Provost Rice," which featured a line that I will always treasure: "Condi leaves a legacy as a powerful administrator who cares about students." Even the minority communities— particularly the black community—showed their appreciation with a wonderful farewell event, complete with gospel versions of my favorite hymns.

As for the faculty, I'm not so sure. I'd made a lot of tough decisions with directness and without showing much patience for the veto groups that populate a university faculty. Many colleagues, such as Lucius Barker, a black professor who had helped me diversify the faculty, called to say that they'd miss my clear and unapologetic leadership. Nonetheless, I'm sure that many others were relieved when, in the announcement of my decision to step down, I made clear that I was done with university administration. The fact that I'd signed on to help Governor George W. Bush in his run for the Presidency of the United States convinced everyone that I meant what I'd said. But I was absolutely truthful when, at the event held to honor my service, I said that being provost of Stanford was the best job I'd ever had.

CHAPTER THIRTY-SIX

The Governor's Campaign

THE EVENING after Stanford's event in my honor, my father and I had dinner. He was a little pensive but jokingly said that maybe I'd have more time for dinner now that I was no longer going to be provost. Hearing that, I made a silent vow to see him more.

"So, what are you going to do for an encore?" he asked. While I loved the university, I couldn't quite imagine just going back to the faculty after having been provost. I explained that I liked management and the private sector and thought that I might try to combine the two. Daddy asked if I'd decided that foreign policy no longer interested me. That wasn't the case but I did want to be involved in international affairs in a somewhat different way, perhaps through global finance. I'd been in some conversations with Goldman Sachs and J. P. Morgan and was considering investment banking.

"Aren't you going to help George W. Bush?" Daddy asked.

"Yes, but that won't be full-time," I said.

"Sure," Daddy said incredulously—and presciently.

My association with Governor Bush had begun in earnest in August 1998. President George H. W. Bush called to invite me to spend a little time with him and Mrs. Bush in Maine. They had hosted me several times before at their wonderful family home in Kennebunkport. The weathered, shingle-style house, done in calming pastel chintz, has an elegant yet understated decor, and a spectacular view of the ocean. I'm not all that fond of being in the water, but I love to look at it. There isn't a prettier place to view the Atlantic than Walker's Point. I loved going there and readily accepted.

This time would be different. The elder Bush didn't hide his desire to get me together with his son George, just so we could get to know each other better and talk a little about foreign policy.

When the then-Texas governor told me that he'd likely make a run for the White House, his presidential bid struck me as having long odds for success. The Clinton years had been morally tarnished but peaceful and relatively prosperous. The governor was untested and would likely face a real pro in Vice President Al Gore. I was too polite to say these things, but I sure thought them.

George W. Bush was still a few months from being reelected as Texas governor in a landslide victory, carrying 68 percent of the vote. He told me that he was confident of reelection and that if he won impressively (which he fully expected), he'd likely run for the Presidency. He wanted to start thinking about what to do in foreign policy if he got elected. Throughout the weekend, while fishing (he fished, I sat in the boat and watched) or exercising side by side in the small family gym on the compound, we talked about Russia, China, and Latin America. I soon realized that he knew our southern neighbors, particularly Mexico, far better than I did. I made a mental note to read a few articles about Mexico when I got back to California.

But we also talked about other things. He was interested in my upbringing in segregated Birmingham. I was attracted to his passion for improving education for disadvantaged youth. We compared notes on the problems of college admission and affirmative action. I was more traditional in my support of race-based admission, but he'd tried to increase diversity at the University of Texas by other means. He proudly said that he would likely receive half of the Hispanic vote and more than a quarter of the African American vote.

We emailed back and forth several times during the fall, and a couple of days after the election, I received a note from him. From that time on, we began to follow international events together. In March 1999 I received a call from Karl Rove asking if I'd come down to Austin to talk to the governor about the upcoming campaign. When my picture appeared on the front page of the *New York Times* as a member of the "exploratory committee" dedicated to electing George W. Bush President of the United States, my father was the first person I called.

The campaign itself proved professionally fulfilling, but early on I realized that it would require my full-time focus. Foreign policy would be the governor's Achilles' heel against more seasoned candidates in the primaries and, eventually, in the general election. I knew that George Bush would look to me to help answer the inevitable questions about his readiness to assume the mantle of commander in chief.

I was having fun. Anyone who's interested in politics should do a campaign from the ground floor at least once. Early on we got stuck in traffic jams and carried our own bags. Crowds were enthusiastic but, in some places, kind of small. The music track that introduced the governor at campaign rallies included Stevie Wonder's "Signed, Sealed, Delivered." I never understood why that song was chosen, but to this day I can't listen to it without vivid memories of stadiums, auditoriums, and cowboy bars full of early believers in George W. Bush.

I loved the pace and the sense of being a part of an adventure. Life had settled into a nice post-provost pattern and I was quite content. I would discuss the campaign frequently with Daddy. When I arranged to have George W. Bush meet my father during a trip to Palo Alto in the fall of 1999, Daddy was hooked. He peppered me every night with questions about campaign strategy that I couldn't answer. "How in the world did we screw up New Hampshire? George Bush isn't getting through to people that he is going to be different. That's what people need to know." John Rice was a loyal Republican. He loved Governor Bush and my association with the campaign.

Then, in February 2000, Daddy suffered cardiac arrest. I was back home, helping to rally the troops for the California primary in the wake of the disasters in New Hampshire and Michigan. The night before, I'd told Daddy that I would stop by to watch a Stanford basketball game but that I first had to go to a campaign rally in Palo Alto. I called after the rally and almost said that I was too tired and would just go on home. But I didn't. I went to his house and we ate pizza and watched the game. Daddy mentioned that he'd forgotten to pick up his heart medication from the pharmacy. "Oh, I'll get it tomorrow," he said.

The next morning I was getting ready to do an interview with a reporter named Ann Dowd for a profile of me. Ann had gone to interview my father that morning and was in the house when suddenly my father had the attack. She called 911 and then my longtime assistant, Marilyn. I was in a meeting, but Marilyn burst in and said that something had happened to Daddy and he was not breathing. I rushed out and sped to his house. It looked like a scene from *ER*. Daddy was on the floor and they were shocking his heart. I heard the medic say, "I have a weak pulse." We all rushed to the hospital and waited. It hadn't been a heart attack, but his heart had stopped long enough to cause what his physician called an "anoxic brain event." Essentially, he'd been deprived of oxygen to his brain and was now in a coma. No one could say what the prognosis was.

Daddy continued in a coma for about a week and then he began to stir. But he'd sustained significant brain damage. A few times we were asked those awful questions about life-sustaining support. Here I have to say that I was weaker than my stepmother, who was prepared to go to extraordinary lengths to keep my father alive. I just wasn't so sure and prayed every day and night for guidance about what to do.

Then one day I was in his room and the basketball game was on television. I thought I could see him tracking the game with his eyes. Nurses and doctors said that this was something families often imagine. But a physician who was also my good friend stopped by, and I asked her to watch him for a moment. "No doubt," she said, "he's tracking." Not long after, Daddy began to improve, and eventually he was transferred to a nursing home for long-term care.

Soon after, I resumed my campaign activities. I called several times a day to check on Daddy. Friends such as Louis Olave, the long-term partner of my dear friend Chip, took daily shifts to sit with my father. Lytton Gardens had wonderful, caring attendants, especially Carmen, my father's favorite nurse. But nursing homes are woefully understaffed. Thus, I never trusted the quality of care enough to leave him alone, even for a minute.

Sometimes Clara or my aunt Gee, my mother's sister, who'd come out to help us, would put Daddy on the phone. He seemed to know that he was talking to me. I tried never to be away from home for more than seventy-two hours, returning to help oversee his multiple therapies and feeding tubes or struggle with Medicare and insurance. And I would endure those terrible episodes when he would yell out for what seemed like hours. This was, according to the doctors, a good sign that the brain was repairing itself. To me it sounded as if my father were being flung into the depths of hell.

By the summer, Daddy's condition had improved somewhat more and we moved him home. We found wonderful caretakers, including a huge but loving Tongan man named Tai. Daddy seemed to understand what was being said to him, but his responses were often off track. Yet at least he was home, where we could sing together and share the occasional flashes of lucidity that would come. Sometimes he'd amaze us all. On Thanksgiving as we gathered around his bed, my uncle Alto said, "Who is going to give the blessing?" Without missing a beat, Daddy reached somewhere deep into the recesses of his memory and prayed.

He never fully recovered, but he fought to live. Several times he was near death and refused to go. As I watched this giant of a man who'd loved me more than anything in the world approach the end, it was hard to find much good in life. It seemed so unfair that I could no longer share stories of the campaign with my father. Here I was at the height of my professional career and my father couldn't enjoy it with me. Not surprisingly, my absences from home became a source of guilt, and the campaign, which had been such a wonderful magical mystery tour, became something of a slog.

I kept going and told myself that Daddy undoubtedly approved of my decision to keep my commitment to the campaign. The pace of the campaign kept me away from home more than I would've liked. But slowly the governor was climbing in the polls and clearly had a real chance to be President. After the debates that fall in which Governor Bush fought Al Gore to at least a draw on foreign policy, it was in the hands of the voters. I felt that I had done all I could do.

CHAPTER THIRTY-SEVEN

Florida

I FLEW DOWN to Austin the afternoon of the election. By the time I arrived at the Four Seasons Hotel, the news stations were chalking up state after state in the Gore column. By the time I made it downstairs to watch with a few Bush friends and family, everything was going against us: Michigan, Illinois, Pennsylvania, and Florida were all gone. I sat there with Doro Bush Koch, the governor's sister, and watched in dismay. "Let's change places," I said to Doro, employing a superstition from my days as an athlete and a sports fan: if your team is not winning while you're sitting on the right side of the sofa, move to the left. Yes, I know it doesn't matter, but it can't hurt.

We did change places. Almost magically, NBC News reported that we had won Georgia. Then Jean Becker, the elder George Bush's assistant, got a call. Jean had been a reporter, and a friend from *USA Today* called to tell her that they were about to reverse the call on Florida. Within what seemed like minutes but was much longer, the TV screen suddenly began showing "George W. Bush, 43rd President of the United States." It was quite a moment, and immediately I just wanted to call my father. I decided not to, fearing that he would be too disoriented to share the moment with me.

I jumped in a minivan with other Bush supporters for the trip to the capitol for the victory speech. It was freezing cold in Austin and we stood on the square, rocking to "Y'all Ready for This" from the Jock Jams album, and hugging each other. But something was wrong. Al Gore hadn't conceded. I could also see the big screen displaying CNN's election coverage. The margin of victory in Florida was shrinking very fast.

Then Karen Hughes, who was with the Bushes, called her husband, Jerry, and reported that Gore had withdrawn his concession. After another hour or so, we all shuffled back to the minivan and went back to the hotel. There was confusion but not really despair. I went to bed and woke to the news that Florida would be contested.

When I spotted Fox News reporter Carl Cameron in the lobby, I asked him, "What's going on?"

"I thought *you* might know," he said, and then went on to tell me that there would likely be a recount.

I also ran into Bob Blackwill. "You know what this is like? It's like eating a really spicy meal before bed and having a bad dream. You think to yourself, 'Must have been what I ate last night. Boy, I'm glad to wake up from that one!'"

But of course it wasn't a dream. I stayed in Austin a few days. I hung out near Karl Rove, trying to understand what was really happening via his sophisticated county-by-county analysis of our chances in Florida.

Governor Bush called the morning after the election to say that he wanted me to be national security advisor, but we'd obviously have to wait a bit on any announcement. It was surreal, but we went through the motions of planning a foreign policy transition that might never happen. One particularly bad idea was to have a photo op of the governor and me sitting in front of the fireplace discussing foreign policy. It looked like a faux Oval Office shot and was properly ridiculed. I decided to go home to California.

The return to California gave me a chance to spend quality time with my father. I watched the ups and downs in Florida, my mood swinging with every court decision. Sometimes Daddy seemed to be tracking, becoming agitated and shedding tears when the news was bad.

I left on December 8 to attend a meeting of the foreign policy team in Washington. We were planning for the transition in case there was one. After the session, Steve Hadley, who had worked with me on the campaign, and I were sitting in the conference room of his law office when we got word that the Florida Supreme Court had ordered a manual recount. We walked outside toward the restaurant for dinner. "Steve," I said, "I would have loved to serve with you. You would have been a great deputy national security advisor." I flew home to California the next day believing that it was over. When I got off the plane and into the car, my driver, Mary Reynolds, gave me an update. The Supreme Court had by a 5–4 decision issued a stay, halting the manual recounts and setting a hearing for the matter on Monday, December 11. This meant that the judges in the majority were likely to rule in favor of Bush on the merits of the case, certifying Bush as the winner of Florida's electoral votes. George W. Bush would indeed become the 43rd President of the United States.

That night I went to a surprise birthday party for George Shultz at the Bohemian Club in San Francisco. The mood was very festive, and everyone congratulated me on my appointment. It hadn't been announced, but it had been assumed for a long time that I would accompany the governor to Washington as national security advisor. I accepted the thanks, but the next morning I called the governor and told him that I didn't think I could go to Washington. I explained that I couldn't leave my father in his current state. In fact, I'd already told a couple of close friends. I remember a conversation with my friend from my early days at Stanford, Janne Nolan. "People would understand if I said I can't do it because of the children," I said. "They won't understand my obligations to my father."

"Rent a baby," Janne said. We laughed, but she was one of the few who seemed to understand.

The governor called back and said that he understood but that it was important I go. "I'm not asking you to leave your dad alone. He's always been there for you, and you want to be there for him. We'll make it work." We agreed that I'd come to Washington but travel back to California every two weeks. In my heart I knew that it wasn't a practical solution, but I wasn't prepared to leave my father alone.

CHAPTER THIRTY-EIGHT

"The Saints Go Marching In"

THREE DAYS before Christmas I went to have dinner at the home of my good friend and sports buddy Lori White. I stopped by to see Daddy on the way, and he seemed in pretty good spirits. I called a few hours later as I was leaving Lori's house, and Daddy got on the phone.

"I'm going home," he said.

"Daddy, you are at home," I answered.

"No, it's time for me to go home."

I knew in my heart what he meant, and it terrified me. My father, a Presbyterian minister and a man of great faith, believed that at the end of our earthly existence, God calls us home to eternal life.

I rushed to his house. He seemed fine, and I left. I drove the ten minutes to my house. As I walked in the door, Clara was calling. Daddy had stopped breathing. We rushed to the hospital. This time the physical and mental damage were irreparable. On Christmas Eve, after slipping into a coma, my father died.

I'd told Daddy just after the election that George Bush wanted me to go to Washington and become national security advisor. He was able to communicate his understanding, but he also cried, and I couldn't tell whether they were tears of joy for my achievement or tears of despair because he knew that we would be separated. With his death he resolved my dilemma. Was it coincidence? I've always prayed that it was, because I can't bear to think that John Wesley Rice Jr. deliberately did this one last thing to make sure I fulfilled my dreams. Honestly, it would have been just like him.

The funeral for my father stood in stark contrast to the private service for my mother. John Rice loved people and people loved him. Jerusalem Baptist Church, where Clara worshipped, was filled to the rafters. Jonathan Staples, the Jerusalem pastor, gave the eulogy. He was yet another young man whom my father had befriended and mentored. I made certain that there was a Presbyterian minister participating, given my father's long association. Frank VanderZwan from Menlo Park Presbyterian, my church, had worked with my father in outreach to East Palo Alto. Clara and I sang "In the Garden," a song that my father remembered and sang until the very end.

> *I come to the garden alone,*
> *While the dew is still on the roses;*
> *And the voice I hear, falling on my ear,*
> *The Son of God discloses.*

And He walks with me,
And He talks with me,
And He tells me I am His own;
And the joy we share as we tarry there,
None other has ever known.

The service ended with a little jazz ensemble playing "When the Saints Go Marching In" for this son of Louisiana.

We laid Daddy to rest at Alta Mesa Memorial Gardens, not far from the Stanford campus, on December 28. A few years before, I'd moved my mother's remains from Denver to the same cemetery. When I decided to do so, my father was very pleased. But he reminded me that the grave is not really a Christian's final resting place. "The Lord's eternal home is the final destination," he'd say. At the end of Daddy's life, I was comforted by my faith in the truth of what he had said and my belief that he and my mother were united again.

I LEFT for Washington about a week later. There was so much to do as the new national security advisor. I told myself that I couldn't afford to be debilitated by my grief. I just powered through the meetings, the briefings, the calls each day, determined to do what needed to be done. Yet ever since my mother's first bout with cancer I had wondered how it would feel to live without my parents. We had been so close. Would I ever feel whole again?

Oh, how I missed them. At the inauguration in 2001, I ached to have my parents sitting on the Mall watching George W. Bush take the oath of office, ushering me into the White House as well. When I landed in Moscow aboard a plane that simply said "The United States of America," I wanted to send them the photograph. Visiting the Holy Land, I thought of how much my father would have relished walking in the footsteps of Jesus Christ. Sitting in the Presidential Box at the Kennedy Center, I thought that my mother would have loved to have seen *Aïda* there and that my father would have hated it but gone along for "Ann's sake." And, of course, in 2010 I wanted my father to know that the New Orleans Saints had won the Super Bowl. He would have *loved* that!

But often it has been their presence, not their absence, that I've experienced. I could almost see John and Angelena Rice at the door of my West Wing office as national security advisor, and again hovering over me as I flew into a combat zone in Baghdad or Kabul as secretary of state. "You are well prepared for whatever is ahead of you," I could hear them say. "Now don't forget that you are God's child and He will keep you in His care." They remain by my side. And I feel today, as before, the overwhelming and unconditional love of the extraordinary, ordinary parents that I was so blessed to have.

A Note on Sources

I CONSULTED SEVERAL sources to supplement my own recollections of the events that shaped my life experiences. In recalling my early childhood in Birmingham, I benefited greatly from interviews with friends and neighbors as well as from former students and colleagues of my parents. I am grateful to Eva Carter for helping to organize some of the interview sessions that brought me back to Alabama, and I am thankful to the following people for sharing their own memories of my mother and father: Carolyn Armstrong, Deborah Cheatham Carson, Margaret Cheatham, Gloria Dennard, Harold Dennard, Ann Dowling, Lillian Ford, Raymond Goolsby, Linda Harris, Willie Harton, Helen Heath, Eugenia Henry, George Hunter III, Vanessa Hunter, Edythe Williams Jones, Ann Lampman, Jim Lampman, Dannetta Thornton Owens, Ricky Powell, John Smith, Julia Emma Smith, Leola Smith, Carole Smitherman, John Springer, James Stewart, Elaine Thompson, Carol Watkins, and Cora Williams. I am also grateful to Harold Jackson, Sheryl McCarthy, and Amelia Rutledge for helping to clarify my recollections of their achievements.

To help reconstruct the historic events of the early 1960s in segregated Birmingham, I consulted Clay Carson, professor of history at Stanford and director of the Martin Luther King Jr. Research and Education Institute, who provided valuable insights and perspectives. I also drew upon Glenn Eskew's remarkable *But for Birmingham: The Local and National Movements in the Civil Rights Struggle,* which was particularly valuable in helping me to recall details of the "selective buying campaign," the 1963 municipal elections, the "Children's Crusade," and the May 11 riots. Stanley Robinson at the Birmingham Park and Recreation Board provided a number of helpful articles from the *Birmingham News* and the *Birmingham Post-Herald* on the city's segregated recreational facilities. Jim Baggett at the Birmingham Public Library's archives department and Wayne Coleman at the Birmingham Civil Rights Institute provided me with key documents and photographs from this era.

I gained a number of insights on Daddy's teaching and leadership at the University of Denver after reviewing his papers stored in the Special Collections division of DU's Penrose Library. I am especially grateful to Steve Fisher, curator of the university's Archives and Special Collections, and Jennifer Thompson, associate dean at the Josef Korbel School of International Studies, for making these documents available to me. I am also grateful to Jim Berscheidt, associate vice chancellor for university communications, for supplying me with photographs from my time in Professor Korbel's classroom. I also reviewed articles about my father and his courses that appeared in the *Denver Post,* the *Denver Clarion,* and the *Rocky Mountain News.*

In writing about my tenure at Stanford, I consulted materials and multimedia from the Stanford News Service, the *Stanford Report,* the *Stanford Daily,* and the *Palo Alto Weekly.* Assistant University Archivist Aimee Morgan helped to track down facts and historical information.

A partial list of sources appears below.

Bush, George. *Public Papers of the Presidents of the United States: George Bush, 1989–1991,* 4 volumes. Washington, D.C.: United States Government Printing Office, 1990–1992.

Bush, George, and Brent Scowcroft. *A World Transformed.* New York: Alfred A. Knopf, 1998.

Branch, Taylor. *Parting the Waters: America in the King Years, 1954–1963.* New York: Simon & Schuster, 1988.

Eskew, Glenn T. *But for Birmingham: The Local and National Movements in the Civil Rights Struggle.* Chapel Hill: The University of North Carolina Press, 1997.

Kennedy, John F. "Radio and Television Report to the American People on Civil Rights: June 11, 1963," *Public Papers of the Presidents of the United States, 1963.* Washington, D.C.: United States Government Printing Office, 1964.

Nunnelley, William A. *Bull Connor.* Tuscaloosa: University of Alabama Press, 1991.

Ostermann, Christian F. (ed.). *The End of the Cold War.* Cold War International History Project Bulletin, issue 12/13. Washington, D.C.: Woodrow Wilson International Center for Scholars, 2001.

Rice, John W., Jr. "Black Studies Programs at the University of Denver, 1969–1970." Report to Chancellor Maurice B. Mitchell, University of Denver, Denver, CO, June 20, 1970 (unpublished).

———. "The Black Experience in America." Course pamphlets, University of Denver, Denver, CO, 1970–1973 (unpublished).

Zelikow, Philip, and Condoleezza Rice. *Germany Unified and Europe Transformed: A Study in Statecraft.* Cambridge: Harvard University Press, 1997.

ACKNOWLEDGMENTS

Writing this book has been an exceptional journey, allowing me to revisit memories of my extraordinary, ordinary parents and our family and to reconnect with the communities in which I grew up and worked: Birmingham, Tuscaloosa, Denver, South Bend, Palo Alto, and Washington, D.C. I want to thank those who have contributed to this effort and who have helped me to recount and, in some cases, learn anew my family's story.

First and foremost, I could not have done this work without my family. My aunt Gee, my uncle Alto and his wife, Connie, and my late aunt Mattie spent countless hours helping to reconstruct the narrative of the Rices and the Rays. My father's first cousin, Philip Rice, and my cousins Lativia Ray Alston, Yvonne Ray German, Albert Ray, Patrice Ray Cathwright, Denise Bonds Williams, and Connie Rice contributed greatly to this endeavor, as did my stepmother, Clara Bailey Rice, and my stepbrother, Greg. Edythe Williams Jones, my maternal grandmother's cousin, who is ninety, used her still-ironclad memory to enrich my understanding of our family story. Many of the photographs included in this book surfaced thanks to the willingness of friends and family—particularly Yvonne, Clara, Louis Olave, and Chris McNair—to search hard and long for the best images of our lives together.

I was able to spend numerous hours immersed in old memories, both good and bad, with my childhood friends Deborah Cheatham Carson, Freeman Hrabowski, Carole Smitherman,

Vanessa Hunter, and Velda Robinson and with my dear friend Mary Bush. Thanks to the tireless efforts of Eva Carter, one of my father's "youth fellowship kids," Westminster Presbyterian Church hosted a day of remembering with Carolyn Armstrong, Margaret Cheatham, Gloria and Harold Dennard, Ann Downing, Linda Harris, Willie Harton, Lillian Ford, Eugenia Henry, Julia Emma Smith, Leola Smith, Elaine Thompson, and Cora Williams, all members of my father's congregation. I am also grateful for the stories Carol Watkins shared with me about my mother.

I want to thank the city of Fairfield and the Fairfield Industrial High School Alumni Association for hosting a wonderful lunch at which I met several of my parents' first colleagues and students, including members of Daddy's football team and girls and boys basketball teams. Their stories of my parents' early life together were largely unknown to me until that session. And thanks to the great Willie Mays for sharing his memories of my mother and father.

Similarly, Eva and the staff of the Hoover Library in Hoover, Alabama, arranged a session at which my father's and mother's colleagues from the Birmingham Public Schools and many of the students in the youth fellowship and Cavaliers programs participated. It was wonderful to hear the firsthand testimony of Raymond Goolsby, Helen Heath, George Hunter III, Dannetta Thornton Owens, Ricky Powell, John Smith, James Stewart, and John Springer. I will always remember my moving encounter with the Reverend Fred Shuttlesworth, and I thank his wife, Sephira, for making our recent reunion possible.

Ronald Carter, Robert Bolton, and Bridgette Johnson sent me a copy of my father's 1946 yearbook from Johnson C. Smith University in Charlotte, North Carolina. Jim Baggett of the Birmingham Public Library's archives department, and Wayne

Coleman of the Birmingham Civil Rights Institute, helped me document the historic events of the civil rights era. And my friend and colleague, historian Clay Carson, graciously read the portions of the manuscript that dealt with that period.

I talked, too, with many family friends in Denver, South Bend, and Palo Alto, including my father's great mentor, the late John Blackburn, and my college buddies Jim and Ann Lampman and Debbie and Rich Griffin. I benefited greatly from the efforts of Steve Fisher, the curator of the Penrose Library Archives and Special Collections at the University of Denver; Jennifer Thompson, associate dean at the Josef Korbel School of International Studies; and Jim Berscheidt, associate vice chancellor for university communications at DU.

Randy Bean, Chip Blacker, Mariann Byerwalter, Nancy Hubbell Biffar, Gerhard Casper, Susan Ford Dorsey, Mary Edmonds, Jendayi Frazer, Wendy Frieman, Steve Krasner, Tim Warner, Mia Jackson, Louis Olave, Jane Robinette, Gene Washington, Lori White, and Amy Zegart all contributed stories that brought my graduate school days and early professional life into sharper relief. Aimee Morgan, the assistant university archivist at Stanford, and Michele Futornick of the Stanford News Service were helpful in tracking down facts and photographs of my time at the university. Bonnie Burlbaw at the George Bush Presidential Library and Museum as well as Colin Powell and members of his staff, especially Peggy Cifrino, assisted me in compiling photographs from my time in government.

I could not have completed this book without the support of the Hoover Institution and Stanford University. I particularly want to thank Director John Raisian and my friends Tom and Barbara Stephenson, who are the generous benefactors of my fellowship.

I have been blessed with the help of a wonderful staff. Colby Cooper and Anne Lyons followed me to Stanford from Washington, bringing not just their invaluable experience but also an unwavering commitment to helping me reestablish my life in California. This book could not have been completed without the efforts of Caroline Beswick, who keeps me on schedule and on time, and my trusted assistant of more than a decade, Marilyn Stanley, who never ceases to amaze me with her sixth sense about what needs to be done before I even say it.

My research assistants, Leisel Bogan, Daniel Slate, Dianna Bai, and Jenny Arriola, as well as my student assistants, Taylor Jackson, Emma Welch, and Natalie Davies, were true bloodhounds in unearthing materials for the book.

And what can I say to Theo Milonopoulos and Cameron Bell, except thank you for your patience and care in checking and rechecking every detail, reading and rereading every word, and helping to make this book a far better one than it would have been without your exceptional dedication and commitment.

I'd like to thank my team at Crown Publishing and William Morris Endeavor Entertainment, particularly Tina Constable and Suzanne Gluck for their comments and direction. Thanks also to Wayne Kabak for his continuing support and interest in me.

And, finally, I want to express my deepest gratitude to my talented editor, Rick Horgan, who now knows every twist and turn in the story of the Rices and the Rays. Rick has always found just the right touch in helping me to make this a better book while always remembering that this is a deeply personal story—and giving me the space to tell it in exactly that way.

INDEX

READING GROUP GUIDE

for the *New York Times* bestseller

Extraordinary, Ordinary People

A MEMOIR OF FAMILY

CONDOLEEZZA RICE

INTRODUCTION

B Y ANY measure, Condoleezza Rice has built an extraordinary career, becoming the first female National Security Advisor and the first black woman to serve as Secretary of State during a time of seismic shifts on the international landscape. Many public figures have written autobiographies describing hard-won paths to success, but Rice's journey from the segregated South to the world's most exalted corridors of power is truly remarkable. Paying homage to her inspiring family, *Extraordinary, Ordinary People* is a portrait of loving parents who taught their daughter to conquer adversity with determination and education. As we meet her elegant mother and vibrant father, Rice introduces us to her community of middle-class blacks who, in the 1950s, stood poised to topple George Wallace's call for "segregation now, segregation tomorrow, segregation forever."

Rice's family of ministers and teachers had forged success on the outskirts of Birmingham, Alabama. Her parents devoted themselves to Condoleezza, undeterred by the racially motivated violence erupting around them. (Rice knew one of the young girls killed in the Sixteenth Street Baptist Church bombing.) She vividly captures a household where she was encouraged to be "twice as good," never allowing herself to be cast as a victim to the humiliating circumstances of segregation. Yet it was also a household filled with joy as her mother immersed the family in fine arts and her father coached her on the finer points of football.

In the midst of Birmingham's struggles, the Rices moved to Colorado, where Rice wandered into a class on international politics at the University of Denver and discovered her passion for foreign affairs. After completing his graduate studies, John transitioned from a life as a Presbyterian minister and became an assistant dean at the University of Denver. Rice describes his unfailing support as she followed in his footsteps into academia, earning a Ph.D., becoming a tenured professor at Stanford, and later serving as the university's provost. Soon recognized as a leading Cold War scholar, she played a key role in forming U.S. policy as the Soviet Union collapsed, and she went on to become invaluable in both Bush presidencies. Rice recalls each achievement as a tribute to her parents as well.

Brimming with wisdom about families, careers, and history, *Extraordinary, Ordinary People* is destined to inspire future generations of leaders for years to come. We hope that the following discussion guide will enhance your experience of Condoleezza Rice's captivating journey.

Questions and Topics for Discussion

1. Discuss the memoir's title. What led John and Angelena and their ancestors to strive for excellence? What gave them

the drive to rise above the ordinary? What family legacies have shaped your identity?

2. How did Rice's book enrich your understanding of black society in the segregated South, especially in middle-class communities like Titusville?

3. As educators, what did Rice's parents know about helping students excel in school? Do you think most American parents today share the Rices' approach, determined to deliver the best possible education no matter what the obstacles are?

4. Rice observes that in some cases she was more proficient than many whites in her knowledge of European culture, from classical music to history. Why did her parents immerse themselves in European culture, despite Europe's domination of the slave trade in previous centuries? How did her father reconcile this with his campaign to increase African studies courses at the University of Denver?

5. Discuss your family's recollections of the Civil Rights movement. If you had lived in the shadow of Bull Connor, would you have marched with Reverend Shuttlesworth and the SCLC, or would you have worked for change in less visible ways?

6. What did you discover about Jim Crow politics by reading Rice's book? Did John Rice's experience with voter registration surprise you? In "College Years," Rice writes about her dislike of identity politics and the fact that Jimmy Carter's foreign policy caused her to favor Republicans. How does her approach to party politics compare to yours?

7. What role did faith play in the Rice family? What does it say about religion in America that Rice's father distrusted the Kennedys because of their Catholicism and preferred an intellectual Presbyterian style of worship rather than a charismatic Baptist one?

8. How was Rice affected by being an only child? How did the three close-knit family members influence one another over

the years? How were Condoleezza and John sustained after Angelena's death?

9. Consider the tremendous sacrifices, financial and otherwise, that the Rices made for their daughter. What rewards did they hope she would reap? Was there someone in your life, not necessarily in your family, who "invested" in you in some way?

10. What prevented Rice from becoming bitter after her many encounters with racism? What sustained her love for America?

11. In "Leaving the South Behind," Rice describes her mother's adjustment to life in Colorado, where she had difficulty finding a job and missed the refinement of her southern friends. What did Angelena teach Rice about being a successful woman? To Angelena, what were the qualities of an ideal woman?

12. As Rice described her young professional life, what common ground did you see between the world of Stanford/Palo Alto and the world of Washington, D.C.? How did a career in academia and the think tank RAND prepare her for a career of public service?

13. What universal human experiences did Rice observe as a witness to both the Civil Rights movement and glasnost? What aspects of her life story transcend ancestry?

14. In "Tough Decisions," Rice writes about her strong support for including race as a factor in college admissions. Do you agree with her approach? What can society and institutions do to foster even greater numbers of minorities in higher education, the foundation for stepping into a leadership role?

15. What aspects of Rice's story surprised you the most? How does her personal voice compare to her image as a public figure?

AN INTERVIEW WITH CONDOLEEZZA RICE

Q. You were clearly a little girl who possessed a rich imagination and many creative talents. Do you think the arts can benefit all young people, regardless of the careers they choose later?

A. I have long believed that arts education is an integral and indispensable part of a school's curriculum. I cringe when I hear music and the fine arts described as "extracurricular"—the term implies that arts education is somehow "extra" and therefore expendable when it comes to budget cuts in education. When I cofounded the Center for a New Generation in East Palo Alto, I worked to make arts education part of an extended learning day for highly motivated, underprivileged students. I am continuing that work today through my work with the Boys and Girls Clubs of America, where I serve on the organization's national Board of Governors.

At a very early age, music became a kind of language for me. I could read music before I could read prose. Studies have shown that playing music enriches the mind just as much as it does the soul by activating regions in the brain that also appear to be used in language acquisition and mathematics. The fine arts also serve as a kind of universal language that reaches across cultures to promote common understanding and shared experiences. Every young person should have the opportunity to benefit from the kind of education that the arts are uniquely suited to provide.

Q. How did your community in Alabama define success? What do you think your success, and that of your ancestors, says about the role of nature and nurture?

A. In the face of humiliating conditions in the most deeply segregated big city in America, the adults in my community encouraged young people to become "twice as good" as their white counterparts by taking full advantage of educational and cultural opportunities offered to them. By mastering the finer elements of "white" culture even better than "they" could, the thinking was that "they" might not like you, but "they" had to respect you. The adults also reminded us that although we could not control the degrading circumstances we confronted in Birmingham, we could control our responses to them. There was no room for victims. Through a combination of education, faith, community, and family, my parents and so many others in our community inspired us to pursue our highest aspirations.

Q. You write that your father emphasized intellect when he was a minister. How has this combination of mind and spirit sustained you?

A. My father often took a cerebral approach to his ministry, partly because he himself was an educator. He encouraged me to wrestle with theological questions and to challenge him as I navigated the mysteries of my faith. Because of my father's approach, reason and faith were not enemies of each other for me but, in fact, complementary, with each enriching the other. As I write in *Extraordinary, Ordinary People,* this more intellectual approach sustained me and has allowed me to experience my faith more deeply than I otherwise would have. I have been able to avoid complacency in my faith by continuing to struggle with its meaning and seek greater understanding of the spirit and promise of eternal life.

Q. What did you learn about trust and commitment from watching your parents' marriage? What helped them endure as a couple?

A. My parents inspired me with their unconditional love and devotion to each other. As teachers, they shared a passion for education and were committed, despite their modest means, to providing me with anything that could remotely be called an educational opportunity. Even in areas where they didn't always have common interests, they still found ways to take part in each other's lives. My father endured long car rides full of Mozart and Beethoven, and my mother dutifully joined our outing to the family's first professional football game—a truly watershed event. They faced many of the same challenges that ordinary couples face, but their deep commitment to each other and their only daughter allowed us to persevere through even the most difficult of circumstances. When my mother passed away at sixty-one from breast cancer, my father and I leaned on each other and our faith to remind us that she remained with us in spirit. I have felt her presence throughout my life, and I continue to feel both of them watching over me to this very day.

Q. In "My Rookie Season," you write about the importance of seeking out mentors regardless of whether they share one's background ("Sally Ride never would have been an astronaut if she had waited to see a female in that role"). Do you continue to have mentors, or are they just for rookies?
A. One is never too experienced to have mentors, and that is certainly the case for me. I was blessed throughout my professional life to have a number of individuals whom I admired and who gave me opportunities to succeed. Josef Korbel, my advisor at the University of Denver, inspired my passion for Soviet affairs and international politics more generally. Brent Scowcroft, the nation's National Security Advisor under Gerald Ford and George H. W. Bush, mentored me in my early years in government and ultimately became the model I sought to emulate when I myself held that office.

Today, I admire deeply my mentor and close friend George Shultz, who served as the nation's sixtieth Secretary of State under President Ronald Reagan. In addition to his diplomatic prowess, business acumen, and intuitive wisdom on leadership and negotiation, I admire George for his willingness to invest in me at a time

when I was just an assistant professor. His guidance and friendship is something that I continue to treasure to this day.

Q. Educational institutions across all levels—from public elementary schools to higher education—are once again facing
serious budget shortfalls. What advice do you have for decision
makers who have to make the kinds of tough choices you made as
provost of Stanford?

A. We as a nation cannot continue to accrue budget deficits by
throwing money at the problem. When I first became Stanford's
provost, the university was facing a budget deficit of about five
percent. Given that I was responsible for budgetary matters, I
consistently reminded my colleagues that, unlike the federal government, I could not print money and that the university would
have to live within its means.

We need innovative solutions to improve K-12 education,
and I currently co-chair a task force on education at the Council on Foreign Relations that is working to develop such options.
From my perspective, one of the most effective ways to drive in-
novation in education will be to increase "competition" among
schools and educators in ways that will benefit our students. This
requires that we increase opportunities for parents of all socioeconomic backgrounds to choose the schools they feel most
appropriate for their children. By enhancing school choice, principals and educators could be driven through funding incentives
to demand higher performance from their teachers. Teachers, in
turn, should be rewarded for effectiveness in their teaching, not
merely the length of time they have spent in front of a classroom.
Although I am an ardent defender of the tenure process at the
university level, I believe that the tenure system at the secondary level does not adequately reflect a merit-based approach and
consequently does not serve our students.

Q. When you were a young American, you faced obstacles of race, gender, unequal education, and parents who had to work long hours to build a middle-class life. What do you think the greatest obstacles and challenges are for young Americans in the twenty-first century?

A. We are facing a real crisis in this country when I can look at a child's zip code and tell you whether he or she is going to get a good education. As growth in the world's economy continues to demand more skilled workers, the United States risks falling behind other nations in maintaining even basic literacy and arithmetic proficiency among our children. Nearly one in four students who take the U.S. military's entrance exam do not pass, given the poor state of our country's educational system. The crisis in K-12 education is truly the greatest national security challenge this country faces.

Compounding this issue is what President George W. Bush has called "the soft bigotry of low expectations" that is preventing underprivileged and minority students from reaching their full potential. The widening achievement gap in our country threatens to leave behind an entire generation of students because of an implicit and patronizing bias that suggests their dire circumstances simply make it impossible to help them succeed. We are failing to deliver for these students the basic promise of equality of opportunity that is vital to the American experience. Without that, America will have lost its core principle that makes our country the envy of the world.

Q. What did segregation as well as Cold War politics teach you about leadership? What leadership lessons can a reader gain from *Extraordinary, Ordinary People*?

A. Among the most important lessons I learned from my experiences enduring segregation and observing the unraveling of the

Soviet Union were the importance of vision in leadership and the universal aspirations of all people for freedom. Leaders in both the Civil Rights movement and the Cold War succeeded in part because they articulated bold visions of what a world should look like after segregation barriers fell and the Berlin Wall crumbled. It would have been easier to cave to expectations that segregation would not end in my lifetime or that Germany would not unify for more than one hundred years. And yet, because of the bold visions of our leaders, Germany unified in two years to become one of Europe's strongest economies, and the United States elected its first African American to be president of the United States soon after two African Americans had served as Secretary of State.

Additionally, these experiences reinforced for me the idea that freedom is a universal aspiration. I often recall how my father was unable to register to vote in the South. Segregationists had long considered blacks too "childish" to participate in politics. Similarly, Soviet leaders assumed they knew what was best for their people by imposing the strong hand of communism to redistribute wealth and opportunity in a bankrupt vision of equality. Any illusion about the aspirations of people in Eastern Europe and the Soviet bloc were wiped away by the hundreds of thousands of impatient patriots protesting in squares and staring down Soviet tanks as they clamored for democracy. This same spirit—this universality of freedom—has driven Arabs into the streets today to topple authoritarian regimes. These experiences have reinforced for me the importance of leaders to stand for the proposition that every man, woman, and child deserves to live in freedom.

Q. Your book poignantly describes the constant support you, John, and Angelena provided one another. Who are the members of your support team these days?
A. I continue to be blessed with close family and an extraordinary

group of friends. Since leaving office, I have reestablished my life in northern California and reconnected with many of the individuals mentioned in these pages. I often spend the holidays with my aunt Gee, and my cousin Lativia and her husband, Will, have recently moved close to me in the Bay Area. I am also extraordinarily fortunate to have resumed my professorship at Stanford, where I have the great privilege of teaching and interacting with students. Their vitality and intellectual curiosity renew my faith in the promise of the next generation that will serve our country.

Q. Will your next book pick up where this one leaves off?
A. My next memoir will indeed resume where *Extraordinary, Ordinary People* left off and reflect on the foreign policy decisions I helped shape during a consequential period in our nation's history. I hope that once the memoir is published, readers will find it as informative and engaging as the book they currently hold in their hands.

ABOUT THE AUTHOR

Raised in Alabama, CONDOLEEZZA RICE became the sixty-sixth U.S. Secretary of State and the first black woman to hold that office. Prior to that, she was the first woman to serve as National Security Advisor. She is a professor at Stanford University.

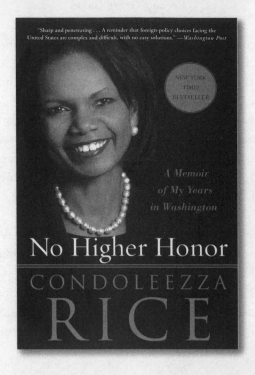

"Sharp and penetrating . . . A reminder that foreign-policy choices facing the
United States are complex and difficult, with no easy solutions." —*Washington Post*

NEW YORK
TIMES
BESTSELLER

*A Memoir
of My Years
in Washington*

No Higher Honor

CONDOLEEZZA
RICE

FOR EIGHT YEARS, Condoleezza Rice influenced national and international policy at the highest levels.
No Higher Honor is the memoir of her years as National
Security Advisor and Secretary of State for the Bush
Administration, an expansive personal chronicle of the
moments and personalities that shaped one of the most
politically significant decades in world history.